Selections from the Ileana and Michael Sonnabend Collection

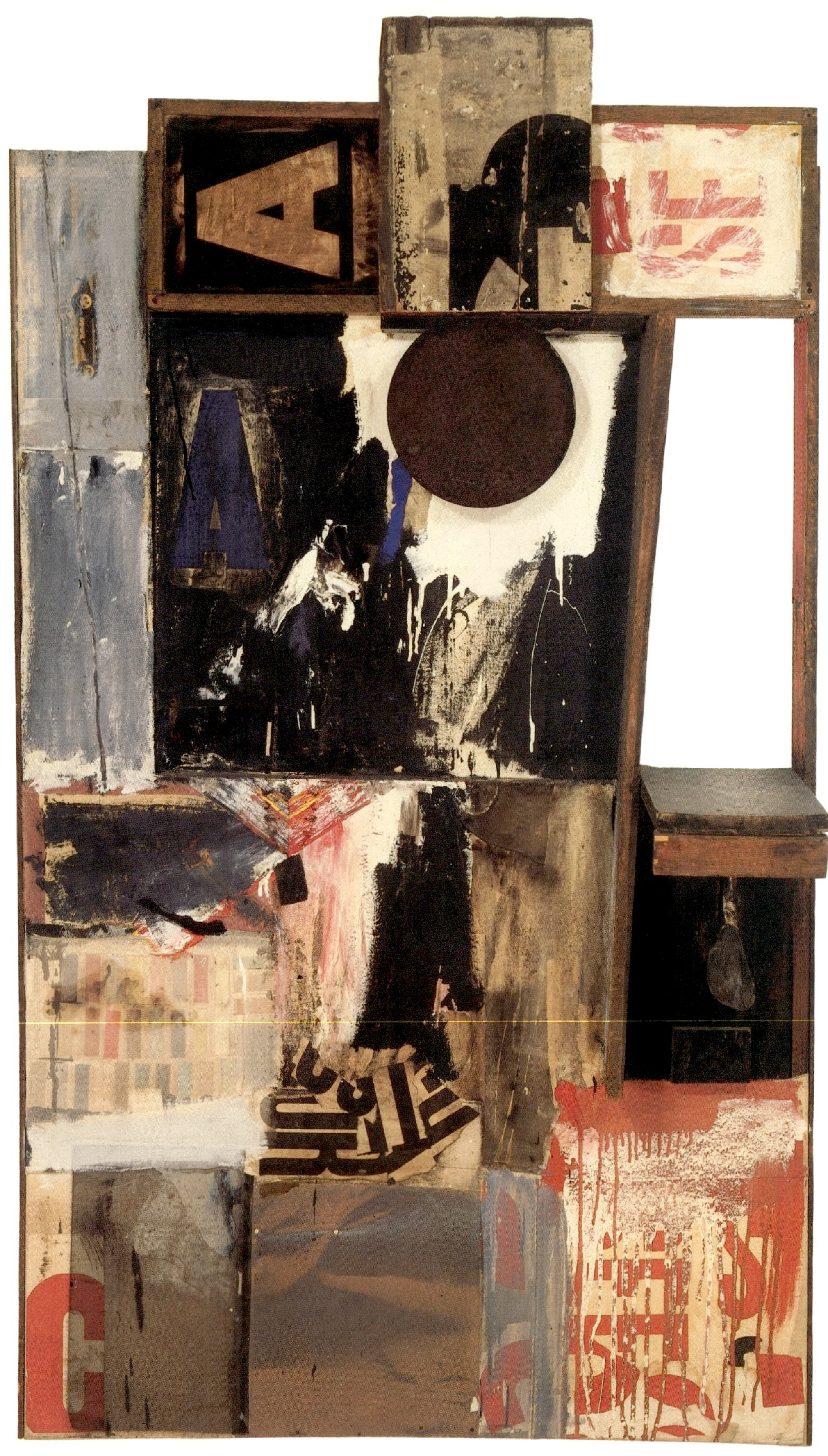

Selections from the Ileana and Michael Sonnabend Collection *Works from the 1950s and 1960s*

BY SAM HUNTER

and Jonathan Bloom, Malcolm R. Daniel, Isabelle Dervaux, Julia Hicks, John Otte, Erica Wolf

with an essay by Robert Pincus-Witten

THE ART MUSEUM, PRINCETON UNIVERSITY

This catalogue has been supported by the Publications Fund, Department of Art and Archaeology, Princeton University.

Designed by Bruce Campbell
Set in type by Columbia Publishing Company, Inc.
Printed by Schneidereith & Sons

ISBN: 0-943012-06-6

The Art Museum, Princeton University
Princeton, New Jersey 08544

Cover illustration: Jasper Johns, *Number 8*, 1959, encaustic on canvas, 20 × 15″. Photograph by Clem Fiori.

Frontispiece: Robert Rauschenberg, *Magician II*, 1959, combine painting, 65½ × 38¼ × 16¼″. Photograph by Clem Fiori.

Published in conjunction with the exhibition "Selections from the Ileana and Michael Sonnabend Collection: Works from the 1950s and 1960s."

The Art Museum, Princeton University
February 3–June 9, 1985

Archer M. Huntington Art Gallery
The University of Texas at Austin
September 8–October 27, 1985

Walker Art Center, Minneapolis
November 23, 1985–March 9, 1986

Contents

6 **Acknowledgments**

7 **Introduction** *Allen Rosenbaum*

15 **Ileana and Michael Sonnabend**
Robert Pincus-Witten

21 **The Sixties: A Revolution in Art**
Sam Hunter

35 **Arman** *Malcolm R. Daniel*

38 **John Chamberlain** *Sam Hunter*

40 **Christo** *Malcolm R. Daniel*

43 **Jime Dine** *Malcolm R. Daniel*

50 **Jasper Johns** *Isabelle Dervaux*

58 **Roy Lichtenstein** *Julia Hicks*

66 **Robert Morris** *Isabelle Dervaux*

70 **Claes Oldenburg** *Jonathan Bloom*

76 **Robert Rauschenberg** *Sam Hunter*

85 **James Rosenquist** *Erica Wolf*

88 **Frank Stella** *John Otte*

92 **Cy Twombly** *John Otte*

96 **Andy Warhol** *Erica Wolf*

104 **Tom Wesselmann** *Julia Hicks*

110 **Checklist**

Acknowledgments

This exhibition was proposed and organized by Professor Sam Hunter, Department of Art and Archaeology, Princeton University. The catalogue is the result of an informal seminar given by Professor Hunter with Princeton undergraduate students Jonathan Bloom, Julia Hicks, and Erica Wolf, and graduate student Malcolm R. Daniel; John Otte; and Isabelle Dervaux, a graduate student from the Institute of Fine Arts, New York University. Robert Pincus-Witten has provided personal notes from his long association and intimate friendship with Ileana and Michael Sonnabend.

We greatly appreciate the cooperation, support, and good cheer of Antonio Homem, director of the Sonnabend Gallery, and also the assistance, in the gallery, of Michele Fleidler, David Nolan, and Nick Sheidy.

Eight of the works in the exhibition are on loan indefinitely to The Baltimore Museum of Art, and we are grateful to Arnold L. Lehman, Director, Brenda Richardson, Assistant Director for Art and Curator of Painting and Sculpture, and the staff for their cooperation in making these works available for this exhibition.

For The Art Museum we wish to thank Harriet Senie, Associate Director; Bitite Vinklers, Editor of Publications; Robert Lafond, Registrar and Coordinator of Museum Operations; and Anna Greczyn, Secretary to the Director.

And finally we wish to thank Ileana and Michael Sonnabend for allowing us to make their collection available to students and also to present the exhibition to a larger public.

This catalogue was generously supported by the Publications Fund of the Department of Art and Archaeology, Princeton University.

A.R.

Introduction

by Allen Rosenbaum

The selection of works of art from the 1950s and 1960s in this exhibition is only an indication of the richness of the collection of Ileana and Michael Sonnabend; by no means does it represent the full range of the collection. Mrs. Sonnabend has indicated that a selection of works in their collection from the 1970s and 1980s could provide yet another exhibition. Such a remark is not prompted out of pride of possession as much as it is a statement of her continuing commitment to contemporary art, her keen interests as a collector, and her vitality as one of the foremost art dealers today.

Professor Sam Hunter, in his selection of the works for the exhibition and in his essay, has chosen to emphasize the 1960s, a period Mrs. Sonnabend helped to shape through the early presentation both in New York and Europe of many now internationally recognized artists. This period—the late 1950s and the 1960s—and the artists included in this exhibition are those with whom Mrs. Sonnabend is still very closely identified, despite her continuing important activity in contemporary art. After her divorce from Leo Castelli in 1959, and her marriage to Michael Sonnabend, in 1962 she opened the Galerie Ileana Sonnabend in Paris, where she showed the works of these artists and made them known in Europe. The Sonnabends were determined that the work of such artists as Robert Rauschenberg, Jasper Johns, James Rosenquist, Jim Dine, Roy Lichtenstein, Tom Wesselmann, Claes Oldenburg, Andy Warhol, and George Segal, unlike that of the Abstract Expressionists, be shown in Europe as it was being created.

It is, of course, a temptation in the context of this catalogue also to emphasize the involvement of Ileana Sonnabend in the Castelli Gallery in the choice of artists, so remarkable as to suggest a certain infallibility. By her own statement, it was "Leo's gallery,"[1] her husband's business—this attitude perhaps prescribed by her European and social background as well as her natural reticence. But hers and Leo Castelli's partnership was a strong and close one, and has perhaps been best described by Robert Rauschenberg: "Ileana was more sensual and imaginative, while Leo was more analytical and art-history-aware, and it was the tension between their two approaches that made the gallery."[2] She herself has said, "I once told Leo, 'You know, both of us are such adolescents.' Leo laughed and laughed. 'That's true,' he said. 'And nobody knows it but us.' "[3]

She was Ileana Schapira, the daughter of one of the wealthiest Rumanian industrialists, and Leo Castelli was the son of a well-to-do family from Trieste, expected to pursue a career in banking. Hers was an early attraction to art: she tells how, as a young girl, bored by shopping with her mother and sister, and therefore a bother to them, she was relieved to be delivered to the Kunsthistorisches Museum in Vienna when it opened in the morning and retrieved only at closing time.

On the Castellis' honeymoon in Vienna, she asked to have a work of art instead of a diamond ring as a gift from Leo. The visit to the gallery where they chose a Matisse watercolor made a very vivid impression on her: she remembers a hushed elegance, a place where art was greatly respected, and a gallery director who patiently and gently guided them, through what she describes as almost a rite of passage, to the choice of the Matisse.

In 1935 the Castellis moved to Paris, where Leo had taken a position with the Banca d'Italia. They lived a high-spirited life in Paris, and in 1939 Leo opened a gallery in the Place Vendôme with the architect and interior designer René Drouin. Through the painter Leonor Fini, whom Leo Castelli had known as a child in Trieste, they were introduced to the Surrealist circle—Max Ernst, Salvador Dali, Pavel Tchelitchew, Meret Oppenheim, and others, many of whom showed their fantastic furniture designs there; the original intention of the gallery was to show furniture designed by Drouin and contemporary artists. Ileana remained somewhat aloof from this venture, except for participating in the brilliant artistic society attracted to the gallery.

The Castellis were staying at Ileana's father's house in Cannes when France fell to the Germans, and they eventually left the country for Casablanca to await visas for the United States. Throughout, their relocations and dislocations were always cushioned by her father's wealth, and some *douceur de vivre* was experienced even during the anxious wait in Morocco. After a tortuous journey, the Castellis arrived in New York in March 1941, and by the fall of 1942 they were installed in the townhouse which Ileana's father had bought on East 77th Street, and which also became the first home for the gallery.

The Castellis, as if by natural affinity, became part of what is now a legendary world of artists, critics, and art dealers—Willem and Elaine de Kooning, Jackson Pollock and Lee Krasner, Sidney Janis, Sam Kootz, Harold Rosenberg, Clement Greenberg—in New York and in East Hampton, where they had taken a house. They attended meetings of The Club, the association of artists which met on East Eighth Street. What Ileana Sonnabend liked about The Club, despite certain factions, was the sense of solidarity among the artists.

When asked about those days, especially East Hampton, she is nostalgic, but not without some reservations about the lifestyle into which she was drawn.

> Well, some of it was wonderful. But I wasn't bohemian enough to be quite happy with a situation in which there was an absolute, total invasion of my space. People would get so drunk they would absolutely lose control of themselves, and I don't know that I enjoyed that very much. Heaven knows, I didn't enjoy very much the day after a party, finding people camping on the lawn, in a corner of the house—with children, with girlfriends and boyfriends and whatever.
>
> I did enjoy a lot living with John Graham, my stepfather. [Mrs. Sonnabend's parents were divorced after they came to New York.]

For the painter John Graham she felt "a certain affection and fascination." She recalls that he "had a very strange attitude about his work —one day it was worthless and the next day it was far too good for anybody else to possess. He was a very extravagant person too. He destroyed a lot of his work and he gave a lot away." She also recalls that she liked listening to Harold Rosenberg. Looking back on that period of her life, Mrs. Sonnabend remarks, "They were crazy times. It seems to me that I've only had crazy times. Perhaps life now is not quite crazy enough."

Despite Leo Castelli's venture with Drouin in Paris, his long flirtation with opening a gallery in New York, arranging exhibitions, and dealing in paintings sent to New York by Drouin has been attributed to his reluctance to actually being "in trade."[4] As for Ileana, no matter to what extent she shared and supported Leo's interests, it was perhaps natural that it would be her husband who would enter into the world of affairs. De Kooning was eager for Castelli to open a gallery, which he would have joined. Her answer was: "I think Leo will open a gallery and that you won't be one of the artists."[5] This remark was an indication of the Castellis' strong commitment, which both have held to, to show emerging art despite their ability to draw on established artists, such as de Kooning, or to continue dealing comfortably in such modern masters as Léger and Mondrian, which Drouin had been providing. They were waiting for a direction, and certainly had a desire to make their own mark as dealers. The gallery opened in 1957. After some early exhibitions, that mark was made with the first shows of the work of Jasper Johns and Robert Rauschenberg.

It is worth retelling in brief the well-known story of the Castellis' first visit to Rauschenberg's studio, where they were distracted from their purpose by meeting Jasper Johns, who had brought up ice for drinks, and by a visit to his studio on the floor below. Leo Castelli had been very excited about a painting by Johns, *Green Target*, which he had recently seen at The Jewish Museum in New York, and he seized the opportunity. Ileana, characteristically, bought one of

Johns's paintings during the visit to his studio, and a show was arranged for Johns at the Castelli Gallery. It was Ileana whom Rauschenberg encountered at the gallery when he came shortly thereafter to inquire if the Castellis were still interested in giving him a show. "I was very embarrassed," she recalls, "and suddenly aware of how much he had been hurt."[6] Her relationship with Rauschenberg has been the closest and the most sustained among those with the artists with whom she has worked; at the time of the writing of this introduction, I received an announcement from the Sonnabend Gallery of a show of new works by Rauschenberg.

Ileana herself claims that, despite her closeness with many of the artists, she was not very actively involved in the running of the Castelli Gallery, but during a period when Leo was ill she had to take over. She very happily, and somewhat nostalgically, reminisces:

> I became very friendly with Allan Stone and Dick Bellamy and Ivan Karp. We used to go visiting studios, and then we would visit each other and exchange impressions, and those were very exciting times. Sometimes we'd start around five o'clock, when the galleries closed, and we would go on until two o'clock in the morning seeing studios.
>
> So we became very friendly with a group of artists—with Andy Warhol and with Jim Dine and with Bob Morris and with Rosenquist and Lichtenstein, and I was really enthusiastic about their work and we bought things.
>
> And when I separated from Leo, I had a very hard time because I was already so used to the art world and my way of life, and I was sort of at loose ends, but then I married Michael and we decided to go to Rome to spend a year and then come back and see whatever. And when we left, we went with a lot of documentation about Rauschenberg, about Johns, about all the Pop Art people.
>
> First we went to Paris with Rauschenberg, because he had a show there, and it was a very awkward moment—awkward politically—because of the panic created by the Algerian situation, and so we arrived and Paris was absolutely deserted, and the people who were supposed to meet Bob at the airport with money and with arrangements for rooms didn't show up. So we all went to the hotel and had a very good time there.
>
> Then the gallery people appeared, but it was somewhat disorganized and somewhat difficult for Bob, so we gave him moral support and we enjoyed it a lot. And that's where it started—where I thought, Well, it's really important for this art to be shown in Europe while it's happening.
>
> After a year in Rome, we found out that Rome was not really the place. It is now, but it wasn't then. And I found the attitude towards women extremely difficult to deal with. And so we decided to go to Paris. But in Paris we found more or less the same situation, plus a tremendous chauvinism and a certain hostility towards Americans.

When asked if, in the early sixties, she felt some responsibility to Abstract Expressionism, she replies:

> No, I deplored the fact that it hadn't been shown, but I felt no responsibility. I took the responsibility to have younger artists seen in Europe. And it was very difficult, because in the sixties the French were very chauvinistic and also very depressed. There was no money; it was very difficult for the galleries generally, and even the one gallery where it would have been agreeable to show didn't have any money—couldn't pay for the transport, couldn't pay for anything. After looking around for galleries, and showing slides in hotel rooms to all the critics we knew, to all the journalists we knew, to all the professors we knew, to all the gallery people we knew, we were always told that this art was counter-humanist art, that it was an attack against European humanism. Those galleries that were open were interested only if we were willing to pay for insurance, transport, crating, framing, and everything—then they would be willing to try. At that point Michael said, "Well, that's silly—by the time you pay all that, we might as well show ourselves." And so we looked for a space.
>
> We were helped by René Drouin. He knew of a gallery in a hotel, very well located; the woman who owned the hotel tried to run a gallery, but she was not really qualified and so she decided she would rent it on a monthly basis.
>
> I had no experience with the French at all, and it's quite a different system, all the details of shipping and bringing things over. Michael helped me a lot. It was, even in Paris, as a woman, not that easy.
>
> We took the place for six months and started showing, and had a lot of success and a lot of controversy from the beginning.

Actually, according to the art critic Annette Michelson, the opening of the Sonnabend gallery in Paris was a somewhat perplexing disappointment: no one came, and the situation remained a mystery until it was explained to the Sonnabends that they had chosen a holiday for the opening. But, again according to Michelson, "What did become apparent—and this, of course, had been foreseen by Leo—was that there was, as always, an audience in Paris, and that it simply had to be recognized and informed. To observe the course of the first three years of international activity was, then, instructive and refreshing. Above all, Ileana Sonnabend and her associates were, as Leo is in New York, 'there': that is to say, accessible and hospitable to the students, artists, writers, intellectuals and anonymous art lovers who came in steadily increasing numbers, well before the collectors, museum officials or members of the cultural bureaucracy. The importance of this generously informal and indefatigable accessibility should not be understressed . . . ."[7] And she remembers Michael Sonnabend enthusiastically engaging visitors to the gallery. According to Ileana Sonnabend, "Michael was a very good press agent," but also assumed an increasingly active role in running the gallery.

But the collectors, the museum officials, and the members of the cultural bureaucracy did come to the gallery: Edi de Wilde, director of the Stedelijk Museum in Amsterdam; Hammacher of the Hague; Alan Bowness, now director of the Tate Gallery in London; the art critic John Russell; Bryan Robertson of the Whitechapel Gallery in London; Pontus Hultén, at the time director of the Moderna Museet in Stockholm; and Count Panza, the great Italian collector of American art. Also André Malraux, the cultural minister of France, and Miró and André Breton came, to see exhibitions of the work of Jasper Johns, Robert Rauschenberg, Claes Oldenburg, Jim Dine, George Segal, Roy Lichtenstein, Andy Warhol, and others.[8]

Ileana Sonnabend is quick to remind you that she didn't show only Pop artists in Paris, but that she was also interested in Minimal Art and showed Dan Flavin, Larry Bell, Don Judd, and Robert Morris. "It took people a little while to understand Minimal Art, but in Europe you know people have more of an intellectual approach to art. This kind of art is still much more understood and more appreciated there than it is here, where people have a more emotional approach."

Ileana Sonnabend has been called the "American arts ambassadress in Paris,"[9] and recently she was decorated by Jack Lang, the French minister of culture. Certainly the climate of interest and the receptivity to American art in Europe, which she did so much to establish, contributed to Rauschenberg's triumph at the Venice Biennale in 1964, when he received the International Grand Prize for Painting, and was the first American in the history of the Biennale to win this award.

The organizer of the American representation at the Venice Biennale was the late Alan Solomon, who was then the director of The Jewish Museum in New York, and was clearly an important figure for Ileana Sonnabend. During his tenure at The Jewish Museum, he organized an extraordinary series of exhibitions, most notably the retrospective of Robert Rauschenberg in 1963 and that of Jasper Johns in 1964.

Ileana Sonnabend was very close to Solomon, even though she was in Paris while he was in New York. She feels that he taught her "moral courage."

> He came and said, "I have this opportunity for a year at The Jewish Museum. I know that after a year they are going to throw me out, but I want to do some things and I really don't care if they throw me out, so I'm going to do them." And I thought that was a very wonderful attitude. And when he came to Venice with so many of the American artists I had shown in Paris, I realized we really felt the same way about art. And there was a tremendous reaction against the "American imperialists taking over"—where were the humanist values? French people came to me saying I brought the Trojan Horse, crying because Rauschenberg had won the prize. And Alan said to me, "You should be more proud. You should say, 'Yes, I did that because it was worth doing.' " In Europe now I have a lot of friends. But I think at the beginning people didn't know what I was doing over there. They considered me like a little shopkeeper maybe. No, not a shopkeeper—yes, well, maybe a satellite.

It is perhaps with Alan Solomon's example in mind that, when asked how she wishes her contribution to be regarded, her answer is mainly one of responsibility to herself. She concentrates very hard before saying, "I think I want to be as true to myself as possible, and I'm ready to pay the price." Elsewhere she has said,

> I have a reputation for being outspoken. I'm supposed to be very difficult, which is not really true. But outspoken, yes. Sometimes I'm a little brutal: I had to learn how when I arrived in Paris, where women were still at a real disadvantage. It was not so easy to be a woman in the so-called business world. Many artists also thought they could maneuver women easily, so I had to be a little more blunt than I would perhaps otherwise have been. I was taken advantage of so many times by so many people that I developed a defense. It also had to do with being American; Americans are supposed to be naïve children to be taken advantage of. I was a target of all this. Today I am not bothered by what could be called "reputation," nor do I act in order to be loved. Instead I prefer to be appreciated for having acted in a certain way or done certain things. You also have a lot of enemies, but you simply bear with them. Luckily, I have kept good friends as well.[10]

In 1970 the Sonnabends opened a gallery in New York on Madison Avenue. Ileana recalls,

> I never really intended to stay in Paris. I always intended to come back. What happened was sixty-seven, sixty-eight were very difficult years in Paris because everybody was politicized, nobody was interested in art, young people didn't come to galleries. Collectors were very much afraid of spending money, and especially of tax people who were hounding them.
>
> I hated the uprisings. I was alone because Michael was in New York. We lived right next to Place Saint-Michel, and the apartment was full of tear gas all the time. It was very unpleasant. And that is really when I decided maybe it was time to go back home but I didn't want to leave altogether.

A very happily and proudly remembered moment in Paris, in 1973, was when Michel Guy, the minister of culture—"a wonderful man," in Ileana Sonnabend's words—gave her and the gallery director, Antonio Homem, carte blanche to do whatever they wished for a month in the Musée Galliéra in Paris. This included art, music, dance, video and film, and artists' performances. American artists included Robert Morris, Bruce Nauman, Robert Rauschenberg, Vito Acconci, and Mel Bochner, and among the Europeans were Kounellis, Poirier, Paolini, Becker, and Simone Forti. "Rauschenberg had a wonderful room, a whole environment." And there were concerts, of music and dance, by Philip Glass, Joan Jonas, Trisha Brown—"lots of good people" who were performing in Paris for the first time. This extraordinary celebration brought to Paris for a very brief season some of the excitement and optimism of the contemporary art scene which existed in New York. However, Antonio Homem remembers that the events were poorly attended and sometimes there were so few people on hand for concerts and performances that one had the sense of private, somewhat Medician, entertainments. He also recalls, good-naturedly, that many of those in Paris who envied the vitality of New York at the time and lamented the dearth of such avant-garde activity in Paris today claim a certain nostalgia for this brilliant episode despite their indifference then.

Michael Sonnabend had been running the New York gallery while Ileana remained in Paris with Antonio Homem. The intention was to show artists in New York who would be new to it—Europeans such as the Italian Arte Povera artists—Merz, Anselmo, Zorio, and Calzolari—and American artists from the West Coast—John McCracken and Robert Graham. And so the Sonnabends began the long business of building the New York gallery and in that process were as important in introducing current European art to America as they had been in presenting current American art in Europe the decade before.

> I show many Europeans today at my gallery in New York. Even before, I didn't think so much in terms of American art only; I never believed that art should have a nationality. I thought of the Americans as a group of people doing sensational work, work that had to be seen. Later, I began finding interesting artists in Europe and tried to arrange shows for them in New York. Again, I found the possibilities practically nonexistent. Nobody wanted to deal with European artists, young ones in particular. Paul Klee or Léger, that was a

different matter. It was upsetting to see such chauvinism on both sides.

Opening a gallery in New York was really the reverse of my Paris situation, partly because I wanted Europeans to be seen here, if they were good, but also because the center of gravity of the art world had shifted to New York.[11]

"Michael wanted a space in SoHo, and when the building at 420 West Broadway came up for sale he thought we should buy in," Ileana recalls. The Sonnabend Gallery there opened in 1971 with a show of drawings by the English artists Gilbert and George, who performed their "Singing Sculpture" for the length of the exhibition. The Sonnabends still had their lease on the uptown gallery, and as the center of activity was shifting to SoHo, Ileana decided to use the uptown gallery for exhibitions of Art Deco furniture and objects of the twenties and thirties, which she had been collecting privately for some years.

I had a liking from the start for the outlandish. When I go to Paris, I still have to see what they have. Since these things were not really well known here, we thought it would be interesting to do a series of shows focusing on the designers of the period, and so there were exhibitions, one-man shows, of Ruhlmann furniture, Lalique glass, and silver by Jean Puiforcat. We had some wonderful shows then, I must say. Did we sell? Too much! We thought we were expensive, but we found out soon after that you couldn't buy at the price we were selling. At that point we stopped. We have some things left. I do live with some of them, and it's a great pleasure, and I'm sorry not to have a big enough apartment. At the same time, we became interested in photographs and had shows, mostly of that period, including August Sander, Cecil Beaton, Horst, and Hoyningen-Huene. It worked well and people were very interested.

Art for Ileana Sonnabend is heroic, and ideally she would represent only artists who engage her on that level. She clearly has a predilection for the theatrical and mysterious, and for "things . . . that make me look for their meaning."[12] And if, as a dealer, she feels she contributed to the heroic enterprise of making art by bringing works to public attention, she also feels a responsibility which goes deeper than her commercial concerns.

How can I say this without sounding too arrogant—there are dealers and there are dealers. We respect people who have commitment, and the rest are shopkeepers, which is all right too. I don't have models. But I do respect a lot of people. I greatly admired Curt Valentin, and he was very important to me. I admired his commitment, his marvelous commitment, and he had wonderful shows, beautiful things really. What I liked in him was that he would talk to everybody and explain everything. He had so much enthusiasm and he would take the time, although he was very busy.

In answer to the skepticism with which dealers' collections are sometimes viewed—that they comprise works that couldn't be sold and that are still for sale—Ileana Sonnabend's reply is that often she finds that the most interesting things are not sold because they are more difficult, and those are the things which have interested her most. She is acquisitive, quick to buy the work of an artist she believes in, and sometimes she finds herself in conflict with her clients, as in the case of a painter she currently represents and finds very exciting, Terry Winters. "It's very difficult for me to keep anything because there is such a demand. I finally got a painting, and then two or three days after I bought it I got a letter from a museum that they wanted that painting and wouldn't I sell it to them, though they understood that it was in my collection. In such a case, I really would be competing with the collectors and museums, and I try not to do that. But this artist will do many more wonderful things, and I try to wait until everybody is satisfied."

"We sell everything," Ileana Sonnabend says when asked if she still has the Matisse watercolor she was given on her honeymoon. Once Dr. Peter Ludwig, the great German collector of American art, came to the Sonnabend Gallery; when he asked the price of a work, he was told by Mrs. Sonnabend that it was not for sale. He countered that everything was for sale if the price was right, even her bed. And she, in turn, had to agree, but that he would have an easier time buying her bed.

NOTES

1. Unless otherwise indicated, statements by Ileana Sonnabend are from conversations with Allen Rosenbaum, which took place in New York in October 1984.
2. Quoted by Calvin Tomkins, "Profiles: Leo Castelli," *The New Yorker*, 56 (May 26, 1980).
3. Ibid.
4. Ibid.
5. Calvin Tomkins, *Off the Wall: Robert Rauschenberg and the Art World of Our Time* (New York: Penguin Books, 1981), p. 140.
6. Ibid., pp. 141–42.
7. Quoted in David Whitney, ed., *Leo Castelli: Ten Years* (1967).
8. Quoted in Laura de Coppet and Alan Jones, eds., *The Art Dealers* (New York: Clarkson N. Potter, 1984), p. 114.
9. Otto Hahn, quoted in *Leo Castelli: Ten Years*.
10. *The Art Dealers*, pp. 116–17.
11. Ibid., p. 114.
12. Ibid., p. 116.

Ileana and Michael Sonnabend

by Robert Pincus-Witten

For the greater part of the last half century the Sonnabends and the Castellis—families once linked by marriage, now by friendship—have fascinated the art world as well as me personally. Intensely private people and never selfish, they share an elegant liberality, and the *sprezzatura* cherished by Castiglione as part of his courtly ideal. Publicity and the confessional note are anathema to them, and they despise vulgarity—except as it exists undaunted in unself-conscious art. Through their efforts, the history of contemporary art has been enlarged immeasurably. Much has been written about Leo Castelli, and much about Ileana Sonnabend; of Michael, by contrast, scant detail, though this gentle and impish scholar and filmmaker has been a loved member of the art world for decades. This exhibition, of works selected from the broad spectrum of the Sonnabend collection, offers an opportunity to clarify the importance of the role played by the Sonnabends in the development of contemporary art.

Early Ileana—as a time frame, that is—corresponds to the opulence and privilege of the period between the two world wars; she was born to provincial luxury and the platinum spoon, but her world was also marked by domestic repression and the massing clouds of anti-Semitism.

During the 1920s and 1930s Ileana was the ideal woman of chic, a stylishness reaffirmed when she and Leo Castelli settled into a Neuilly flat, at the most fashionable edge of Paris. She came to know the Surrealists and the displaced Constructivists, as Leo and René Drouin, the architect-designer, opened a first gallery on the Place Vendôme, in the spring of 1939. Bad timing. The occupation of France was but a few months off.

Then war, flight, displacement, but finally a rooting in a far from alien soil. This period was marked by Leo's absence (on assignment for the United States Army Intelligence Branch), motherhood, and studies in psychology at Columbia University, where she met Michael Sonnabend. With the postwar period came Ileana's absorption into the Abstract Expressionist group, with its high increment of Surrealist and Constructivist values, and its world of artists, galleries, dealers, critics, enthusiasts, and backbiting.

Ileana remained through all of this a dutiful helpmeet, as the Castelli lives altered bit by bit, through the 1950s, first across private and then public art dealing. All the lights, lesser and greater, merged with theirs: Lee Krasner and Jackson Pollock, Elaine and Willem de Kooning, Annalee and Barnett Newman (to this day I believe that Annalee Newman remains Ileana's closest friend of that generation), as well as artists whose rank has shifted since the 1950s.

The period was also marked by divorce, Ileana's remarriage, to Michael Sonnabend—and Leo's marriage to Antoinette ("Toiny") Fraissex du Bost—and from 1961 on the inauguration of the sequence of Sonnabend galleries: in Paris, then Paris/New York, last just New York, with the express aim of promoting the new American art values in a Europe mired in early modernist pieties.

In terms of stylistics—that is, the essential core of art—Abstract Expressionism had been superseded by Pop Art, and during the height of the movement, about 1962–64, Ileana came to be dubbed the Mom of Pop, an epithet that still causes her to wince. By now the names of Ileana's artists have become household words—Johns, Rauschenberg, Twombly, Warhol, Lichtenstein, Oldenburg, Rosenquist, and others. In a certain sense, the 1960s represent Ileana's coming of age as a resolutely autonomous force. I see the ever-mounting prestige of the Sonnabend Gallery as representing the definitive break with the imperturbably solemn piousness of Abstract Expressionism.

Naturally all these great art dealers, Ileana, Michael, and Leo, are extremely sensitive to shifts in taste; they have the coltish flair of thoroughbreds, rapidly sniffing at the winds of fashion—but their galloping legs fall firmly to earth. Ileana especially possesses a dedicated irresilience about certain artists once she has come around to their work. At moments I have been critically doubtful. Why, Ileana, do you continue to show so and so or such and such, when you know that your experience has been . . . She smiles inscrutably. She sees something, is committed to something, that eludes me—and which in the end may elude description. But she also knows that someday soon I too will see it.

Having been given the chance to record stray impressions of Leo Castelli to honor his twenty-fifth year in business as well as his seventy-fifth birthday (in *Gentle Snap Shots*, Zurich, 1982), I was delighted when Professor Sam Hunter asked whether I would contribute similar impressions of Ileana and Michael Sonnabend, for this occasion of the exhibition of selected works from their private collection. But a warning: what I find fascinating about the Sonnabends may strike some readers as being curiously inappropriate for a catalogue addressing the art historical milieu of the 1950s and 1960s. The minutiae that captivate me concern private and early formation. What is compelling, I think, is the tragedy of the generation of great European cosmopolitanism, dislocated by the First World War and incinerated in the Second. As survivors, Ileana, Michael, and Leo have a sense of tragedy that has become so internalized by now that, in a Beaumarchais-like way, their poignant experience of the world makes them laugh lest they weep. What strikes me is the vivacity and excitement of their shared memories, revealed to me from, as it were, that last beautiful springtime before the failure of Europe in 1914–18 and its reduction to ash in 1939–45. An irony is that, though for me the Sonnabends and the Castellis are madly European, their real achievement has been the creation of the quintessential American modernist position.

A second warning: since my notes are journal excerpts, the occasional burr in my epistolary tone is more likely mine than that of my subjects. What is absent from my record is their irradiating modesty, kindness, and humor.

8 March 1980

In a rare aphoristic mood, Ileana says: "Peggy Guggenheim has been an enormous literary influence on me. After reading her memoirs, I was more convinced than ever not to write mine." Of course, Ileana is often morbidly shy, a feature of her character she at times turns to advantage—when wishing, for example, to avoid harsh confrontations. Then, too, Ileana is rarely confidential and only in terms of the briefest passing comment. Her conversation consists mostly in listening. She loves to listen. She never advises or gives opinions. But if one listens carefully to her, a stray detail is sometimes revealed as if by accident. She seems to say without saying.

17 May 1972

Dinner last night with Ileana, Antonio Homem (Ileana's Paris director), Ealan Wingate (gallery director here in New York); Mel Bochner and Dorothea Rockburne showed up at Rocco's, in the Village. Eventually Ileana warmed to the conversation. What were her happiest moments, I asked. Her greatest insight into people? Her moments of triumph? What does she regard as the cardinal human quality? Those kinds of questions.

So far as I can make out, Ileana was born in Rumania at the beginning of the First World War to a liberal-minded, Jewish industrialist family, the Schapiras: Mihail, her father, and Marianne, her mother.

Ileana converses quietly in a haunting, fluty speech. She is humorous, oblique, bemused, essentially an aesthete, a creature of senses and impulse. The point is the good living of life, not the shoring up of wealth. Though she has never been poor, money is but a means to pleasure, and the art world is the most pleasurable world she knows.

She speaks often of and with affection for Leo and is unwavering in her admiration for his sense of justice. "But, do not for a moment think it was Leo who left me," she confides—a reflection that veers to memories of her wealthy, tyrannical father.

He, even as a refugee in New York City, owned an apartment on Fifth Avenue overlooking the park, as well as the marble townhouse at 4 East 77th Street, where she, Leo, and Nina settled when they arrived here in March 1941 (this apartment became the original seat of the expanding network of Castelli galleries).

Ileana's childhood memories are marked by a consciousness of her being small—her nickname was Mausi—and of being in competition with her sister, Eve—issues less significant in memory than her rejection by school companions because of her family's Jewishness. She also has an amusing memory of her betraying an elderly nanny, whom she falsely denounced to her father as the culprit who spilled ink on the carpet, as if he could not have guessed.

She remembers herself in young womanhood as stylish, foolish, snobbish, and heartless, though I take the last three adjectives to be flirtatious exaggerations. In 1942, she began to study psychology at Columbia University. There she met Michael Sonnabend, who was working toward a Master's degree in the art department. Ileana never completed her degree, nor did Michael. Neither did Leo, who was at Columbia University at the beginning of the Second World War doing graduate work in economic history. Now she regards herself as wholly unpsychological.

She met Robert Rauschenberg in 1951 during the Ninth Street Show curated by Leo. During the hanging, Rauschenberg arrived with the artist Susan Weil, then his wife. He struck Ileana as the handsomest man she had ever seen. "Who is that prince?" she asked of Leo. Her relationship with Rauschenberg is highly important. She clearly loves him with a deep affection that has lasted these past thirty years. The candy Lifesaver cast in sculpmetal which she wears around her neck every day as a talisman is perhaps the charm and emblem of their relationship. Rauschenberg gave it to her at the time that Ileana left Leo. I've seen her panic when this token is misplaced.

Some of her happiest moments were passed in the summer of 1952 in the Hamptons, when she and Leo were sharing their house with her mother and John Graham, and Bill and Elaine de Kooning. Jackson Pollock, whom they saw often, is in memory the most charismatic artist for her. She recalls a moment of great terror, like that occasioned by her flight from the Nazis, that took place when, during a party, Pollock strode purposefully into the Atlantic, in an apparent suicide attempt. Ileana returned to ease only when the Abstract Expressionist group present at the scene was able to drag him back to shore and calm him.

3 March 1984

Last night a sumptuous *menu gastronomique* at La Chanterelle. The service moved ceremoniously, but over coffee Ileana suddenly warmed to memory and spoke of East Hampton, of Jackson Pollock, whom she loved, of Willem de Kooning, whom she loved less—putting in a good word for the pluck of Elaine de Kooning, who managed well in a taxing personal situation.

Of The Club, the social center of the Abstract Expressionists, she remembers that she frequently arrived early to clean up the previous week's mess. That's hard to imagine, Ileana sweeping and washing up. She said that the critics and artists were always angry with Robert Motherwell, because he was consistently more knowledgeable than they. Leaving herself out—"I was mute at the time"—she remembered that Motherwell, Matta, and Leo formed a kind of clique. "They were accused of being 'Frenchified.' " The reference to Matta and Surrealism led Antonio Homem aptly to dub the movement transposed to America as "Ballet Surrealism."

16 March 1984

Wonderful lunch with Leo, Ileana, Antonio Homem, and David Salle. Nominally the latter was there because his show was being installed at Leo's but really because he wanted to hear for himself what happens when we all get together. And this time, David had quite a nostalgic earful, as Leo and Ileana have never waxed quite so retrospectively before, in a sentimental frame of mind doubly inspired by the glasses of wine Leo had drunk prior to our tardy arrival.

The recollections were sparked by a reference to Count Ciano, Mussolini's foreign ambassador, who is alluded to in an essay on de Chirico I have been working on. "What was his first name?" I asked. At length Antonio came up with the right answer—Galeazzo—but, by that time, the others were well into souvenirs of Vienna, Budapest, and Trieste.

Leo fixed on the subject of nannies. Frances Grundy, Nina's nanny, had arrived in Vienna a week after Nina was born, fresh from the Nordland Institute in London, as *pimpante* and starched as ever a nanny was. Still alive, Frances lives in Washington, where she continues to look after children. She had called Leo the day before to remind him that it was on March 12, 1941, that they had all arrived in New York together, forty-three years ago now, with snow on the ground. Leo was then thirty-four. So you see how it went.

Leo's own nanny, in Trieste, was a certain Maria Sanolini Friuli. True, I had my Gudrun; but Ileana's list was topping: Mlle. Pédusseau, Mlle. Prual, Mlle. Chidiac, and a certain Jeanette Echevary, who had an affair with her father's brother, uncle Leo. And did Ileana say that Mlle. Prual had been the mistress of Emile Faguet, the *boulevardier* critic? Another nanny was called "Irma the Mandolinista," who it seems introduced Ileana's cousin Richard to the erotic mysteries, while the children attempted to peer through the frosted nursery windows. Mausi, being smallest, could not even catch a glimpse, but knew it was wonderful whatever it was.

5 January 1977

With Ileana, Antonio, and Ealan for a late supper at the Russian Tea Room. I was talking of my mother and of the sadness of the music-hall turn I had seen in a theater with her. Ileana rose to the bait, if bait it was, and she suddenly began to talk of her parents, her father, her sister, Eve.

Her mother was an ardent Zionist. Ileana always felt defeated by her sister, since she felt Eve was "beautiful" and she not. Utterly untrue. Eve was surrounded by beaux, Leo one of them. Did not Leo's subsequent attentions convince Ileana of her own beauty? "No, not really." She always felt bested, won out.

The mystique of parental perfection burst for Ileana when it dawned on her that her father had affairs with the governesses. Her parents divorced here in New York, Marianne subsequently marrying the great painter John Graham. Both parents are now dead, her father dying shortly after her mother, not paradoxically of a broken heart. At the time of their divorce, he realized that after all he had loved her best and suddenly missed her in an anguished and terrible way.

14 January 1977

I had forgotten the most arresting detail of Ileana's recollections: "I met Leo. He was not like the others. He was on the move. He was going to get out of Rumania and I was going to get out too, so I married him." I know Ileana not to be ruthless but, as things boil down to memories, they lend themselves to simple ruthless phrases.

12 November 1976

Always poor, Michael Sonnabend worked his way over to France after World War I, arriving with only a few dollars in his pocket. At the station he asked the porter, an émigré Russian, *un bleu* named Lebedeff, with thin hair combed sidewise over a bald head, where the "Y" in Paris was. The luggage carrier led him there. But the "Y" in Paris was at the time, and still may be for all I know, only a business office, not a dormitory. Perplexed as to what the next step would be, Michael ended up boarding with the porter's family.

By degrees Michael fell in with the acquaintances of this post-revolutionary expatriate. He was fascinated by the intellectual hobos among the Russian's circle of acquaintances. Chief among them was a certain Thouvenin, a chauffeur, an ordinary taxi driver, whose claim to celebrity was that he personally knew Bibi la Purée. And who was this celebrated Bibi? Why, Verlaine's bootblack! He had once even shined the shoes of Oscar Wilde. With these voluble hangers-on, Michael would walk along the Seine down to the Marne, walking and talking all night. When Michael began to make "big money" through the arranging of tours for Americans in the 1920s and 1930s, returning to Europe to visit battle and grave sites, he always remembered the taxi driver by hiring him as chauffeur for the tourist cars (Thouvenin fell to his knees exclaiming, "There is a God!").

Ironically, at the early moment in Paris when Michael was just eluding a borderline misery, Ileana (then unknown to him) would visit Neuilly, her parents having rented some *grand résidence* for the family and the retinue of governesses and maids. Michael at that time had moved on to the Quartier Latin. Until he had a few sous in his pocket, he slept at a student hostel, not as a proper lodger but as a stowaway in the washroom. After the concierge locked up at night, he would emerge from the *cabinet* to sleep on chairs. Because he had so little money, Michael spent his first day in the Queen City not daring to leave the métro and traveling from station to station. At the subway platforms, he would exclaim: "So this is the Opéra!" "So this is the Place de la Concorde!"

Michael's saddest story. Immediately following Dylan Thomas's death, a memorial reading of work by the poet was scheduled at Columbia University. Walking hurriedly to the service, Michael passed a Babbitty Rotarian dropping off a pimply youth at Columbia's Hamilton Hall—a plain father leaving an indifferent son at the sill of the university to Begin Life. Twenty paces past them, Michael began to cry. The point of the story is clear: some poignant pervading sense that Michael's life had come to naught because no father had been interested in giving him purpose or vocation. This reading is false; I know scarcely any person who has made such a success of sheer living.

7 November 1976

There is a reference I want to embroider—Michael's being a perpetual student. Doubtless many people who have seen Michael scribbling notes into tiny notebooks have wondered what these *carnets* might contain. Well, yes, they are the notes of a transient day—filled with the concerns of an international art market—the do, call, fix, get, the names, numbers, collections, prices, locations of things to do. We all have our radiating network of responsibilities—we all make such lists. But what is interpolated in these *aides-mémoire*? The answer is poetry and, in a way, one poet's poetry, Dante's. There is no line in Dante, no allusion, no rhyme that is not meaningful to Michael. That he should feel so greatly the deprivation of formal education is ironic, like some vast universal joke, so deep is Michael's learning. Michael has conquered foreign languages to colloquialism (though his Buffalo inflection can still be detected in his speech), and foreign history, and foreign culture.

29 January 1977

In Michael's pocket are folded yellow sheets covered with scrawl. I ask what the notations are. "Oh, I am translating Michelangelo's sonnets."

19 February 1982

We talked about Dante, and Michael quite astounded me. He'd just finished translating the *Purgatorio*, his favorite above either *Inferno* or *Paradiso*. "Not a poetical translation. I could never do that. I could never imitate the complex rhythmic structures in English. But a commonsensical translation for the viewers of 'Donahue.' Just a good simple translation. It's not even pretty. If it's ever published it should read 'lighting by Sonnabend.' That's it, translated the way a play is lit."

Michael, well in his eighties now, delights me with long quotations from Dante cited in Italian. He then renders each passage into English. His preferred passage occurs when Dante explains what poetry is, an explanation that Michael sees as the source of Wordsworth's emotion recollected in tranquillity. He thinks it's from the Circle of Gluttony, canto 24, where Dante first discovers the *dolce stil nuovo*.

I asked him of whom in the *Purgatorio* Ileana reminds him. As Pia in canto 5, who is at first modestly concerned about Dante the poet, instead of immediately going on about her sins. "When you return from your long journey and are rested . . ." she says. It is Pia's concern for Dante that identifies her in Michael's mind with Ileana. And then he quoted the famous terzet "*Siena mi fe'; disfecemi Maremma*," the one about the evil husband, who, suspecting his gentlewoman of adultery, exposes her to the noxious vapors of the swamp, the maremma. When she does not succumb to the fumes, he tosses her from the tower window.

Paradiso, Michael feels, is too abstract, too exquisite. He cannot quite grasp a mentality that discriminates among thirty-six kinds of light. All this is reported with his characteristic animation, teeth clicking in his gray stubbled jaw. The leprechaun is a Dantephile.

The Sixties: A Revolution in Art

by Sam Hunter

In a fast-breaking sequence of artistic developments at the end of the fifties and in the early sixties, the Abstract Expressionists, who had worked passionately to overcome public antagonism to avant-garde art, found their rising star eclipsed by a group of vanguard upstarts. Artistic styles rooted in popular imagery and blatantly subservient, as it seemed, to commercial models suddenly emerged to defy both the elevated ideals and the abstract styles that identified Abstract Expressionism.

The fruits of a widening public acceptance clearly promised by the triumphal European tour of the Museum of Modern Art exhibition of Abstract Expressionist work in 1958, organized by Dorothy Miller and Alfred H. Barr, Jr. and called "The New American Painting," had hardly been tasted when the old avant-garde's preeminence was sharply challenged. First came the remarkable success of Robert Rauschenberg and Jasper Johns in the late fifties, followed by the eruption of Pop Art in a series of controversial, if publicly appreciated, group and personal exhibitions beginning in 1962.[1]

The same years introduced Frank Stella's seemingly mechanized and immaculately fashioned black-stripe paintings, innovations that signaled an equally threatening and critical shift away from Abstract Expressionist philosophical values and pictorial methods in the realm of abstraction. Robert Rosenblum, a sympathetic and discerning critic of the contemporary avant-garde as well as a distinguished art historian, has vividly evoked the heady sense of emancipation these abrupt changes brought to his generation, in a recent reminiscence:

> For me and many of my contemporaries, Rauschenberg, Johns, Stella swiftly became the Holy Trinity that led us from the Old Testament to the New, liberating us from the burden of living under the oppressive yoke of the coarse and sweaty rhetoric of Action Painting, whose supreme deity, de Kooning, suddenly loomed large for many younger spectators and artists as a conservative force, a tyrant of past authority who demanded the instant embalming of any youthful, liberated spirit. Loving most of de Kooning's work as I do today, in 1984, I am still puzzled to recall how antagonistic I felt about it in the late 1950s, a tribute, I guess, to the overwhelming grandeur it had achieved as a suffocating father-image. And I recall that even when, as an Oedipal challenge, Rauschenberg in 1953 erased a de Kooning drawing or presumably destroyed in 1957 the parental image of spontaneity by almost exactly replicating *Factum I* with *Factum II*, he still seemed not to have exorcised that demon, whose heart could only be stopped, so it then seemed, with a stake driven by Johns' flags and Stella's stripes.[2]

By the early sixties the prevailing angst[3] and the ego-centered Sturm und Drang that marked the work of the older generation had begun to diminish. As new artists made their way more easily, thanks in large measure to the efforts of the Abstract Expressionists to overcome public mistrust, artistic values shifted from the drama of the "act" of painting to an interest in exploring the social and physical environment of objects and popular culture.[4] Moreover, the younger artists were less affected than the Abstract Expressionists by the heroic and militant moods arising from the experience of the Depression and the war years, which had conditioned the Abstract Expressionist outlook, both aesthetically and politically. Rauschenberg, for one, found it impossible to work within the older framework of expressionistic struggle and torment, partially in response to his own, more objective, artistic apprenticeship at Black Mountain College in the fifties under Josef Albers, who had announced, "Angst is dead."[5]

A new attitude of even-handedness, or indifference to competing political ideologies, became the rule in avant-garde circles. The rejection of Abstract Expressionist militancy and social alienation was expressed by Allan Kaprow, the primary inventor of Happenings and one of the first artists to see Pollock's paintings in environmental and materialistic terms rather than interpreting them as antisocial gestures directed at an uncomprehending middle class. Kaprow wrote:

> The modern artist is apolitical, like some predecessors, but he does not have their anxiety of ideological betrayals, so typical of the 1940s. International affairs lack essential issues; in practice Communism and Capitalism look alike.[6]

In their two major manifestations, and polarities—abstraction of a more objective, formalist character and an art of popular imagery—the dominant styles of the sixties reflected a matter-of-fact and detached view of the artistic object and process. Harold Rosenberg, a champion of engagé and committed Action Painting, rooted in Existential self-definition, noted the shifting climate of ideas:

> Instead of being . . . an act of rebellion, despair or self-indulgence on the fringe of society, art is being normalized as a professional activity within society.[7]

Although Rauschenberg, Johns, and the succeeding Pop artists, in particular, were taken to task for supporting, with their presumably imitative forms and commercial icons, the shallow and predatory values of a rampantly consumerist society, they by no means identified with bland and settled middle-class values. In the early fifties, Rauschenberg and other young artists in music, dance, and theater as well as the plastic arts turned to the iconoclastic spirit of Duchamp in order to free themselves from the oppressive influences of the recent past. For painters that meant Abstract Expressionism, which, through increasingly academic and mannered painterliness at the time, began to seem irrelevant and unauthentic. Particularly through the reintroduction of objects into works of art, whose presence ironically posed the art/life paradox, the younger artists returned external "reality" to art. The rebellion occurred separately but virtually simultaneously in Paris and New York: under the aegis of "New Realism" in Paris—the rubric invented by Pierre Restany, a critic for the Paris group—and in the form of the "combine" paintings begun by Rauschenberg in New York about 1953. Restany explained the aims of the Paris group as "quantitative instead of qualitative expression, [with] respect for the intrinsic logic of the materials it employs."[8] In another characterization he wrote:

> What they offer us is an entire aspect of the real, captured in its objective integrity, without transcription of any sort. Never, at any moment, is it a question of re-creation, but on the contrary of an expressive transmutation.[9]

Prominent among the members of this group were Yves Klein, Tinguely, Arman, and Spoerri. In 1958, Christo arrived in Paris and met Restany and members of the New Realists, but his association, he has averred in conversation with the author, was "marginal and brief," although he exhibited with them twice, in 1962 and 1963. It was probably through the New Realists, however, that Christo came to his first, primitive use of found objects and then to wrapping objects, so reminiscent of Man Ray's celebrated photograph of a wrapped sewing machine, *The Enigma of Isidore Ducasse*, 1920.

In New York the first public manifestation of the exhaustion of Abstract Expressionism as a collective impulse was the appearance of a more inclusive environmental art, beginning in the mid-fifties, which took into account the impact of popular culture, and mass-produced objects and their discarded fragments. The new critical, aesthetic, and philosophical issues raised in consequence were summarized and brilliantly focused by the important exhibition organized in 1961 for The Museum of Modern Art by William Seitz called "The Art of Assemblage." In the catalogue Seitz declared:

> The current wave of assemblage . . . marks a change from a subjective, fluidly abstract art towards a revised association with environment. The method of juxtaposition is an appropriate vehicle for feelings of disenchantment with the slick international idiom that loosely articulated abstraction has tended to become, and the social values that this situation reflects.[10]

And Allan Kaprow, in a manuscript of 1960, prophesied the power of the randomness and vitality of the great modern city, with its refuse-filled streets, to condition the art of our time, when he advocated ". . . a quite clear-headed decision to abandon craftsmanship and permanence" and then recommended "the use of obviously perishable media such as newspaper, string, adhesive tape, growing grass or real food," so that "no one can mistake the fact that the work will pass into dust or garbage quickly."[11]

By associating his recommended mode of artistic assimilation of refuse from the urban junk heap with the humbler expressions of historical art, Kaprow raised once again the critical issue of art and anti-art which had been so central to Dada:

> The eternal problem of what may be (or become) art and what may not. The intellectual's typical disdain for popular culture, for the objects and debris of mass production, is as always a clear instance of aesthetic discrimination: *this* is fit for art; *that* is not. Such high-mindedness is not at all different from the seventeenth century's belief in the greater value of "noble" themes over genre ones.[12]

The artist who deserves priority in a discussion of American assemblage art is Robert Rauschenberg, for, with his creative energies and artistic innovations, he probably did more to transform the character and practice of American art in the fifties than any other single figure. Rauschenberg had encountered John Cage and joined his circle in his student days at Black Mountain College. He most probably would have warmly seconded Allan Kaprow's later reaction to Cage's instruction, when Kaprow attended the composer's seminars at The New School for Social Research in New York in the late fifties:

> The best thing that happened to us in Cage's class was the sense he gave that "anything goes," at least potentially . . . . The main thing was the realization of possibilities.[13]

Rauschenberg contributed a slide show and hung his paintings in the "concerted action" which Cage performed with the help of Merce Cunningham, David Tudor, and Charles Olsen at Black Mountain in 1952, an early attempt at theatrical synthesis of the arts which was arguably the major prototype for the Happenings invented by Kaprow, Oldenburg, Dine, and others in the sixties. These informally staged events dramatically broke down historical genres in art and the barriers between art and life, making possible, among other things, the introduction of objects, emblems, and content from popular culture in painting and sculpture. George Segal, who also attended some of Cage's New School lectures, ranked the composer with Picasso and Duchamp as the artist "most basically responsible for the new permission in the air to incorporate non-art materials into art."[14] And in a letter written by Rauschenberg to Betty Parsons at the time he was collaborating in Cage's staged musical event, the young artist described his paintings made at Black Mountain College that summer as non-art, "because they take you to a place in painting art has not been." Then, in environmental terms reminiscent of Cage's aesthetic, he denied that he was their artist. "Today," he wrote, "is their creator."[15] In their different ways, his truly remarkable "combine" constructions *Dylaby*, *Magician II*, and *Hymnal* blatantly use nontraditional materials and object fragments to call into question the hierarchy of distinctions between the fine arts and waste drawn from the urban refuse heap. Rauschenberg skillfully submerges these alien materials in his spontaneous, gestural painting passages, so reminiscent of de Kooning, and yet allows them to remain identifiable. At the same time, the materials and derelict objects (note especially the decorative molding in *Interior*, with its somewhat precious Victorian associations) can be overtly nostalgic, even while they allude to the cycle of the object's life from manufacture and function to decay and waste. Rauschenberg's combines, indeed, can be legitimately understood on one level as a commentary on a culture where planned obsolescence, as many have observed, is not only an economic catch phrase but a state of mind.

Rauschenberg's perhaps best-known statement, an obvious allusion to the Dadaists' determination to efface the boundaries between an artifact and its source, is this:

> Painting relates to both art and life. Neither can be made. I try to act in the gap between the two.[16]

If Rauschenberg bridged the "gap" between art and life, Jasper Johns, with whom he was closely associated from 1955, mined the rich ambiguities and intellectual resonance of that no man's land between image and idea, concept and representation. Johns made far-reaching innovations in the art of his time with his painting series of flags and targets, first exhibited in 1957, and the subsequent maps, numbers, rule and circle devices, and other motifs. Together they created radical new forms and options of representation for American art by questioning past assumptions about the nature of representation.

In his first small *Flag*, 1954–55, Johns transformed the familiar stars-and-stripes image into an abstract painterly device on a thickly pigmented field of off-white, an overall configuration inevitably suggesting relationships both to Rothko's stark and impassive frontality, and to the layered brushstrokes of de Kooning and Guston. Operating in a new way, as an abstract visual sign divorced from its functional meanings, the flag provoked confounding questions: was it an object or a painting or both? With such ambiguities Johns managed to combine representation and abstraction in a fresh synthesis—a problem which de Kooning, Pollock, and the other Abstract Expressionists could not satisfactorily resolve.

Johns is also an exquisite and expressive draftsman, and his two more considered drawings in this exhibition have a special status as independent works of art, although they also prefigure or amplify motifs found in his paintings. The tiny *Flag* drawing in pencil of 1954 was made after the painting in the exhibition. Even in an expressive form as reductive and formally rigorous as *Flag*, Johns has taken pains to restore to illusion its traditional prerogatives. Despite the tangled and cumulative overlays of graphic marks, which seem to simulate Abstract Expressionist brushwork in another modality, he never quite obliterates the flag image. In typically Johnsian fashion, however, the issue is left suspended in a poetic state: we can never be certain which meaning presides more decisively—the purely abstract articulation of form or the literal presence of the faintly discernible stars and stripes.

Pop Art made its dramatic, public debut in 1962 with a number of individual and group shows of work by Roy Lichtenstein, Claes Oldenburg, James Rosenquist, Andy Warhol, Tom Wesselmann, and Robert Indiana. Warhol had his first one-man show that year at the Ferus Gallery in Los Angeles; Oldenburg and Rosenquist held their first one-man exhibitions at the Green Gallery, New York, and Jim Dine showed at the Martha Jackson Gallery, also in New York. In November of 1962 most of these artists and the European New Realists and emerging Pop artists were represented in the then controversial exhibition entitled "The New Realists," which was held at the Sidney Janis Gallery, New York. The term "Pop Art," coined by the critic Lawrence Alloway in 1958—in a somewhat different, British context—became *de rigeur*, supplanting such earlier descriptive tentatives as Common Object Art[17] or Anti-Sensibility Painting,[18] which represented the first efforts to come to terms with the radical shift in imagery, technique, and cultural attitudes. The reaction to these early shows was stunning, especially in the Abstract Expressionist group.

An offending shock was experienced by many established artists and almost all their sympathetic critics, confronted by an apparently vulgar, vernacular imagery, which seemed scarcely transformed from its sources—newspaper comic strips, billboards, commercial brand symbols. Some common ground with New Realism and assemblage, with their derelict object fragments and mediating paint passages, had seemed possible. But the bright commercial accents, banal subject matter, and seemingly slavish imitations of the products of a consumer society clearly alienated the defenders of high art and the older avant-garde, and no compromise in values could be contemplated. The rather astonishing emergence, however, of a number of strongly defined and individualistic personalities among the Pop artists, and their similar pattern of development, soon made it impossible to ignore this remakable movement or to view it merely as a passing fad or as entertainment.

With his impartial and almost offhand visual reportage of violent public events, supermarket counter imagery, gruesome scenes of highway carnage, and blandly rendered movie stars, Andy Warhol came to signify exactly the kinds of compromise with the pervasive mass media, and an apparent indifference to the values of high art, that could be counted on to wound the Abstract Expressionists most deeply. Warhol cavalierly breached the limits of the outrageous and the perverse in a 1963 interview with G. R. Swenson, when he responded to a series of sober questions with a kind of ghoulish, mock seriousness and advocated totalitarian conformism and regimentation as an artistic strategy:

> "Someone said that Brecht wanted everybody to think alike. I want everybody to think alike. But Brecht wanted to do it through Communism, in a way. Russia is doing it under government. It is happening here all by itself without being under a strict government; so if it is working without trying, why can't it work without being Communist? Everybody looks alike and acts alike, and we're getting more and more that way.
>
> "I think everybody should be a machine.
>
> "I think everybody should like everybody."
>
> *Is that what Pop Art is all about?*
>
> "Yes. It's liking things."
>
> *And liking things is like being a machine?*
>
> "Yes, because you do the same thing every time. You do it over and over again."[19]

As a commercial artist in the fifties, Warhol had worked for I. Miller Shoes, perfecting his impersonal and naïve style of draftsmanship. A later variant, turned to a different cultural purpose, was embodied in his Maybelline drawing, an advertisement parody with Hedy Lamarr's visage. A rare pre-Pop icon, it anticipates his obsessive Marilyn image of the early sixties. Beginning with experimental monotypes in the late fifties, Warhol gradually came to favor silkscreen technique (a strategy Rauschenberg only later adopted), which aptly expressed his growing preoccupation with a machine-like and depersonalized reproduction process.

Warhol's *Four Marilyns* is a mature and characteristic Pop expression, offering the viewer a repeated, modulated icon of a profane subject, floating on an ethereal, multicolored ground. The gravity of the central image seems to arrest the transience of a once topical but now nostalgic subject, and evokes the brief and touching cycle of fame and notoriety of the Hollywood celebrity. Warhol's approach to contemporary imagery was to use his canvas, much as he did film, as a random and continuous medium. An important part of his subject matter was the reproduction process itself. The coarse scrim of silkscreened halftone dots gave his images a visual roughness (they often seemed "printed" out of color register) that identified them as crude media products. Since Warhol's presentation is straightforward, and even literal, the viewer is thrown back onto the surface marks, blotchy paint, and imperfect color registration, which enliven and artistically assimilate the banal or disturbing subject matter.

Roy Lichtenstein also focused the viewer's attention on medium and artistic process, despite his deliberately vernacular and cartoon-inspired style, by overstating his hand-painted Ben Day screen dot simulations. This strategy played a conspicuously formal role in establishing composition and design, and distracted attention from a banal subject matter. Thus, even in such classic images as the dramatic *Eddie Diptych*, inspired by comic books, or *Non-Objective II*, with its allusion to high art, the subjects are not so much cartoons or Mondrian's abstract art as the commercial or artistic styles in which these images have been made known to a mass audience through mechanical reproduction. (Walter Benjamin had predicted the profound impact on the values of high art of the ubiquitous mechanical reproduction some decades earlier.)

Lichtenstein's meanings expand beyond the actual scenarios of his selected comics (romance and action, especially), his visual quotations from a particular, admired modernist pioneer, or even the implications of a populist reappraisal, as it were, of the inherent cultural and philosophical values of Abstract Expressionism. His stylistic references help us to reconstitute, in valid contemporary terms, albeit screened by the powerful if crude fictions of the mass media, the kind of artistic illusions and meanings, ranging from genre and historical epic to purist expression, that have constantly been reconfigured during the "modern" period in every decade. As Ellen Johnson noted in her recent valuable study, *Modern Art and the Object*, Lichtenstein's sometimes distracting mannerisms in his "comics" style, as an example, become significantly transformed, in scale, inflection, and presence, and finally say infinitely more than either their original sources or a critical or humorous gloss on their models:

> The total work is a powerful, commanding painting at least as far removed from the original comic as Seurat's paintings are from Cheret's posters.[20]

One should add that the "vintage" period look of many paintings in this exhibition of works from the Sonnabend collection, whatever their references—commercial icon, romance comic fiction, or the non-objective styles of high art—also has a remarkable ancillary power to evoke the historical moment in which they were conceived. The repetition of advertising and commercial art forms and images, as the cheap mass-product symbols of a narrowly self-centered material affluence, also suggests specific assumptions, including an attraction/repulsion reflex to the politics of violence typical of the sixties. In Lichtenstein's "despicable" anti-art imagery and mechanical handling, as in Warhol's comparable devices, a clear dissent from public moral codes and standards, and even oblique social protest, can be construed. At least in retrospect, we find not only parody, in an ambivalent, ironic/celebratory view of popular culture, but we see how clearly their art acknowledges (and is thus only a step away from protest and insurgency) the obsessive public and private violence in our culture, and our habitual acquiescence in it, anesthetized by repeated media exposure. Today the pathos of Warhol's *Nine Jackies*, with the mute, sorrowing widow at the President's funeral, still grips us, overshadowing the mechanical image registration.

Harold Rosenberg, the prime polemicist and defender of the Abstract Expressionists, and the scourge of all succeeding tendencies in art, perceived the first collective manifestation of the new and wholesale traffic in mass-culture imagery in the Janis Gallery's "New Realists" show of 1962. Rosenberg noted that the controversial exhibition "hit the New York art world with the force of an earthquake."[21] Reporting on that impact in his regular *New Yorker* column, Rosenberg introduced the Pop artists with some ambivalence, first admiring and then reducing their work to a cultural response rather than considering it as a creative accomplishment:

> The new American illusionist contrivances have a deeper identification with commercial art than plagiarism or adoption of its images. They share the impersonality of advertising-agency art department reproductions . . . . The attempt to purge Abstract Expressionism by polemics against it in the art pages of the press produced nothing more than ideological nagging. The purging of art by works of art based on a different premise is, however, always vitalizing. Those artists, dealers and curators who functioned on the assumption that the look of Action Painting was sufficient to authenticate a canvas were put on notice by the new illusionist objects that any image, including Coca-Cola lettering or the numbers on a pinball machine, could be equally viable. In sum, there is no greater esthetic virtue in copying a de Kooning than in copying the design on a beer can. If you do either, you are talking to the audience about itself, not engaging in creation. In dramatizing this principle, Pop Art has been a contribution to criticism.[22]

In George Segal's *Bus Driver* in the "New Realists" show, Rosenberg discerned an exemplary work, where "the game of illusion reached a pitch of pathos that belongs equally to sculpture and the theater," and he significantly exempted Segal from his major criticism of Pop Art: "Segal was the only exhibitor who used the new illusory combinations to create a new feeling rather than a commentary on art."[23]

Segal's portrait of Michael Sonnabend, 1963, is a second cast, taken of the model's head only, of a figure leaning over a flashy and ornamental pinball machine, which was the central environmental prop in the work entitled *Gottlieb's Wishing Well*, of 1963, shown at Segal's first European exhibition, at the Sonnabend gallery in Paris, at a time when pinball machines had become a craze in Europe. Segal made his first trip to Europe to work on the show's installation, and admitted to a profound culture shock: "What kind of nerve did I have bringing my art to the motherland!"[24]

Segal's isolated "portrait" of Sonnabend, a casting in wet plaster made from his subject and subsequently expressively modified, must be understood in the context of its absent environment. The most vivid identities and energies of human personality and objects are transformed into an aesthetic statement in the larger work despite the high degree of actualism of their representation; both elements of the work are denied the expression of energy, and all effective action is frozen in time. In the total ensemble, a subtle exchange takes place between the ghostly human effigy in plaster and the machine-object, creating a strangely poignant moment of alienation and identification.

Jim Dine remembers exploring, as a child, his grandfather's and father's hardware store, fascinated by the metal tools which later appeared in such works as *Proposed Still Life*. These familiar motifs, as well as bathroom appurtenances (*Four Soap Dishes*), machinery, and fan blades (*Bedroom Light over Flesh Square*), became part of an intensely personal vocabulary of form, producing many powerfully expressive variations. Like the Surrealists, Dine became interested in his own psyche, as it manifested itself through object-symbols, observing:

> I think my work is very autobiographical. What I try to do in my work is to explore myself in physical terms—to explain something in terms of my own sensibilities.[25]

His brilliant early paintings, with their attached objects, and his related environments have a brute physical presence that simultaneously evokes and rebukes the indirection and muted poetic feeling of Jasper Johns's works. Dine's surfaces also extended the paradoxical play between literal experience and illusionistic representation, by regenerating, with a rivaling skill, the painterly direction and physicality of Action Painting, and then assimilating it to a repertory of objects rich in associations of personal use, strength, and, very often, sexual potency.

Eroticism was an important element, but often given a comical turn, in Claes Oldenburg's visionary drawings for public monuments, many of them executed and now existing on public sites; others, such as *"dam fall,"* have proved too mischievously explicit for such exposure. In many ways Oldenburg has been the most audaciously inventive and outrageous of the Pop artists, and he has exercised a wide influence on all manner of expression and ideas in contemporary art. With Allan Kaprow, Jim Dine, Robert Whitman, and Red Grooms, he invented the Happening, which extended Action Painting into a form of spontaneous, expressionist theater. But he is best known for his ersatz food in painted canvas and plaster, which he evolved after 1960. The foodstuffs in the present exhibition are representative of his earliest freestanding sculptural style, when he handled the painted surfaces of freely invented, if somewhat improbable, edibles in a splatter-and-splash technique reminiscent of Action Painting, but still faithfully adhered to the instantly recognizable real-life models.

Truck/Pants is one of Oldenburg's first conglomerate object-sculptures, in relief, and it was motivated by the same desire to break down the barriers between art and life that propelled Rauschenberg into his dramatic inventions in the early fifties. Using impermanent urban litter, in found objects as well as invented expressionist forms, and calling it "Street Art," Oldenburg created associations with the assemblages of Dubuffet, and paralleled that artist's irreverent intention of "celebrating disparaged cultural values." Interestingly, Oldenburg's first urban art production, whose throw-away materials were promoted to the status of art as isolated entities, had its origins in the Happening, where much of his material, simulating wearing apparel and food, was first used as props. Later these objects were removed from the context of the Happening and displayed individually, demanding scrutiny as independent aesthetic realities.

The performance of the Happening called *The Store* took place in a simulated store constructed by Oldenburg in December 1961, called the Ray Gun Manufacturing Co. Here the objects from the performance were displayed as separate identities, marking Oldenburg's new interest in creating plastic objects rather than collecting litter from the street. In his journal notes, later published as *Store Days* (New York: The Something Else Press, 1967), Oldenburg boldly articulates his compelling need to overcome the art/life barriers erected by the preceding generation. With a certain evangelism, reminiscent of Walt Whitman, he called for an *engagé* urban art that dynamically embodies contemporary social realities, no matter how primitivistic the handling or brutal the content:

> I am for an art that is political-erotical-mystical, that does something other than sit on its ass in a museum.
>
> I am for an art that grows up not knowing it is art at all, an art given the chance of having the starting point of zero.
>
> I am for an art that embroils itself with the everyday crap and still comes out on top.
>
> I am for an art that imitates the human, that is comic if necessary, or violent, or whatever is necessary.
>
> I am for an art that takes its forms from the lines of life, that twists and extends impossibly and accumulates and spits and drips, and is sweet and stupid as life itself. I am for an artist who vanishes, turning up in a white cap, painting signs and hallways. . . . I am for an art that is smoked, like a cigarette, smells like a pair of shoes. I am for an art that flaps like a flag, or helps blow noses, like a handkerchief. I am for an art that is put on and taken off, like pants, which develops holes, like socks, which is eaten, like a piece of pie.[26]

James Rosenquist, between 1954 and 1960, worked as a billboard painter, and the experience of creating immense commercial images (often above Times Square) at close range with Day-Glo paint became an important shaping element in his work of the sixties. The image fragments in *Balcony*, juxtaposing a woman's stylized auburn coiffure and a confusingly rotated male hand and fingers, curling from a cuff and sleeve, recall the contradictions of Dada montage or Magritte's uncanny mix of fantasy and banality, both in image and handling. Rosenquist wrenched everyday objects out of context and recognizability, by scale distortion and the abrupt intercession of competing image fragments. It was a mode of perception related to commercial advertising as well as to illusionistic Surrealism. The artist aptly summarized his vision of things and his response to media influence in an interview with G. R. Swenson:

> I'm amazed and excited and fascinated about the way things are thrust at us, the way the invisible screen that's a couple of feet in front of our mind and our senses is attacked by radio and television and visual communications, through things larger than life, the impact of things thrown at us, at such speed and with such force that painting and the attitude towards painting and communication through doing a painting now seem old-fashioned.[27]

Tom Wesselmann's fragmented and monumental body parts, and his still-life drawings of emblematic supermarket objects or household accessories grew out of his interest in cartoon illustration when he studied at the Cincinnati Art Academy, before transferring in the late fifties to Cooper Union in New York. *Seascape #14*, with its heroic-sized foot, can be related to the *Great American Nude* series, begun in 1961, and its partitive anatomical form can also be linked to Surrealist practice. Its antecedents range from Hans Bellmer's disturbing, disjointed doll construction, *La Poupée* of 1936, to the huge, floating lips of Man Ray's *Observatory Hour—The Lovers*, with its alternative erotic reading of the lips as bodies pressed together in a sinuous embrace. Whatever Wesselmann's imagery may be—an open mouth with a cigarette and smoke curling from it, fragmented limbs, or the entire nude on a field of stars and stripes—his depiction of female anatomy, whole or in part, is usually a tough-minded, blatant presentation more fantastic in scale than in mood, like a good deal of contemporary billboard eroticism.

Of his powerful montages with unappealing and ersatz-looking food, as in *Still Life #45*, with its odd conjunction of found and depicted imagery, Wesselmann has commented:

> A painted pack of cigarettes next to a painted apple wasn't enough for me. They were both the

same kind of thing. But if one is from a cigarette ad and the other a painted apple, they are two different realities and they trade on each other; lots of things—bright strong colors, the quality of materials, images from art history and advertising —trade on each other.[28]

While New Realism and Pop Art were radical reactions to Abstract Expressionism, the post-painterly abstraction[29] that emerged in the late fifties and early sixties was, at least in part, a continuation of certain important aspects of it. A new line of color-stain painting, challenging de Kooning's opulent, loaded brushstrokes and intermittent figuration, made its appearance. It seemed to evolve from Helen Frankenthaler to Morris Louis and then took a more rigorous geometric form in the work of Kenneth Noland. There was also an increasing interest among a large group of artists, including Ellsworth Kelly, in symmetry, clear definition of shape, immaculate surface, and formal order, all of which opposed the free-wheeling invention, spontaneity, amorphous forms, and general messiness of the paint surface of Action Painting.

Supported by the critic Clement Greenberg's hardening formalist position, announced in an article of 1962, "After Abstract Expressionism,"[30] and then consolidated in his influential exhibition of 1964 at the Los Angeles County Museum, "Post-Painterly Abstraction,"[31] the anti-expressionist reaction was based on a concern for formal ordering and a classical sense of restraint. The predilections of the emerging abstractionists appeared in a variety of rather different plastic guises—symmetry, pure hues, and rigorous formal composition only imperfectly identified them with past traditions of geometric abstraction in Neo-Plasticism and Constructivism. More significant examples and authentic precedents could be found in the geometric art of David Smith's last *Cubi* style, and in the diverse Color Field painting of Still, Newman, and Reinhardt.

While Reinhardt was probably not a primary influence on Frank Stella's so-called black paintings, Reinhardt's self-contained, conventionalized, and repetitive art, with its extreme reductions and marginal sensuousness, undoubtedly had an impact on the younger artist. Stella, in fact, was revealed to be one of the earliest collectors of Reinhardt's monochrome paintings at the first New York museum retrospective for Reinhardt, held at The Jewish Museum in 1966. Reinhardt's reduction of painting to a simple cruciform composition of equal trisected squares and a single, if modulated, hue, and his insistence on creating painting that was "purer and emptier and freer than any previous art"[32] embodied probably the first consciously programmatic statement of the Minimalist position, some time before the movement was officially baptized.

Stella's first significant black paintings aspired, like Reinhardt's monochromes, to an art of pure formal essence, purged of all extra-visual meaning or significance. The small untitled work in the present exhibition, from the Benjamin Moore series, with its regular, maze-like linear path and monochrome bars of black on unsized canvas, eliminates relational structure and the hierarchal ordering of traditional geometric abstraction. By extinguishing pictorial variety, development, and climax, Stella's influential early work opened up new expressive possibilities. Stella has constantly emphasized the simple factuality of his painting: "My painting is based on the fact that only what can be seen here *is* there. It is really an object."[33]

Within the broad current of renewed "painterly" painting that began to appear in the late sixties, there was a growing emphasis on a more sensuous and material expressiveness, in contrast to the austerities of Minimalist painting and sculpture. An important revelation of this aesthetic change was the rediscovered work of Cy Twombly. His paintings of 1956 and 1957 and his later drawings in this exhibition are full of recondite references to the artist's long post-World War II residence in Rome, often recorded in a jumbled composite of painting and drawing which freely synthesizes aspects of Expressionism, Surrealist automatism, and postwar Action Painting in an original amalgam. Like the graphic expression of Rauschenberg, a long-time, intimate friend and influence, the sketchbook freedom of Twombly's linear motifs affirms the spontaneous creative moment, but his nervous scribbles and paint marks also suggest diaristic reminiscences. For Twombly, drawing is both an energizing source of visual creation and an autobiographical memory book of actual events.

Conceptual Art was another dramatic phenomenon of the sixties; it crystallized near the end of the decade, when the sculptor/draftsman Sol LeWitt described the "idea" as "the machine that makes the work."[34] The artist's aim, he wrote in the first published declaration on Conceptual Art, is "not to instruct the viewer, but to give him information. Whether the viewer understands this information is incidental to the artist."[35] However, even before this cerebral movement achieved a systematic program, and recruited a number of converts, it had been broadly hinted at in Robert Morris's lead and sculpmetal reliefs with inscriptions, which extended the Duchampian legacy of visual puns and enigmatic objects in a fresh manner. For example, *Something Else*, of 1963, reveals Morris's fascination with Duchamp's assault on official ideas of measurement and order in his *Three Standard Stoppages*, a classic interrogation of received ideas, calculated to undermine the credibility of standard, authorized measurement. Similarly, Morris's ironic works subvert official wisdom.

His protean versatility was also apparent at this early stage, in the two antithetical shows he had in 1964–65. The first was of the sculpmetal reliefs, with their complex and problematic meanings; the second consisted of a few large bland geometric forms in gray painted plywood, scattered through New York's Green Gallery. Morris called them "blank forms," which anticipated radical Minimalist styles and simplistic forms on a monumental scale. By the summer of 1967, tiring of his own Minimalism in large box-like metal and plywood forms, he created his first felt pieces. They embodied an entirely new rationale, which he described in an influential article in *Artforum* in 1968 as "anti form."[36] But these large-scale, soft, draped forms also had an inadvertent conceptual bias, since they depended completely on a given space for their definition, and not exclusively on their creator. They were thus at the mercy of both accident and the forces of gravity, adding a typically Duchampian nonchalance to the other elements determining their configuration.

The late fifties and early sixties spawned a proliferating variety of movements, styles, and artistic phenomena, of such complexity as to defy a summary characterization in a brief introduction. Generally, formalist art, and a new kind of commercial genre painting and sculpture, rooted in popular culture and the media revolution, represented the major polarities of expression. A number of challenging new tendencies gathered force at the end of the decade, centered in earthworks, Conceptual Art, performance art, photography in a novel documentary spirit, and primitivistic environmental sculpture of monumental scale made for particular sites, and they tested the hegemony of the two dominant abstract and figurative traditions, by denying the necessity of the material object itself.

While it is always risky, especially in close historical proximity, to construe artists' relations to events outside pure aesthetic concerns (which would include not only politics but the impact of popular culture and technology), it seems clear that the art of Rauschenberg and Johns and many of the Pop artists had political, or at least wider cultural, implications as commentary and social criticism. Peter Conrad, in his book *The Art of the City: Views and Versions of New York*, persuasively argues that Rauschenberg was a kind of Baudelairean dandy playing amid the ruins of the disintegrating city; a *flaneur* and *bricoleur* who nonchalantly built his "assembly and construction of bric-a-brac" from the decaying urban scrap heap, in the "debased and tyrannized"[37] jungle of the modern American metropolis. And in the exhibition catalogue *The Art of Assemblage*, William Seitz as early as 1961 discerned in the new urban environmental art a network of artists "who, quite independently and with no political affiliation, incorporate and represent in their work flags, shields, eagles, and other symbols of democracy, national power and authority, with mild amusement or irony, with concealed resentment and scatalogical bitterness, or simply as totally banal images."[38]

For a moment in the mid-sixties Minimalism and Pop Art seemed to be equally strong, and an uneasy truce was struck between high formalist tradition and the vernacular position that art cannot be divorced from life. Frank Stella conceived of his paintings divested of "the old values . . . the humanistic values," and favored an art that could be appreciated in purely visual terms.[39] Oldenburg and his Pop Art colleagues, on the other hand, developed an art of the environment, recalling the Dadaist dream of a conglomerate, urban *Gesamtkunstwerk*, "an art that imitates the human . . . that takes its forms from the lines of life . . . and is sweet and stupid as life itself."[40] In their early work both groups achieved their desired goals, for the most part, but in the decades after the sixties, ironically enough, abstract art moved toward expressionism and formal disjunctions, and Pop Art became increasingly stylized, synthetic, and formalist.

The turbulence and insurgency of the sixties undoubtedly left their mark on some of the best art of the period, either by the force and character of the images generated, or obversely, by the apparent repression of political or emotive content. Only lately have we been able to perceive the period as "history." The moment is at hand when the passions, divisions, and artistic sensibilities of the sixties will begin to appear as myth in the artifacts of the period, luring a new generation of interpreters to demystify them and to reconstruct, rather than remember or assume, the artistic and historical circumstances that gave them birth.

NOTES

1. Suzi Gablik and John Russell, *Pop Art Redefined* (London: Thames and Hudson, 1969), p. 30.
2. Robert Rosenblum, "Excavating the 1950s," in *Action Precision, The New Direction in New York 1955–60* (Newport Harbor Art Museum, 1984).
3. Alan Solomon, "The New Art," in *The Popular Image* (Washington, D.C.: Washington Gallery of Modern Art, 1963); reprinted in *The New Art*, Gregory Battcock, ed. (New York: Dutton, 1966), p. 68.
4. Perhaps the broadest and most useful definition of popular culture in relationship to Pop Art has been formulated by Lawrence Alloway, who coined the epithet for the artistic style in London in 1955, actually seven years in advance of the movement's public emergence. Writing in the Whitney Museum of American Art catalogue for his exhibition "American Pop Art," he observed: "Popular culture can be defined as the sum of the arts designed for simultaneous consumption by a numerically large audience. Thus, there is a similarity in distribution and consumption between prints, on the one hand, and magazines, movies, records, radio, TV, and industrial and interior design, on the other. Popular culture originates in urban centers and is distributed on the basis of mass production. It is not like folk art which, in theory at least, is handcrafted by the same group by which it will be consumed. The consumption of popular culture is basically a social experience, providing information derived from and contributing to our statistically normal roles in society. It is a network of messages and objects that we share with others" (Lawrence Alloway, *American Pop Art* [New York: Whitney Museum of American Art, 1974], p. 4).
5. Harold Rosenberg, *The Anxious Object: Art Today and Its Audience* (New York: Horizon Press, 1964), p. 13.
6. Allan Kaprow, "Should the Artist Become a Man of the World?" *Art News*, 63 (October 1964), p. 35.
7. Rosenberg, *The Anxious Object*, p. 13.
8. Pierre Restany, "The New Realists," *Art in America*, 61 (February 1963), p. 104.
9. Pierre Restany, unpublished manuscript, Paris, 1961. Cited in William C. Seitz, *The Art of Assemblage* (New York: The Museum of Modern Art, 1961) p. 152, note 83.
10. Seitz, *The Art of Assemblage*, p. 87.
11. Allan Kaprow, "The Legacy of Jackson Pollock," *Art News*, 57 (October 1958), pp. 56–57.
12. Kaprow, quoted in Seitz, *The Art of Assemblage*, p. 90.
13. Cited in *John Cage*, Richard Kostelanetz, ed. (New York: Praeger, 1970).
14. George Segal, "Sculptures, Paintings, Pastels: A Discussion of My Recent Work," Master of Fine Arts thesis, Rutgers University, May 1963, p. 11; unpublished manuscript.
15. Undated letter of the summer of 1952, Betty Parsons papers, Archives of American Art.
16. Robert Rauschenberg, statement, in *16 Americans*, Dorothy C. Miller, ed. (New York: The Museum of Modern Art, 1959), p. 59.
17. "The New Painting of Common Objects" (Pasadena Art Museum, 1962), an exhibition arranged by Walter Hopps and the first museum showing of Pop Art. Cited in Lawrence Alloway, *American Pop Art* (New York: Whitney Museum of American Art, 1974), p. 128.
18. Ivan Karp, "Anti-Sensibility Painting," *Artforum*, 2 (September 1963), pp. 26–27.
19. G. R. Swenson, "What Is Pop Art? Interviews with Eight Painters (Part I)," *Art News*, November 1963.
20. Ellen H. Johnson, *Modern Art and the Object* (New York: Harper & Row, 1976), p. 179.

21. Harold Rosenberg, *The Anxious Object*, "The Game of Illusion: Pop and Gag," reprinted by Collier Books, New York, 1973, p. 63.
22. *Ibid.*, p. 75.
23. *Ibid.*, p. 74.
24. Jan van der Marck, *George Segal* (New York: Harry N. Abrams, 1979, revised edition), p. 81.
25. John Gordon, *Jim Dine* (New York: Whitney Museum of American Art, 1970), p. 6.
26. Claes Oldenburg, *Store Days* (New York: The Something Else Press, 1967), p. 37.
27. Gablik and Russell, p. 111.
28. *Ibid.*, p. 120.
29. A term used by the critic Clement Greenberg for the title of an exhibition he arranged at the Los Angeles County Museum in 1964 that rejected the de Kooning style of brushwork and Action Painting, and since has become synonymous with the more familiar Color Field painting.
30. Clement Greenberg, "After Abstract Expressionism," *Art International*, 6 (October 1962), pp. 24–32.
31. "Post-Painterly Abstraction" (Los Angeles County Museum, 1964), exhibition and catalogue essay by Clement Greenberg.
32. Ad Reinhardt, address, Brooklyn College, n.d. Reinhardt papers, Archives of American Art.
33. Bruce Glaser, "Questions to Stella and Judd," Lucy R. Lippard, ed., *Art News* (September 1966), reprinted in *American Artists on Art from 1940 to 1980*, Ellen H. Johnson, ed. (New York: Harper & Row, 1982), p. 117.
34. Sol LeWitt, "Paragraphs on Conceptual Art," *Artforum*, Summer 1967.
35. LeWitt, *Artforum*, 1967.
36. Robert Morris, "Anti Form," *Artforum*, 6 (April 1968), pp. 33–35.
37. Cited in Alan Trachtenberg's book review, "Muse of the Metropolis," *The New Republic*, June 25, 1984, pp. 37–39.
38. Seitz, *The Art of Assemblage*, p. 89.
39. Frank Stella, interview, *Art News*, 65 (September 1966), p. 58.
40. Oldenburg, *Store Days*, p. 37.

Selections from the
Ileana and Michael Sonnabend
Collection

Arman

With Duchamp as an acknowledged artistic predecessor, Yves Klein as a friend and liberating influence, and the art critic Pierre Restany as a catalyst, Arman (Armand Fernandez) changed roles in the 1950s from a French Sunday painter to an avant-garde New Realist. He had studied at the Ecole du Louvre and the Ecole Nationale des Arts Décoratifs, but it was his friendship with Yves Klein (they hitchhiked through Europe together in 1947) that most profoundly affected Arman, according to Restany.[1]

In 1955 Arman was living in Nice—selling furniture, skin-diving for food to stock the gourmet restaurants, and painting post-Cubist abstractions in his free time. During this year he went to Paris to see Klein's monochromatic paintings, and there began his mature artistic development. He was armed with a knowledge of art history, and even his earliest mature works, the *cachets* (rubber stamps) of 1955–58, reveal lessons learned from Dada, Constructivism, Surrealism, and Abstract Expressionism.[2] Prodded by Restany to abandon the scale of needlepoint, Arman increased the size and complexity of his *cachets*, which gave way in 1959 to the *allures*—the graphic traces of ink- or paint-covered objects flung against paper or canvas. In the course of creating the *allures*, Arman discovered that the objects themselves were often more evocative than the compositions that they yielded. From this revelation grew the two major directions of all his subsequent work: the *colères* (literally "rages"), in which the remains of shattered objects are presented, and the *accumulations*, collections of like objects.

In 1962 Arman had his first one-man exhibition in the United States (the inaugural exhibition at Dwan Gallery, Los Angeles), and in the same year the Sidney Janis Gallery, New York, held "The New Realists" exhibition, which was organized by Pierre Restany and included Arman's work. Arman's *Infinity of Typewriters and Infinity of Monkeys and Infinity of Time = Hamlet* (1962) is an *accumulation* of twenty typewriters. Arman's titles often provide his work with humorous, poetic, or ironic content, and in this case the title suggests a pervasive theme in his oeuvre, and our society: the relationship between quantity and quality. Arman's equation is correct—given infinite time, typewriters, and monkeys, one will randomly peck out *Hamlet*. The message is a self-referential comment on artistic creativity. Just as the "art" will not be the monkey's but belongs to whoever recognizes the meaning of the language, the art in Arman's *accumulations* lies not in the manufacture, collection, or even presentation of the objects so much as in the recognition that such an *accumulation* might have expressive potential. Further, Arman reminds us that, in contrast to the monkey, a human being with artistic imagination "doesn't need infinity in order to create *Hamlet*."[3]

The typewriters are presented as potential instruments of creativity, as archaeological evidence sealed in a box, and as a pattern worthy of aesthetic judgment. Unlike the objects in the work of his American proto-Pop counterparts Rauschenberg and Johns, Arman's objects are not intended to be part of a larger painted image. Arman acknowledges the conceptual nature of his art, but insists that even in his most extreme works his intentions have not been "anti-art." "I have absolutely no desire to renounce aestheticism."[4] Indeed, he believes avoidance of aesthetics to be impossible, stating that even "the most readymade of [Duchamp's] readymades . . . , elevated to artistic presentation, arrives at a certain aestheticism."[5] His work is meant to be viewed frontally, as surface rather than as sculpture, and its visual aspect is carefully calculated. The number of typewriters, their arrangement, and the method of presentation are all designed to create the most effective visual play of form and pattern as well as to reinforce the conceptual basis of the work.

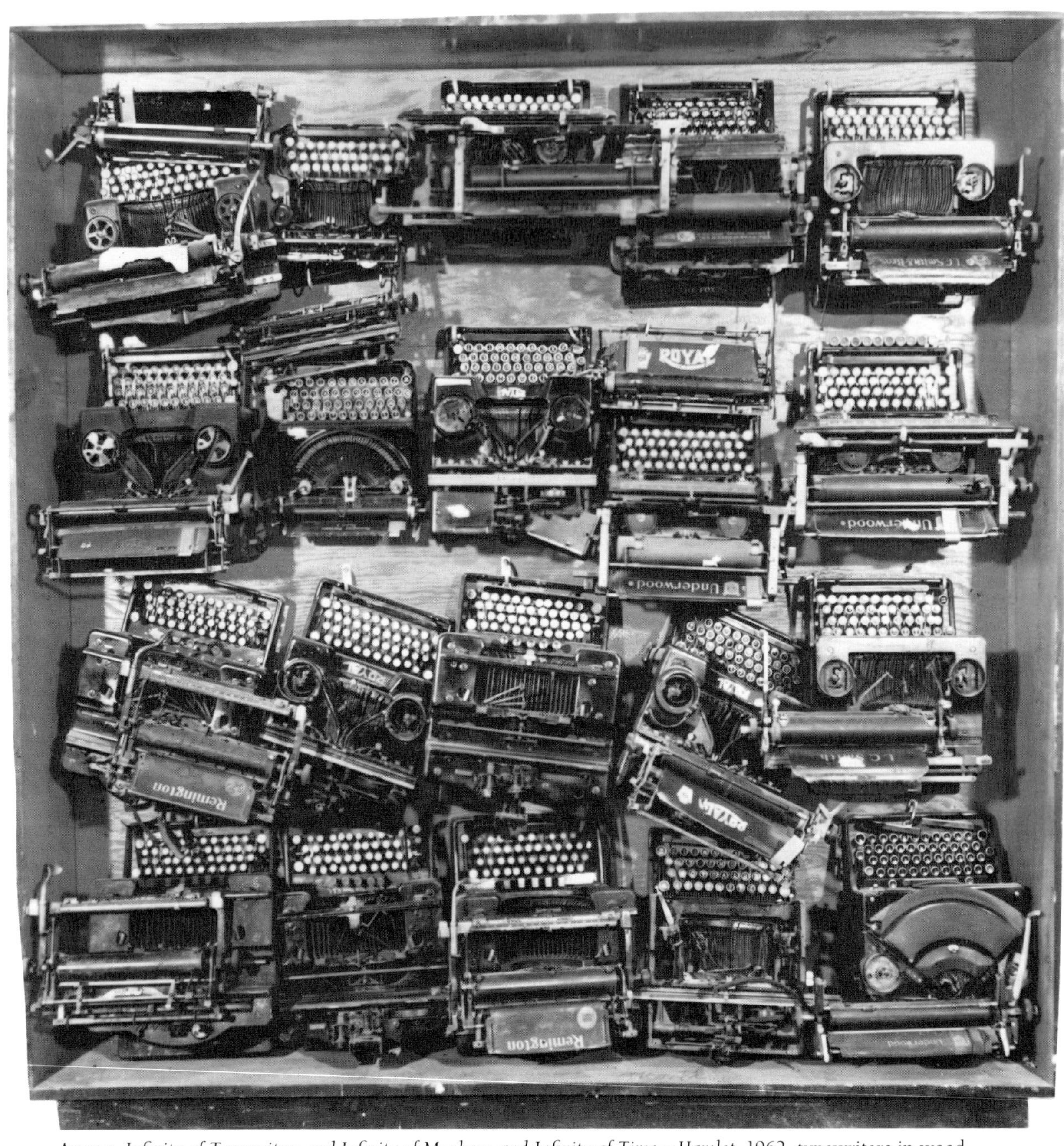

Arman, *Infinity of Typewriters and Infinity of Monkeys and Infinity of Time = Hamlet*, 1962, typewriters in wood encasement, 72 × 69 × 12″.

While the *accumulations* certainly have a formal and conceptual link to the serial images of Warhol and other American Pop artists, there are essential differences between the use of objects and the use of images. Images can be enlarged or reduced (indeed, the humor or irony of much Pop Art relies on exaggeration of scale and consequent monumentalization of the banal), but the use of objects dictates a specific scale and a resulting "critical mass"—the degree of repetition at which each object balances on a fence between individual identity and submersion to the whole. The second distinction is that objects, more than images, retain their associative meanings—their past history—and part of the effectiveness of Arman's work lies in our identification of human needs and emotions with objects.[6] Arman consciously wonders "how many love letters, how many books, bills"[7] were typed on the typewriters of the *Hamlet* piece.

If Pop Art glorified, albeit mockingly, the media presentation and slick packaging of consumer goods, Arman's use of objects puts forth the tenet that our society might be judged by what it discards. This idea found its ultimate expression in his *poubelles* of 1959–60, collections of trash, and in the 1960 exhibition "Le Plein" (Full) at the Galerie Iris Clert, for which Arman filled a section of the gallery with thirty tons of Parisian garbage. This was Arman's answer to the challenge of Yves Klein's exhibition "Vide" (Empty) of 1958, which presented the bare walls of the same gallery.

A 1963 work related to the *Hamlet* piece, a smashed typewriter entitled *The Secretary Might Be Fired*, represents the other great tendency in Arman's oeuvre: destruction. The smashed, split, sliced, burned, and exploded objects of the *colères* present frozen moments of transformation and states of decay, evoking powerful emotional reactions. The meanings of accumulation and destruction are related as part of the life cycle of the object, and, by extension, of the human emotions which we associate with them. Arman has stated, "As a witness of my society, I have always been very much involved in the pseudobiological cycle of production, consumption and destruction."[8]

Malcolm R. Daniel

NOTES

1. Pierre Restany, *Arman* (Milan: Galleria Schwarz, 1968), n.p.
2. In an interview with Alain Jouffroy ("Arman," *L'Oeil*, 126 [June 1965], pp. 25ff.) Arman acknowledges in particular the important influence of the typographic designs of the Dutch printer Werkman, the collages of Schwitters, Pollock's all-over aesthetic, and Duchamp's use of objects.
3. Arman, interview with Sam Hunter, New York, May 29, 1984.
4. Jouffroy, p. 26 (author's translation).
5. *Ibid.* (author's translation).
6. For further discussion of this premise see Henry Martin, *Arman* (New York: Harry N. Abrams, 1973), pp. 22, 36.
7. Arman, interview with Sam Hunter, New York, May 29, 1984.
8. Arman, statement in Martin, p. 56.

John Chamberlain

Born in Rochester, Indiana, in 1927, Chamberlain gravitated to Chicago and its Art Institute, where he studied in 1951–52. Although his major interest was painting in the beginning, he remembers being attracted to the sculpture studio, and to the open metal linear forms and welding techniques of the Chicago artist Joseph Goto, an instructor at the school. At this time Chamberlain also became aware of the work of David Smith, after seeing a sculpture from Smith's *Agricola* series, consisting of a combination of found and shaped metal derived from salvaged farm machinery. De Kooning had just won a major prize at the annual Art Institute show for the painting *Excavation*, which the museum later acquired; the painting made a profound impression on Chamberlain. In this formative stage of his career, the vital painterly abstraction and chromatic power of de Kooning, Kline's single-minded energy and thrust, and David Smith's technical innovations and presence all had a singular impact on Chamberlain and helped foster his own ideas, in conjunction with his later experience of the New York art world.

In 1955 Chamberlain went to Black Mountain College for a year; although he does not recall any particular artists who directly influenced him, he was impressed by the poets—notably Charles Olsen, a faculty member whose method of conferring a fresh perspective on language was to have his students make word collections. Chamberlain later compared his habit of "collecting words" with his collage technique in his wall reliefs and with the random assortment of automobile chassis fragments and chrome that became the composite material of his later free-standing sculpture.

In 1957 Chamberlain made his first free-standing sculpture of auto parts, which remained characteristic of his work from 1957 until 1963, using an abandoned Ford that Larry Rivers had given to him. It was a period when Rivers was also, briefly, experimenting with the construction of a few idiosyncratic but lively welded sculpture figures from scrap metal. *Shortstop* was Chamberlain's first venture, and it has an uncanny resemblance to an infielder's baseball glove. It is typical of Chamberlain's work of the early sixties, although not yet fully expressive in the round, in its energy of bent forms and in rich chroma. Chamberlain has described the complex tension and expansion he sought in these early crude but powerful crushed forms as "the idea of the squeeze and the compression and the fit."[1] Here, and in the untitled sculpture of 1964 in this exhibition, Chamberlain was clearly attracted by a combination of the commonness and the ready availability of scrap metal with its connection to the real world, as well as by the challenge of shaping and transforming these materials without entirely losing sight of their identity as automobile parts.

Chamberlain's first one-man show utilizing auto scrap was held in Chicago in 1957, at the Wells Street Gallery, and three years later he had his first one-man show at the Martha Jackson Gallery in New York, where he had taken up residence. His most important museum retrospective took place in 1971 at The Solomon R. Guggenheim Museum in New York.

In the later years of the sixties he experimented with foam rubber and transparent plastic constructions; he also briefly painted in a lacquer-like technique of thin pigment layers, on flat Masonite board, a series of geometric abstractions before returning to his preferred materials of automobile scrap, from which he has built perhaps his most effective and characteristic composite sculptures.

Sam Hunter

NOTES

1. Phyllis Tuchman, "Interview with John Chamberlain," *Artforum*, 10 (January 1972).

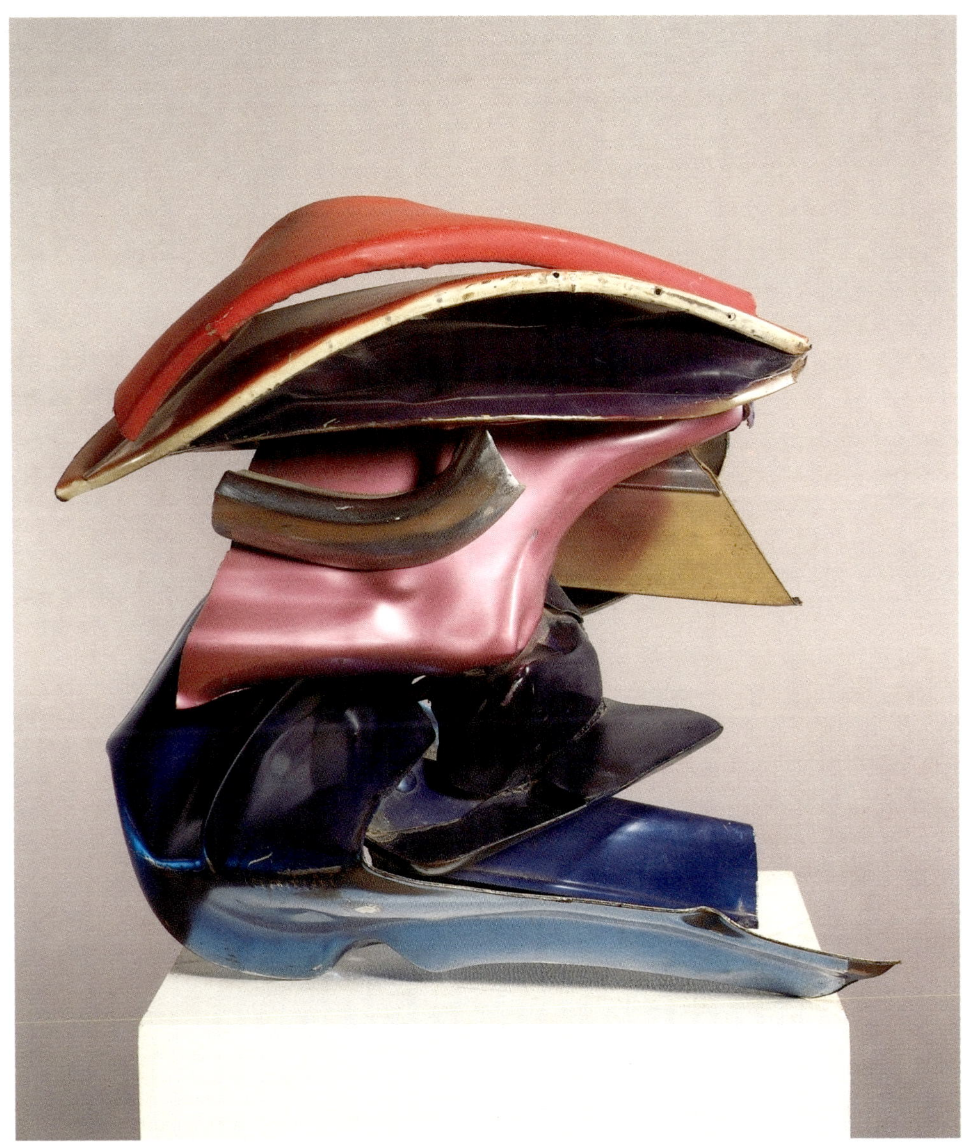

John Chamberlain, *Untitled* (Colonel Splendid), 1964, painted metal, 25 × 23 × 25″. Photograph by Clem Fiori.

Christo

Although best known for such herculean projects as the 24½-mile-long *Running Fence*, the *Valley Curtain*, and, most recently, *Surrounded Islands*—each involving the expenditure of millions of dollars, utilization of advanced technology, securing scores of government permits, and the cooperation of hundreds of workers—Christo has also created art from the most humble of materials (canvas, twine, brown paper, plastic), by simple processes, and on a human scale. Born in Gabrovo, Bulgaria, in 1935, the young Christo found encouragement from his parents for his artistic inclinations; he received private instruction in drawing while the family lived at their country house in the Balkans during the most intense days of World War II. At the Sofia Fine Arts Academy between 1952 and 1956, Christo was trained in the officially sanctioned style of Socialist Realism, which combined populist themes with traditional craft for ideological purposes. More important for his later art, Christo worked in the theater design department and also participated in the propagandistic activities of the Union of Communist Youth; he and his fellow art students painted slogans and billboards around the city and traveled through the countryside instructing farmers in stacking and covering their hay and in positioning farm equipment so as to have the most dramatic visual effect on the Western travelers aboard the Orient Express as it made its weekly crossing through Bulgaria. In this manipulation of the landscape can be found not only the objects and processes but also the philosophical basis of his major projects: the social and political nature of the process, the inclusion of the community, the team effort required for construction, the respectful relationship of art to landscape.[1]

While Christo was in Prague working for the Burian Theater, the 1956 Hungarian uprising threatened freedom in Czechoslovakia and prompted Christo's flight to Vienna. After six months at the Academy there, he went to Geneva, where he found some success as a portrait painter, working in a Neo-Impressionist style. With money earned in Geneva he moved to Paris in 1958, remaining there until his immigration to New York in 1964.

Christo was never formally a member of the Nouveaux Réalistes, the group of avant-garde Parisian artists around Yves Klein in the late 1950s and early 1960s. He did, however, receive encouragement from their spokesman, the art critic Pierre Restany, and he exhibited with them in Munich and at Galerie J in Paris. His Paris work also shows formal and material links with the work of Arman and Spoerri—in the accumulation and presentation of real objects—and conceptual ties with Yves Klein—in the theatrical and transitory nature of his work. Wrapping first appears in Christo's *Inventory* of 1958, a collection of cans, bottles, and drums in the artist's studio, some presented unaltered, some covered with canvas and tied with twine. Other wrapped objects soon followed.

Christo's "packages" resemble the humble parcels of an ordinary person, made with scraps of twine and paper, canvas, or plastic; they are not the flashy commercial packages of contemporary consumer products, the type of packaging which so attracted the American Pop artists. Consumer packaging is meant to excite and entice, to reveal and even exaggerate the character of the contents, to promise, even falsely, the value of what lies within; Christo's packages are anonymous, without words or pictures, obscuring their contents, enticing the viewer through mystery rather than hyperbole. His wrappings transform common and

---

Opposite page: Christo, *Le Diable* (Hand Cart), 1963, fabric, plastic, metal, hand cart, 48 × 40 × 26″.

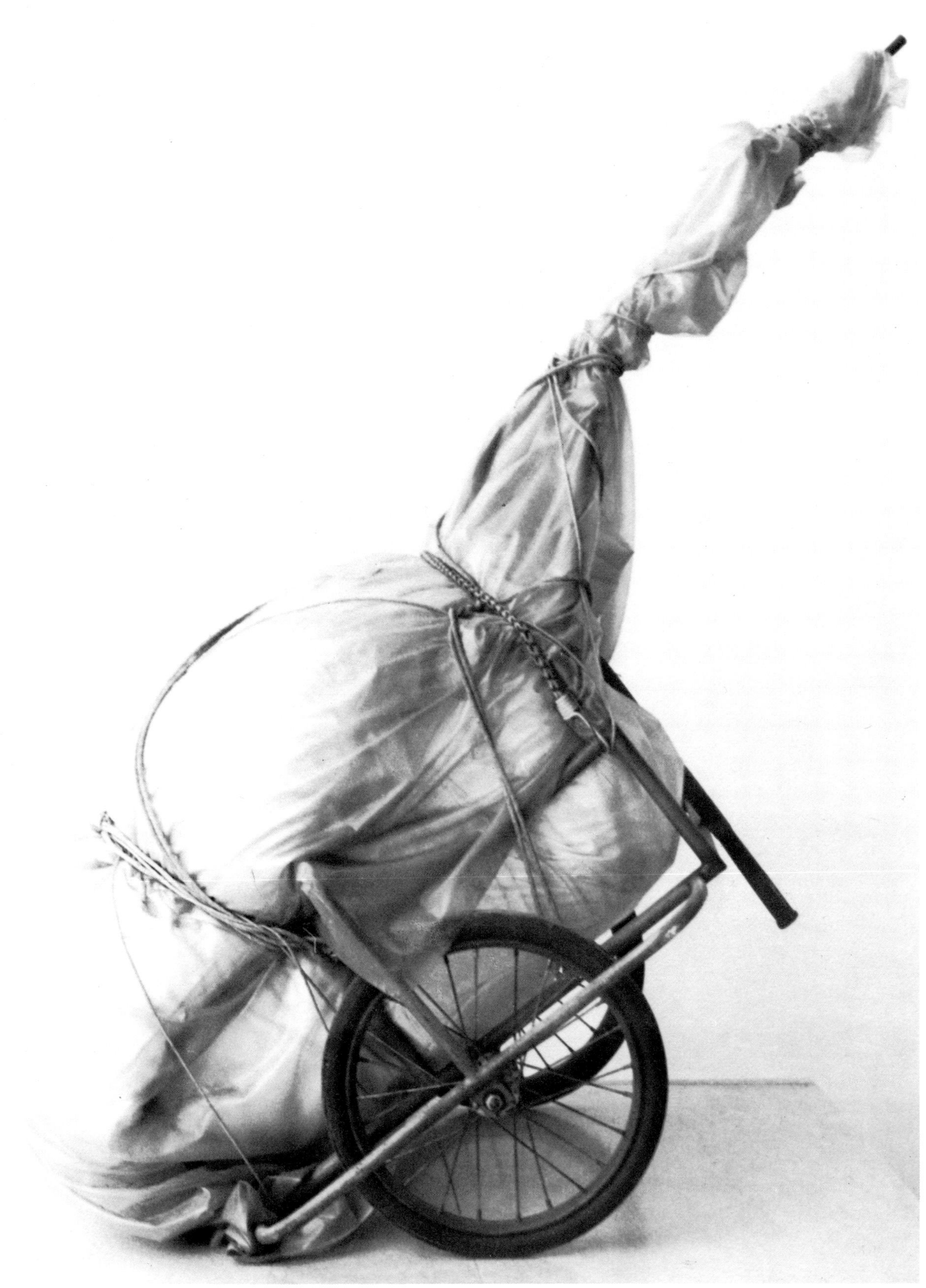

mundane items into objects of great mystery and temptation.

Although formal aesthetic considerations are not Christo's motivating concern, nor the criterion by which he asks to be judged, his work invariably reveals a keen formal sense. In *Le Diable* (Hand Cart), of 1963, the package strains the capacity of the cart and bulges between the ropes which bind it, poking from its wrappings at the uppermost point. Otto Hahn has noted Christo's tendency during this period to juxtapose circular wrapped forms with rectilinear supports, and his observation would seem apt here.[2] Equally important to the work's formal strength is the contrast between the bulky solidity of the package and the open framework of the cart and wheels.

Just as Christo considers the social and artistic process leading to his large-scale projects to be an integral part of the work, the smaller packages clearly reveal the process of their making, as well as the means by which their artistic life might be unmade—or, as some would prefer, the process which would liberate the object from within and resuscitate it.[3] Like an ancient cave painting decaying from the breath of investigating archaeologists, untying Christo's packages and confronting their revealed contents would remove their mystery and destroy the art.

Malcolm R. Daniel

NOTES

1. Jan van der Marck, "Christo: The Making of an Artist," in *Christo: Collection on Loan from The Rothschild Bank AG, Zurich* (La Jolla, California: La Jolla Museum of Contemporary Art, 1981), pp. 53 ff.
2. Otto Hahn, "Christo's Packages," *Art International*, IX (April 1965), p. 26.
3. David Bourbon, untitled essay in *Christo* (Milan: Edizioni Apollinaire, 1966), n.p.

Jim Dine

The humble subject matter and simple manner of Jim Dine's art belie a consummate draftsman and colorist, passionately interested in literature and music, well educated, keenly introspective, and unashamed of lessons learned from the art of de Kooning, Rauschenberg, and Johns.

As a youth Dine took summer courses at the Cincinnati Art Museum. After his mother died and his father remarried, the fifteen-year-old Dine left home to live with his grandparents; determined to become an artist, he painted three nights a week at the Cincinnati Art Academy. After graduating from high school, he spent an unsatisfying year at the University of Cincinnati and a similar six months at the Boston Museum School before enrolling at Ohio University, Athens, from which he received his B.A. degree. Dine vicariously immersed himself in the New York school by reading criticism and clipping reproductions from bound volumes of *Art News* at the university library.

In 1958, at the age of twenty-two, Dine and his wife of one year headed for New York City. There, with Allan Kaprow, Claes Oldenburg, and others, Dine helped invent and participated in the Happenings of 1959 and 1960, which he has described as "painter's theater."

Major critical attention arrived with his first one-man show at the Martha Jackson and David Anderson Galleries in New York in January 1962, an exhibition which featured paintings of articles of clothing, including *Shoe* and *A Black on White Tie/A White on Black Tie*. Clothing, often as implied self-portraiture, is a constant motif in Dine's work, with his series of robes, beginning in the mid-sixties, as the most notable of these images. Soon after the Jackson/Anderson exhibition Dine moved to the Sidney Janis Gallery, also in New York, where he had individual shows in 1963, 1964, and 1967; his work was also exhibited in Paris during the 1960s, by Ileana Sonnabend.

Jim Dine, *Proposed Still Life*, 1962, oil on canvas, mixed media, 84 × 36″. Photograph by Eric Pollitzer.

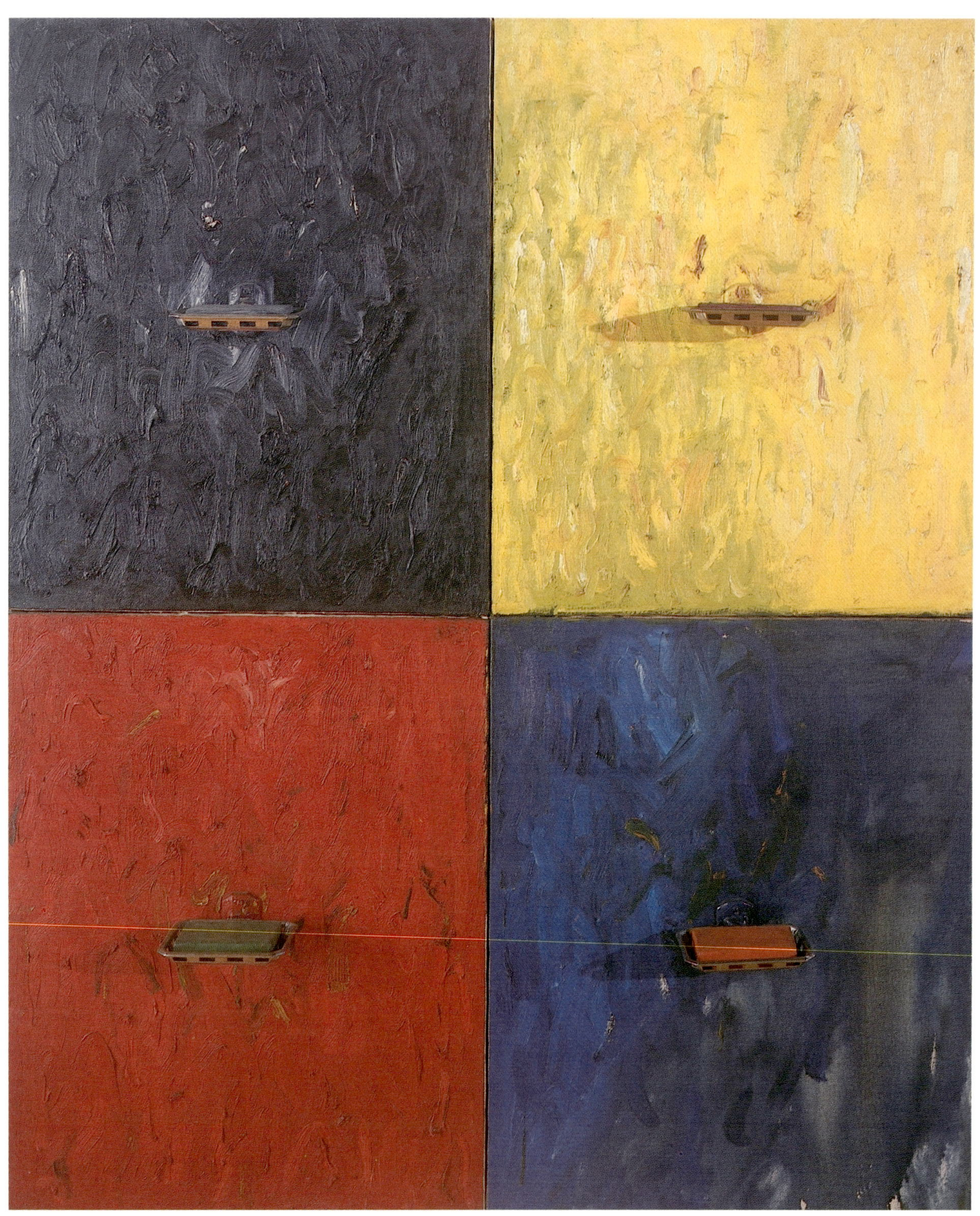

Jim Dine, *Four Soap Dishes*, 1962, oil on canvas with objects, 49 × 41 × 1½″.

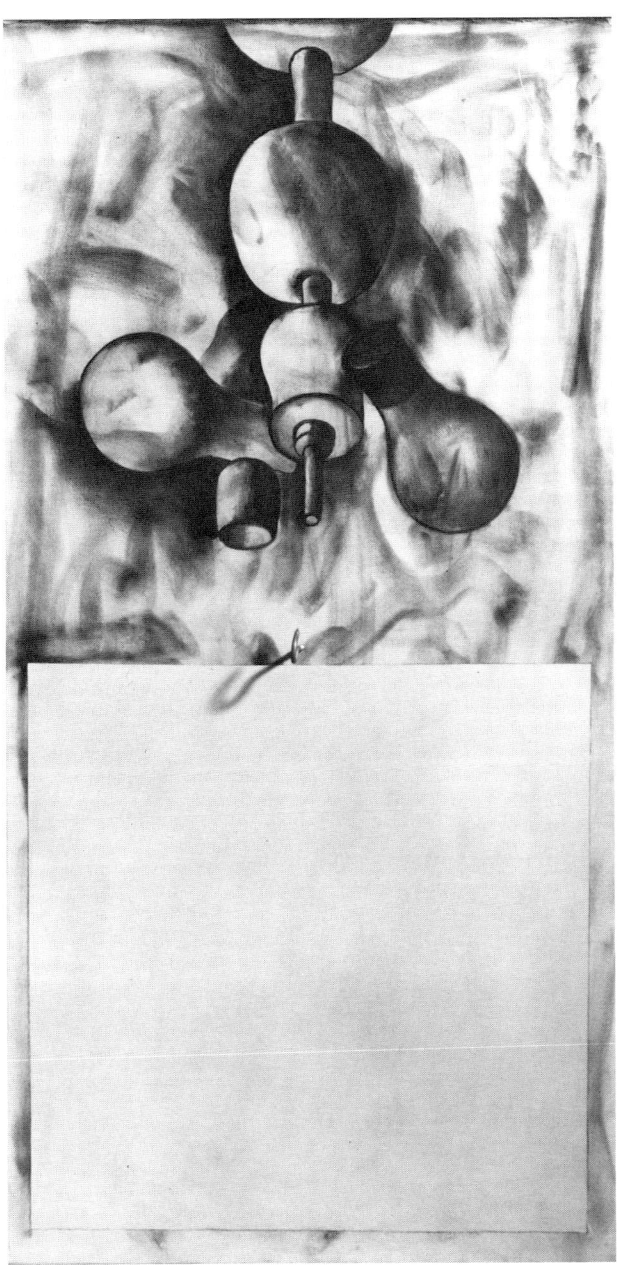

Jim Dine, *Bedroom Light over Flesh Square*, 1965, oil and graphite on canvas, mixed media, 72 × 36″. Photograph By Clem Fiori.

Artists of the preceding generation had abandoned representation in favor of abstraction, believing the depiction of objects to be a literary and trivial pursuit, an unworthy preoccupation of the revolutionary modern artist. For the Abstract Expressionists expressive brushwork and evident process were perceived as more honest and sincere vehicles of a personal and emotional content. The same rapid execution and thick impasto, when found in works such as *Shoe*, seem to be Dine's way of proposing the reverse: that luscious paint handling may be beautiful surface, but that it is the common object described by that brushwork which most powerfully conveys private symbolism, mythic presence, and expressive content. Dine's use of objects (both real and painted) was at least in part a reaction to the emotional catharsis and focus on the act of painting celebrated by Abstract Expressionism, and the same lively response was true of a number of his well-known younger contemporaries. However, few other artists of the period seem to have so consciously and humorously (but not irreverently) parodied the art of their immediate predecessors. At the time of the Jackson/Anderson exhibition, Max Kozloff wrote that Dine "outwits our cherished illusion of the nonrepresentational . . . [showing] us, by the most absurdly obvious jokes, that there is perhaps no such thing as abstract painting . . . . [Abstract paintings] can't help representing anything they remind us of."[1] The 1962 *French Pants* and *A Black on White Tie/A White on Black Tie* masquerade as works by a geometric abstractionist much like Dine's brushy impasto mimics Abstract Expressionism.

Tie and *Bow Tie* include written titles of a deliberate awkwardness directly above or below the painted image. For those who learned from Magritte why "*Ceci n'est pas une pipe*," Dine's "honest" labeling of a false (that is, depicted) reality seems disturbing rather than naïvely straightforward. The empty shelf jutting out at the bottom of the canvas cries out for the actual object described visually and verbally above; the projecting shelves at the bottom of Dine's other can-

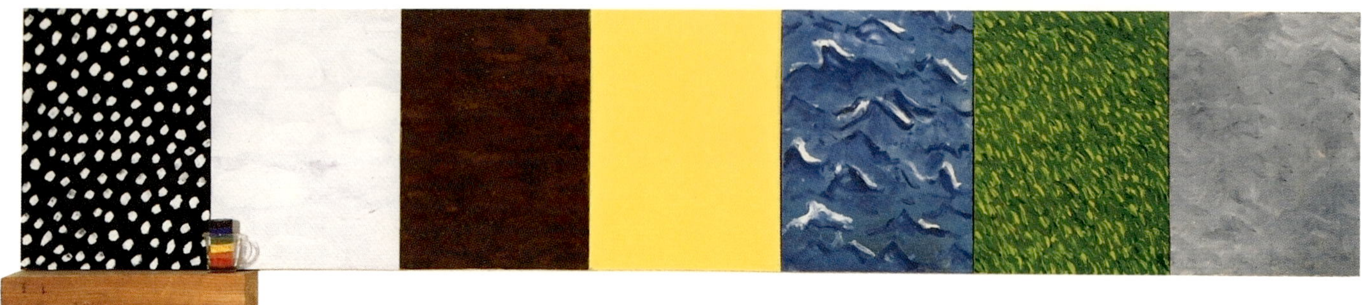

Jim Dine, *Landscape*, 1963, oil on canvas with objects, 27½ × 126 × 6″, each panel 24 × 18″. Photograph by Clem Fiori.

vases all support objects related to the painted image.

Actual objects attached to the painted surface or supported by a shelf are found often in Dine's early work, growing directly out of the assemblage tradition of Johns and Rauschenberg, whom Dine admired and emulated, but with his own strong personal accent. *Four Soap Dishes* (1962) is an arrangement of four equal rectilinear canvases expressionistically painted black (upper left), yellow (upper right), red (lower left), and blue (lower right). Projecting from the center of each canvas is a metal soap dish holding a replica of a bar of soap (actually painted wood) of the complementary color (light gray, violet, green, and orange), and traces of these colors appear also in the background. The dirty and muddied paint surface amusingly contradicts the cleanliness of the subject. A number of Dine's works from 1962 incorporate such wall-mounted objects (sink, medicine chest, shelves, light switch) and present an ambiguous relationship between the painting surface and wall surface, between depictions of rooms and the rooms themselves.

Hardware and tools appear throughout Dine's mature work, in all media. Tools have strong autobiographical meaning for Dine, recalling the years in Cincinnati between the ages of nine and eighteen during which he worked in his father's and grandfather's stores and felt an almost magical attraction to the tools there and to the color charts for mixing paint. In Dine's prints and drawings, single tools are often shown like icons, centered and frontal; actual tools are often incorporated in his paintings, as in *Proposed Still Life* (1962). Centered above a large black field a cluster of colorfully painted tools hangs from a hook. At the bottom the inscription reads

> then a gray screwdriver, then a red hatchet, then a yellow plyers, then a blue vise, then a green drill, then a violet clamp, then an orange level, then a flesh chisel, then a silver

as if these were a small section of a continuum. Like other objects which Dine uses, the tools are symbols for the full range of human emotions: some are violent tools of destruction; others are tools of construction, binding, measurement, and balance. To what extent Dine's conscious symbolic use of objects was enhanced by a period of psychoanalysis (1962–66) can only be guessed, but Dine freely acknowledges the autobiographical basis of his painting and true connection to his introspective processes.

Bedroom Light over Flesh Square (1965) similarly incorporates a personal iconography in which objects take on emotional and sexual meanings, only sometimes decipherable by the spectator. The sexual allusions here are manifold. The work has carnal as well as coloristic con-

Jim Dine, *Black Door*, 1962, painted door, oil on wood, 84½ × 36½″. Photograph by Jon Abbott.

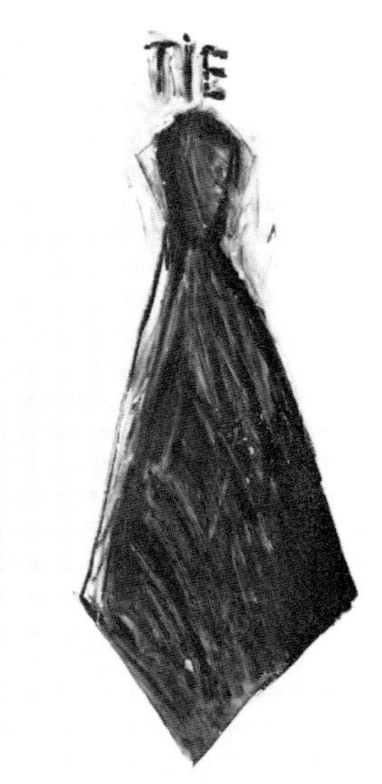

Jim Dine, *Tie*, 1962, charcoal and oil on paper, 26 × 19⅝″ (mat opening). Photograph by Jon Abbott.

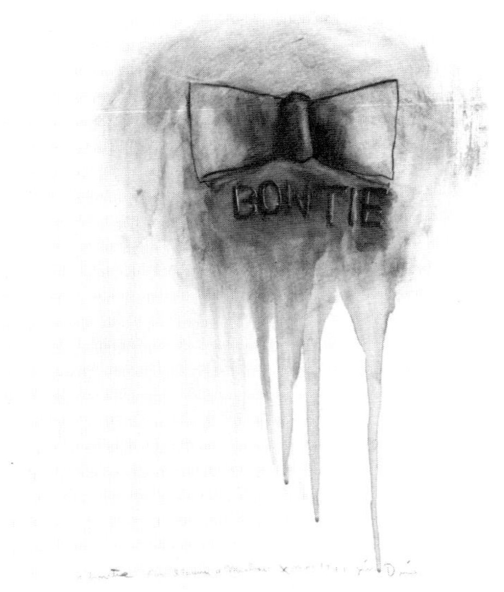

Jim Dine, *Bow Tie*, 1961, pencil and wash on paper, 24 × 18″. Photograph by Jon Abbott.

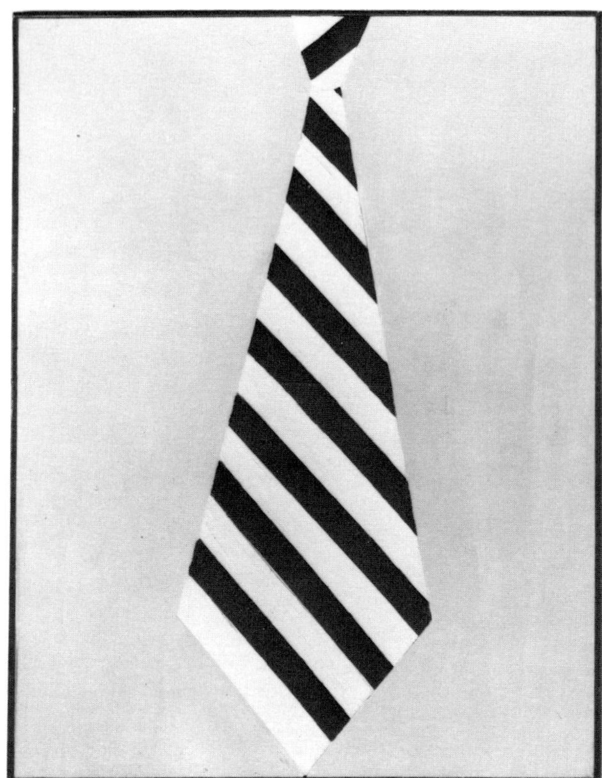

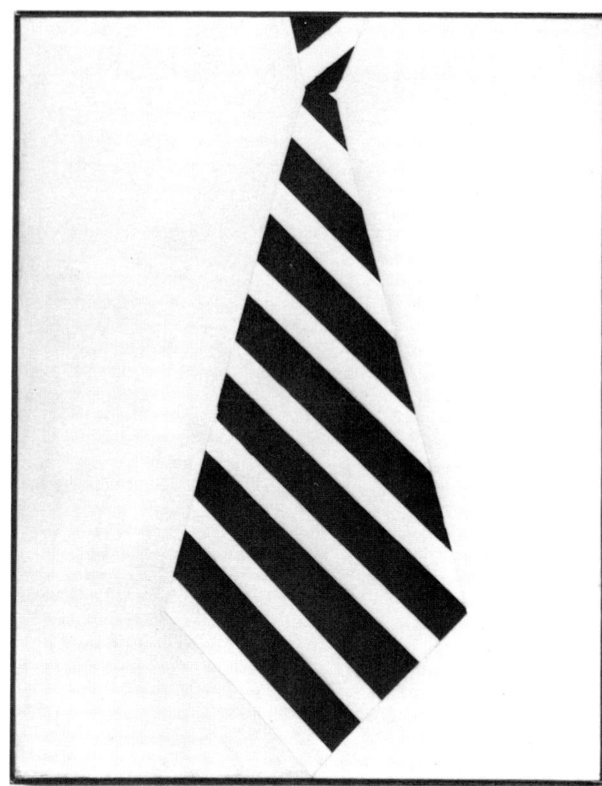

Jim Dine, *A Black on White Tie/A White on Black Tie*, 1962, oil on canvas, diptych, each panel 50¼ × 40″. Photograph by Clem Fiori.

notations, and the flesh square, painted in oil on a canvas otherwise drawn on only with graphite, has a distinctly physical presence. The nakedness of the "flesh" is reinforced through comparison with two contemporary and related works—a triptych, *Walking Dream with a Four-Foot Clamp*, and a diptych, *My Tuxedo Makes and Impresses Blunt Edges to the Light.*[2] In the first, flesh-colored female legs painted in oil parade below charcoal drawings of the bedroom light fixture. On the panels of the diptych, each of which has the dimensions of *Bedroom Light*, the flesh square is replaced by Dine's tuxedo jacket and pants. The light fixture itself is decidedly sexual, both formally and metaphorically: the electricity flows when the male and female elements are properly coupled, or, in the vernacular pun which Dine implies, "screwed" together. Its specific identification as a bedroom light further establishes the scene. The sexual interpretation of the light fixture is further substantiated by association with the superimposed naked female legs in both of the related works mentioned above. Dine's objects function not as hidden narrative (as in Rauschenberg's *Rebus* and *Canyon*[3]) but rather as metaphors for human thoughts, emotions, and desires: "When I use objects, I see them as a vocabulary of feelings."[4]

Malcolm R. Daniel

NOTES

1. Max Kozloff, "Art," *The Nation*, January 27, 1962, p. 88.
2. These two works are illustrated in David Shapiro, *Jim Dine* (New York: Harry N. Abrams, 1981), plates 104 and 106.
3. *Rebus* and other works are deciphered in Charles F. Stuckey, "Reading Rauschenberg," *Art in America*, 65 (March–April 1977), pp. 74–84. *Canyon*, in the Sonnabend collection, is similarly interpreted in Kenneth Bendiner, "Robert Rauschenberg's 'Canyon,'" *Arts*, 56 (June 1982), pp. 57–59.
4. Jim Dine, interview with John Gruen, 1966, quoted in John Gruen, "Jim Dine and the Life of Objects," *Art News*, 76 (September 1977), p. 38.

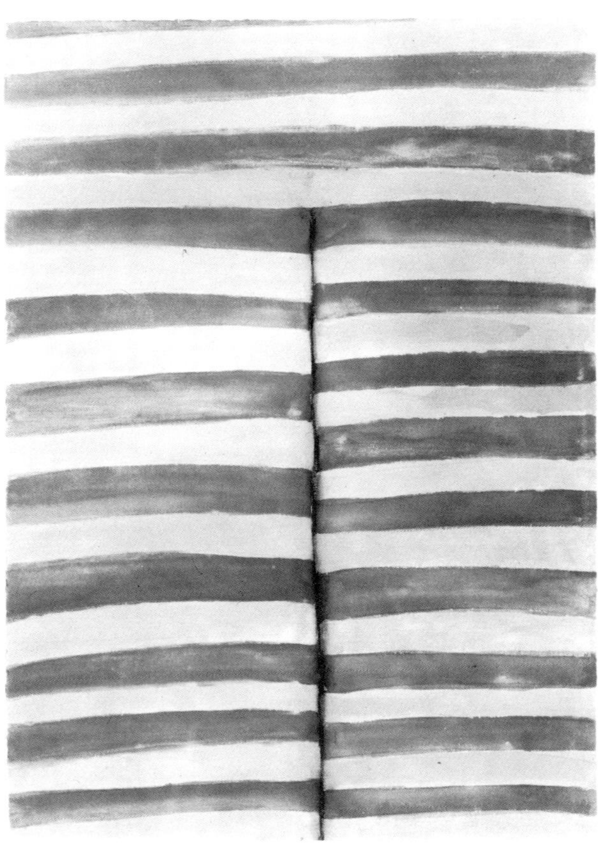

Jim Dine, *French Pants*, 1962, oil on paper, 30¾ × 22½″.
Photograph by Clem Fiori.

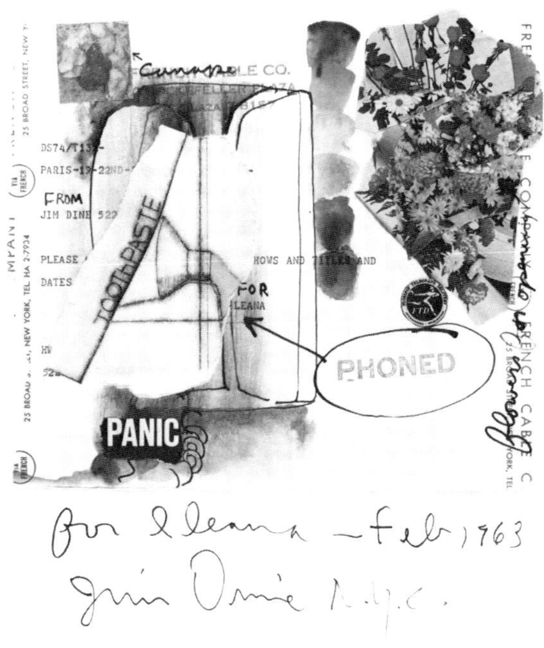

Jim Dine, *Untitled*, 1963, collage on paper, 11 × 8½″.
Photograph by Jon Abbott.

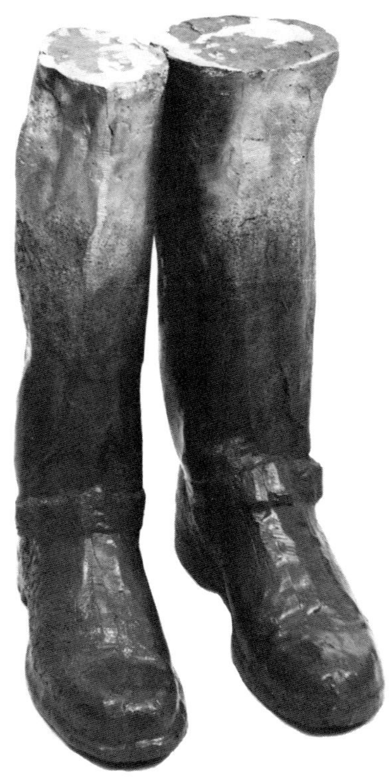

Jim Dine, *A Nice Pair of Boots*, 1965, painted bronze, each boot 16 × 11 × 4″. Photograph by John Goldblatt.

Jasper Johns

Born in 1930 in Augusta, Georgia, Jasper Johns went to New York in 1949. He studied for six months in a commercial art school, spent two years in the army, and then took a job in a bookstore. In 1954 he met Rauschenberg and went into partnership with him on window display jobs for New York department stores. That same year he began making constructions from various materials—wood, plaster, paper collage—most of which he destroyed a few months later. Distancing himself from the dominant Abstract Expressionists as well as from the collages and constructions of his friend Rauschenberg, Johns invented a new imagery and handling, focusing on intellectual content and perception, or, as he said, on "things the mind already knows."[1] The now celebrated series of flags, targets, maps, numbers, and other motifs soon emerged. Johns also adopted the unusual technique of encaustic (wax) painting. His radical conception of the art object, banal imagery, and rare and methodical technical mastery resulted between 1954 and 1960 in a group of highly original and influential works.

Johns's pictorial inventions appear to be real objects, although he uses no traditional illusionistic tricks to establish their verity, such as perspective, modeling, or *trompe l'oeil* effects. The very nature of his subjects—he prefers flat objects or emblems characterized by standard design—creates an ambiguous relationship between the actual object and its representation. Indeed, Johns's paintings and drawings question the nature of artistic representation. At the same time, however, the composition and the emphasis on brushwork focus one's attention on formal qualities, tactile surface, and abstract design.

Johns's characteristic ambiguity is evident in his flag motif. In the first one he painted, the flag covered the whole surface of the canvas: the painting field was thus identical with an actual flag and could be viewed as either one. In *Flag Above White*, 1954, the white stripes have a double role, as image and as field, emphasizing a continuity with the white surface below the depicted flag. The unusual composition thus prevents the viewer from reading the white field simply as a background, and accentuates the duplicity of the white area as neutral ground and nuanced image.

In *Gray Target*, 1958, distancing from the actual object is achieved through the discreet use of gray, which lessens the target's clarity as a distinct image; indeed, the target bands are barely differentiated or visible. This predetermined design allows Johns to concentrate on other formal and expressive features of his work: the delicacy of the brushwork, and the subtle nuances of values and hues. By using encaustic, Johns was able to superimpose several layers of paint without altering the ones underneath, thus enhancing the richness, depth, and luminosity of the surface.

Numbers and letters share with the flag and the target a preordained flat design. Johns was in fact interested in a particular type of commonplace visual element, the commercial stenciled letters and figures.[2] The first numbers, in 1955, were small monochrome units in serried rows. Johns began to execute brightly colored paintings using a different, larger type of stroke and an enlarged, centered image. In *Number 8*, of 1959, Johns applied encaustic on a collage of classified ads from newspapers, a technique he had already explored. Here, the freedom and irregularity of paint application, the large ragged shapes, and the pooled and puddled paint evoke Abstract Expressionist paintings, and, in fact, call to mind the brashness and energy of de Kooning's Woman series. The directness and spontaneity of the improvisational brushwork contrast with the precision of the stenciled figure which Johns used as his model, and with the mechanical regularity of typefaces of the printed ads faintly visible through the painted surface.

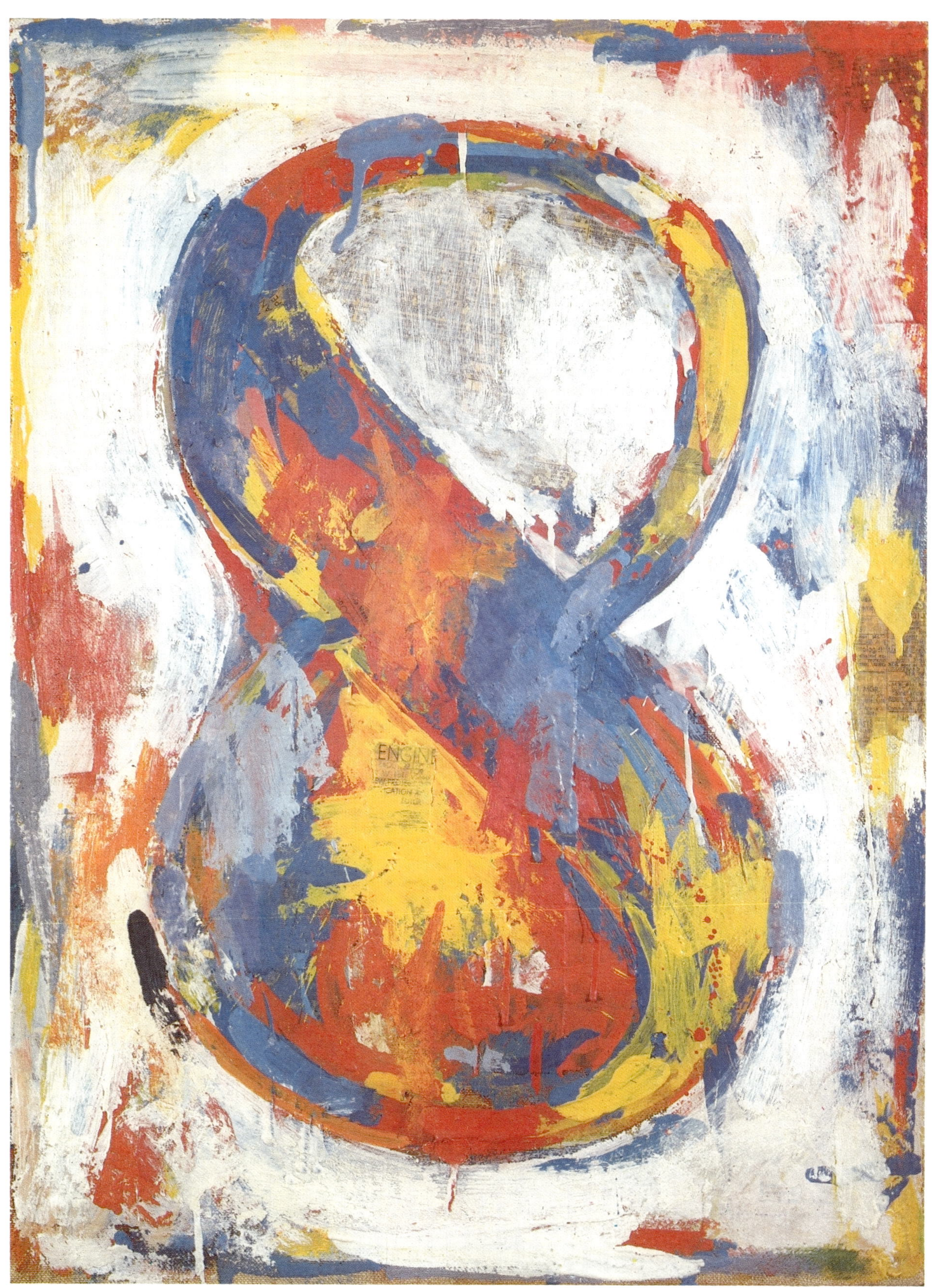

Jasper Johns, *Number 8*, 1959, encaustic on canvas, 20 × 15″. Photograph by Clem Fiori.

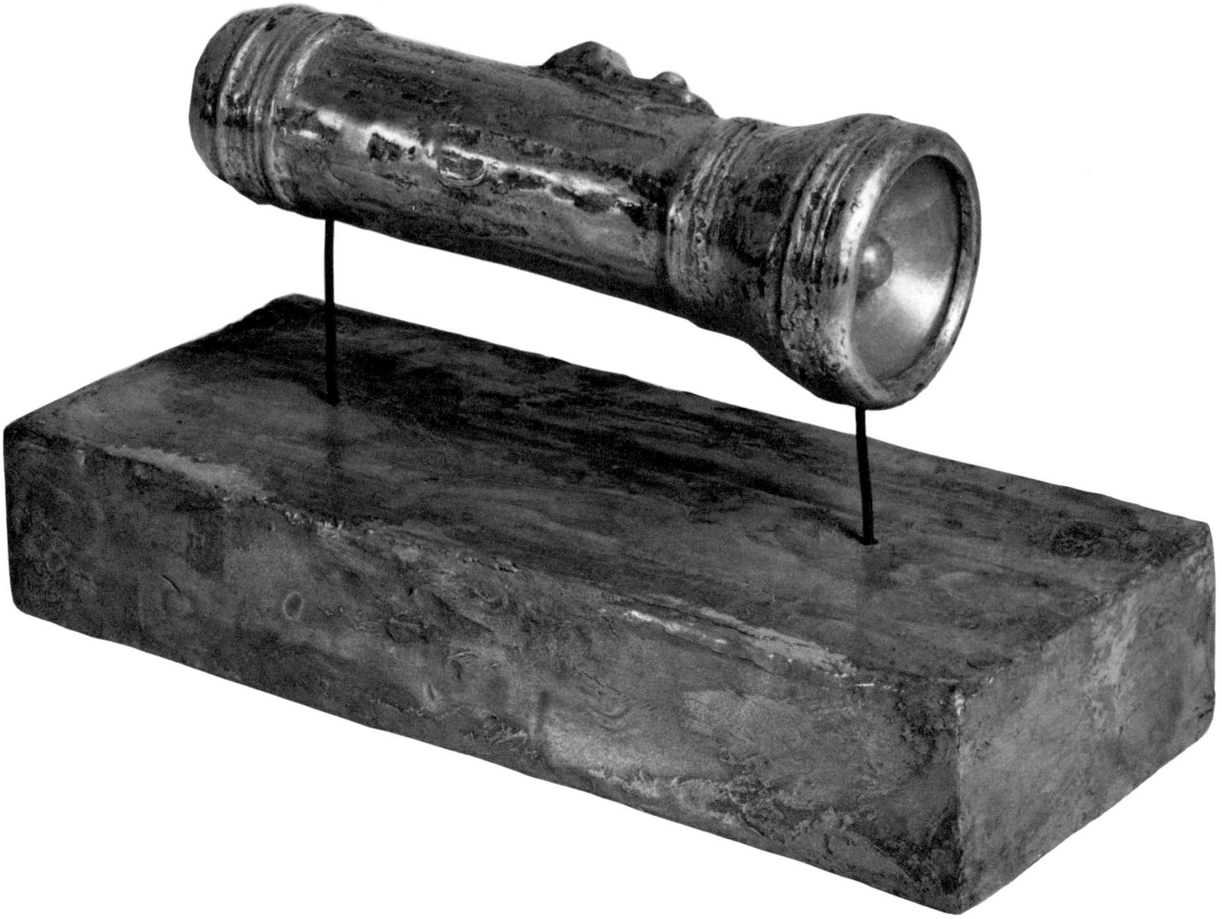

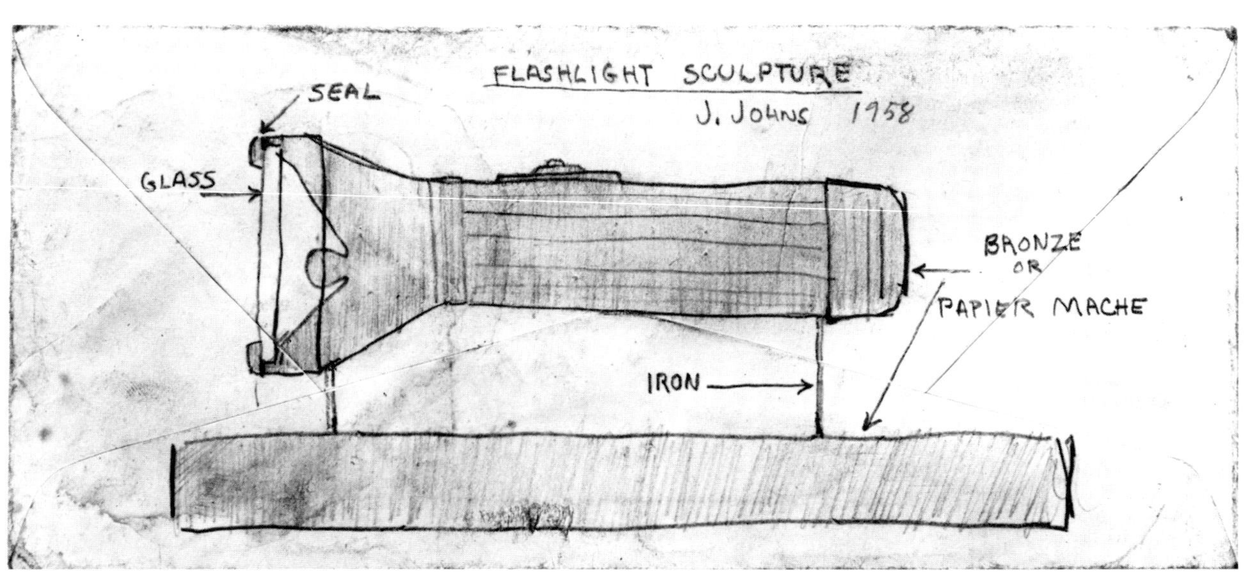

Jasper Johns: Top, *Flashlight*, 1958, sculpmetal over flashlight and wood, $5\frac{1}{4} \times 9\frac{1}{8} \times 3\frac{7}{8}''$. Photograph by Clem Fiori. Bottom, *Sketch for Flashlight*, 1958, pencil on envelope, $4\frac{1}{4} \times 9\frac{1}{2}''$. Photograph by Jon Abbott.

In *Numbers*, 1960, the succession of figures produces a repeated, regular pattern on the surface, without emphasizing a relational hierarchy between the parts, and thus resembles Pollock's "all-over" painting technique. Johns first attempted such visual arrangements of letters of the alphabet in 1956. As in *Gray Target*, the forms of the numbers are more suggestive than clearly drawn, and yet it is surprising how the variety of brushstrokes manages to create an effect of measured regularity. A striking aspect of this painting is its small size. Johns had painted large number series in 1958; the small version, however, is more than a mere reduction. Its small scale, along with the fragility of the medium and the delicacy of the brushwork, gives this work the precious and intimate quality of a miniature. Compared to the large-scale paintings of the Abstract Expressionists and to their revolutionary attack on the principles and practices of painting, Johns's work seems modeled on traditional craftsmanship. The dynamic interplay of brushstrokes in defining and obscuring imagery is fascinating. Although the numbers can be read easily, when one tries to follow their individual contours they are lost in the formal working of the surface and the texture of the paint.

The same ambiguity between revelation and dissimulation of form, precision and a deliberate imprecision, is characteristic of Johns's drawings. Reversing the traditional process of drawing an object against a background, Johns has almost impartially emphasized both the background and the object-image in *Hook*, 1958; the critical image finally emerges clearly in the midst of a dark field of uniform hatchings. In *Flag*, 1954, it seems as if the active and delicate graphite markings were intended to conceal the simple emblem of the American flag. The drawing is covered with layered lines, in generally vertical and horizontal axes, but precisely where one would expect lines —for instance, to define the flag's stripes—there are none. The eye is compelled to struggle to make out the image. *Target* of 1960 signals Johns's increasing interest at this time in the mind and the Dadaist art of Marcel Duchamp, whom he met in 1959. His art became a focus for more intellectual

Jasper Johns, *Flag*, 1954, pencil on paper, 4½ × 3¾". Photograph by Jon Abbott.

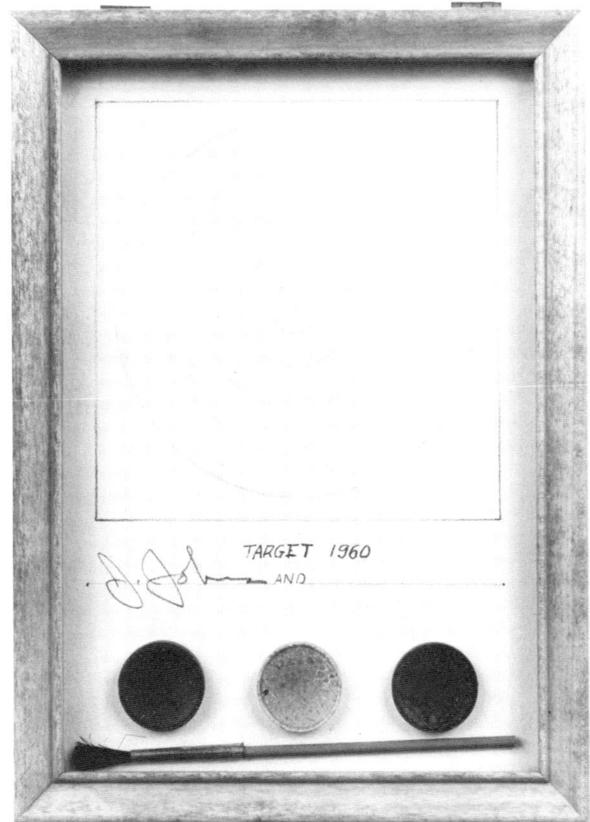

Jasper Johns, *Target*, 1960, pencil with paint brush and dry watercolor cakes, wood frame, 7¾ × 3¾". Photograph by Jon Abbott.

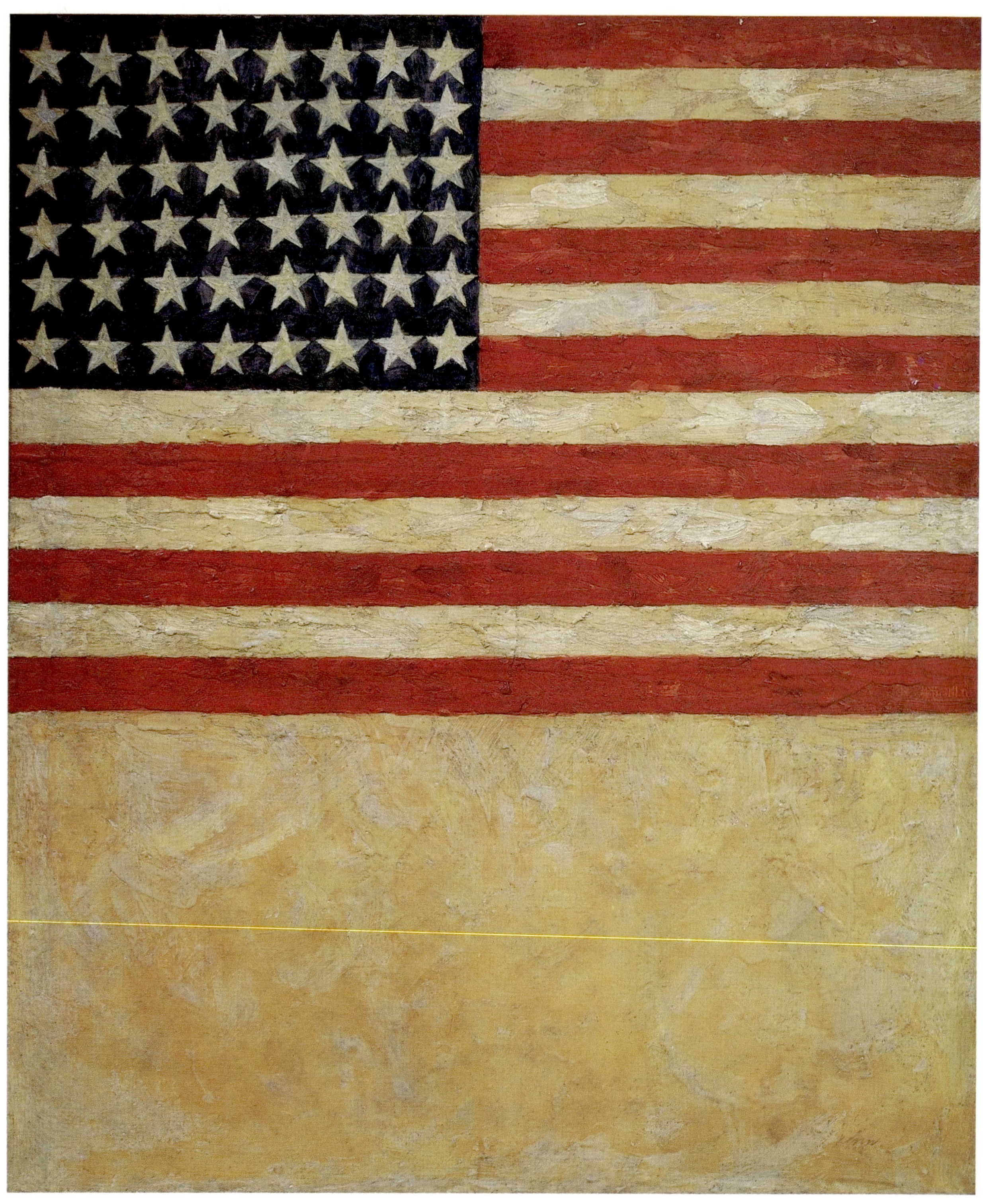

Jasper Johns, *Flag Above White*, 1954, encaustic on canvas, 23¼ × 20″. Photograph by Eric Pollitzer.

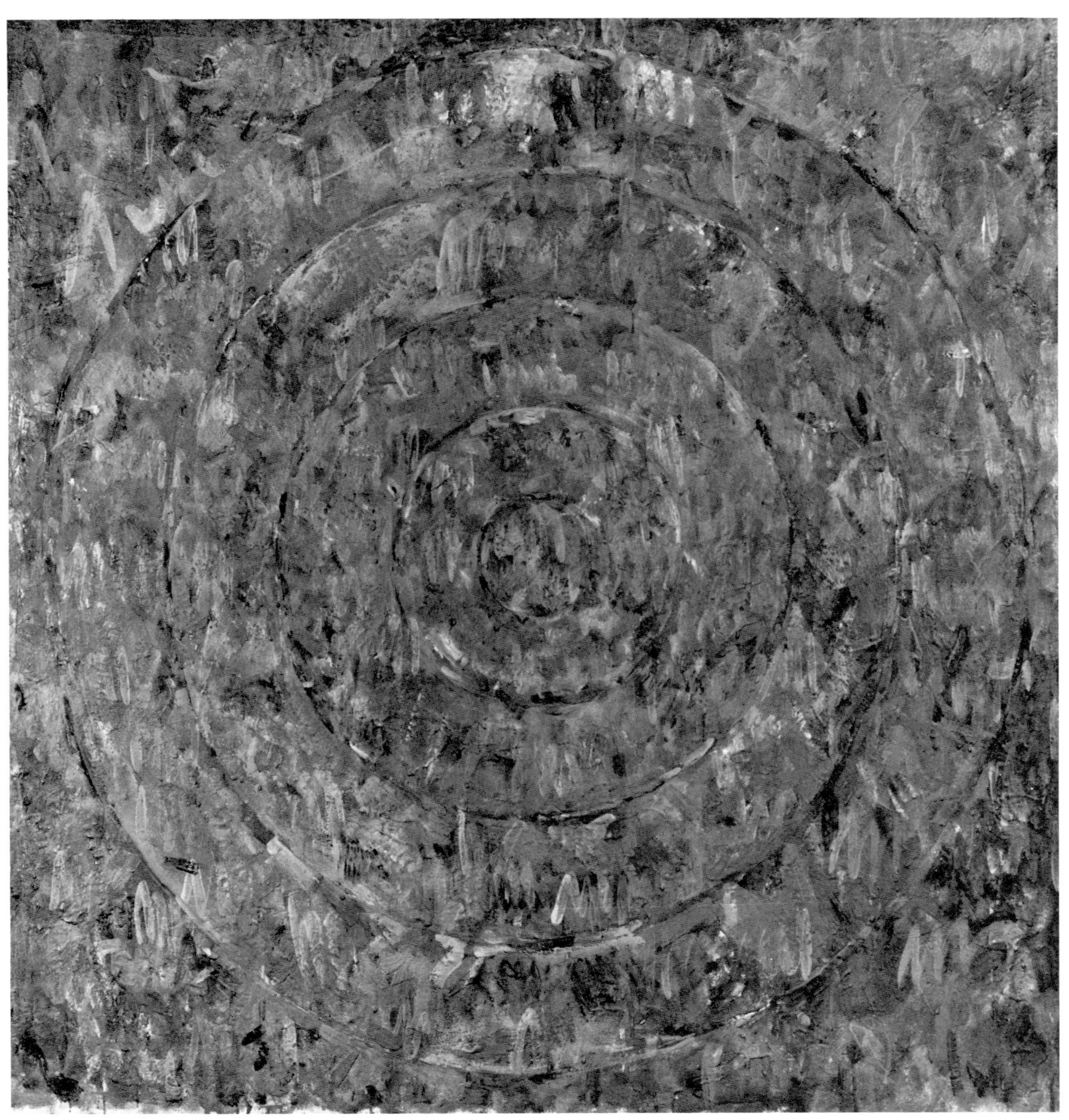

Jasper Johns, *Gray Target*, 1958, encaustic and collage on canvas, 42 × 42″.

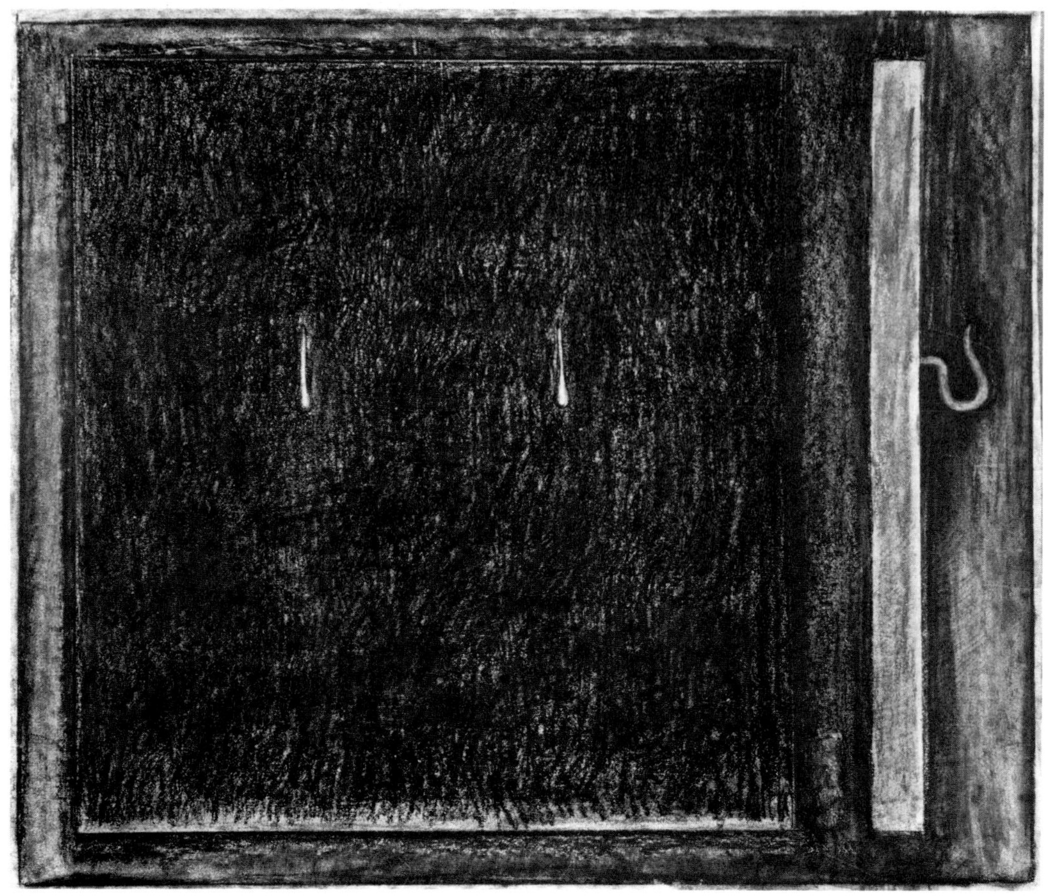

Jasper Johns, *Hook*, 1958, crayon and charcoal on paper, 17 × 20¾″. Photograph by Rudolph Burckhardt.

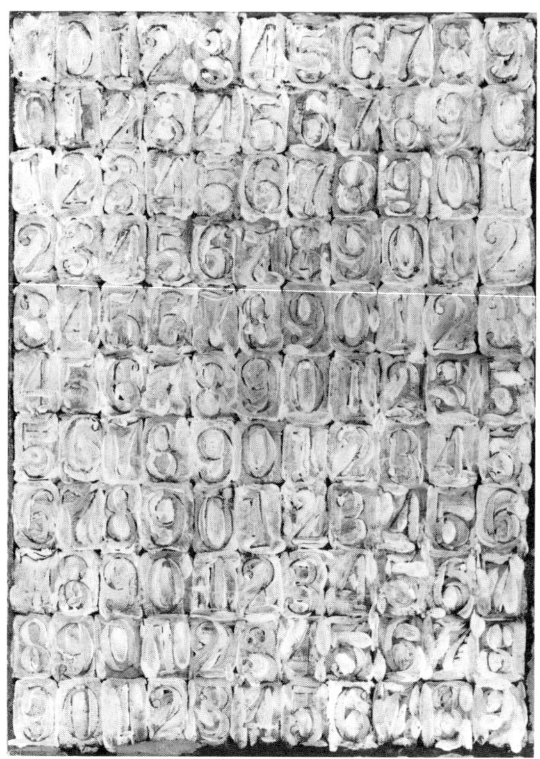

Jasper Johns, *Numbers*, 1960, oil on board, 8¼ × 6″. Photograph by Clem Fiori.

experiment and problematic content. This tiny object, looking somewhat like a toy, is reminiscent of the famous *Target with Plaster Casts* of 1955. The three primary colors of that target are now proposed in the samples, and these samples also recall the colored plaster casts arranged in boxes. The intervention of the artist is now reduced to the conception of the work, which is, actually, a proposal for a painting, with the ultimate realization left, theoretically, to the viewer. The painting is signed by the artist with the word "and," and the "and" is blank, presumably to be completed by the viewer bold enough to color in the target.

Johns's rethinking of Duchamp's concepts also influenced his sculptures. In *Flashlight*, of 1958, Johns used an actual flashlight, emulating Duchamp's readymades. He wanted to use an ordinary flashlight, but it took him a week to find a satisfactory example. He has written, "It made me very suspect of my idea. . . . It turns out that actually the choice is quite personal and is not really based on one's observations at all."[3] In contrast to Duchamp, Johns covered his found object with a layer of sculpmetal, and painted in gray the parts behind the glass shield, including the bulb inside. The flashlight replica was thus transformed to look like an old and worn object, tarnished by use and exposure, even suggesting to some an archaeological sample of the modern world. By coating the flashlight with the malleable sculpmetal, Johns established a continuity with his paintings, where he overpainted the forms of targets and numbers in encaustic. This kind of handling is a constant in Johns's early work, blurring the defining contours and identity of a predetermined design image or a machine-made object. It is extended in *Flashlight II* and *Flashlight III*, where the torch progressively sinks into an amorphous sculpmetal mass, losing all definition.[4]

In the 1960s, Johns's work thus evolved to question the meanings and the validity of illusion and representation. The motifs and artistic issues from the late fifties emerged in more complex compositions, testing our assumptions about identity, memory, and the very making of art, and expanding our responses to art. Flags were paired, with dramatic variations in color or in medium;[5] targets and numbers were reproduced in a series of prints. Strongly rooted in Duchamp's seminal ideas, Johns's work boldly embraced complex interrelations of language, thought, and vision.

Isabelle Dervaux

NOTES

1. Cited by Harold Rosenberg in "Jasper Johns: Things the Mind Already Knows," *Vogue*, 143 (February 1, 1964), p. 175.
2. See Leo Steinberg, "Jasper Johns: The First Seven Years of His Art," in *Other Criteria: Confrontations with Twentieth-Century Art* (New York, 1972), p. 32.
3. Interview by David Sylvester, in *Jasper Johns: Drawings* (London: The Arts Council of Great Britain, 1974), p. 8.
4. See reproductions in M. Crichton, *Jasper Johns* (London, 1977), figs. 30–32.
5. For a study of Jasper Johns's flags, see Richard S. Field, "Jasper Johns's Flags," *The Print Collector's Newsletter*, 7 (July–August, 1976), pp. 69–77.

Roy Lichtenstein

After finishing an undergraduate degree in painting at Ohio State University in 1946 and a master's degree at the same institution in 1949, Lichtenstein taught at the university for two years.

In 1951 he had his first one-man show in New York, at the Carlebach Gallery, which was characterized by a mixture of the energetic style of Action Painting and a dominant western-frontier imagery derived from Remington and Russell. Lichtenstein's early fascination with familiar, if not trite, historical subjects later developed into an interest in a more contemporary American vision, derived from popular culture.

While teaching at the State University of New York at Oswego (1957–60), Lichtenstein experimented with assemblage and Abstract Expressionist style of a gestural character, showing the works at the Heller Gallery in New York. But his period of expressionist painting was short-lived, ending when he began teaching at Douglass College of Rutgers University in 1960, and he soon abandoned strongly subjective tendencies and eliminated autographic, gestural marks in the handling of paint.

At Douglass College Lichtenstein encountered a potent and ambitious group of artists who were incorporating materials and images from popular culture in their work, and who soon became very influential in effecting radical changes in American art. George Segal, Allan Kaprow, Lucas Samaras, and Robert Whitman were originators of Happenings. Robert Watts and George Brecht, also at Douglass College, affected Lichtenstein's development and were soon after associated with Fluxus, a neo-Dada group that produced witty and iconoclastic visual puns somewhat akin to later Pop Art, but of a more enigmatic and intellectual character. Lichtenstein later acknowledged that both Fluxus and the environmental aspect of Happenings—the first one was staged by Kaprow on Segal's nearby chicken farm, in North Brunswick, New Jersey—directly influenced his turning to common objects and the imagery of popular culture. Lichtenstein's drawings, prefiguring his paintings of ordinary household items, as in *Step-on Can with Leg* of 1961, are part of the "kitchen culture" movement in which the artists used simplistic icons from commercial art styles to comment obliquely on the formal basis of art itself.

Because of its familiarity, the subject in Lichtenstein's art became an "object-hieroglyph," with the aesthetic tension centered in the fact that he was almost literally, but with expressive differences, translating the graphic techniques and point of view of commercial illustration into "high" art. The bold highlights and visual contrasts established by the linear abstraction and the emphatic Ben Day dot screens used in the later works, such as *Bread and Jam* of 1963, refer both to the ersatz quality of what we see and to the mechanical reproduction process, which became a metaphor for creative transformation. Lichtenstein's brash and reductive graphic style is both artistic invention and simulation of commercial art styles, including industrial packaging and processing. Although the mechanical printing process is always mentioned in relation to Lichtenstein's pointillist backgrounds, this device carries other equally important references—evoking not only Seurat but contemporary Op Art—and serves the important formal function of operating perceptually to dissolve the painting surface into a vibrant illusion of spatial depth.

As Lichtenstein enlarged his scale and image, he was able to refine his vision and to aesthetically maximize the impact of a particular frame from a cartoon strip. He also began to move toward a clearer social content and conscious cultural stereotypes, such as that of a Hawaiian

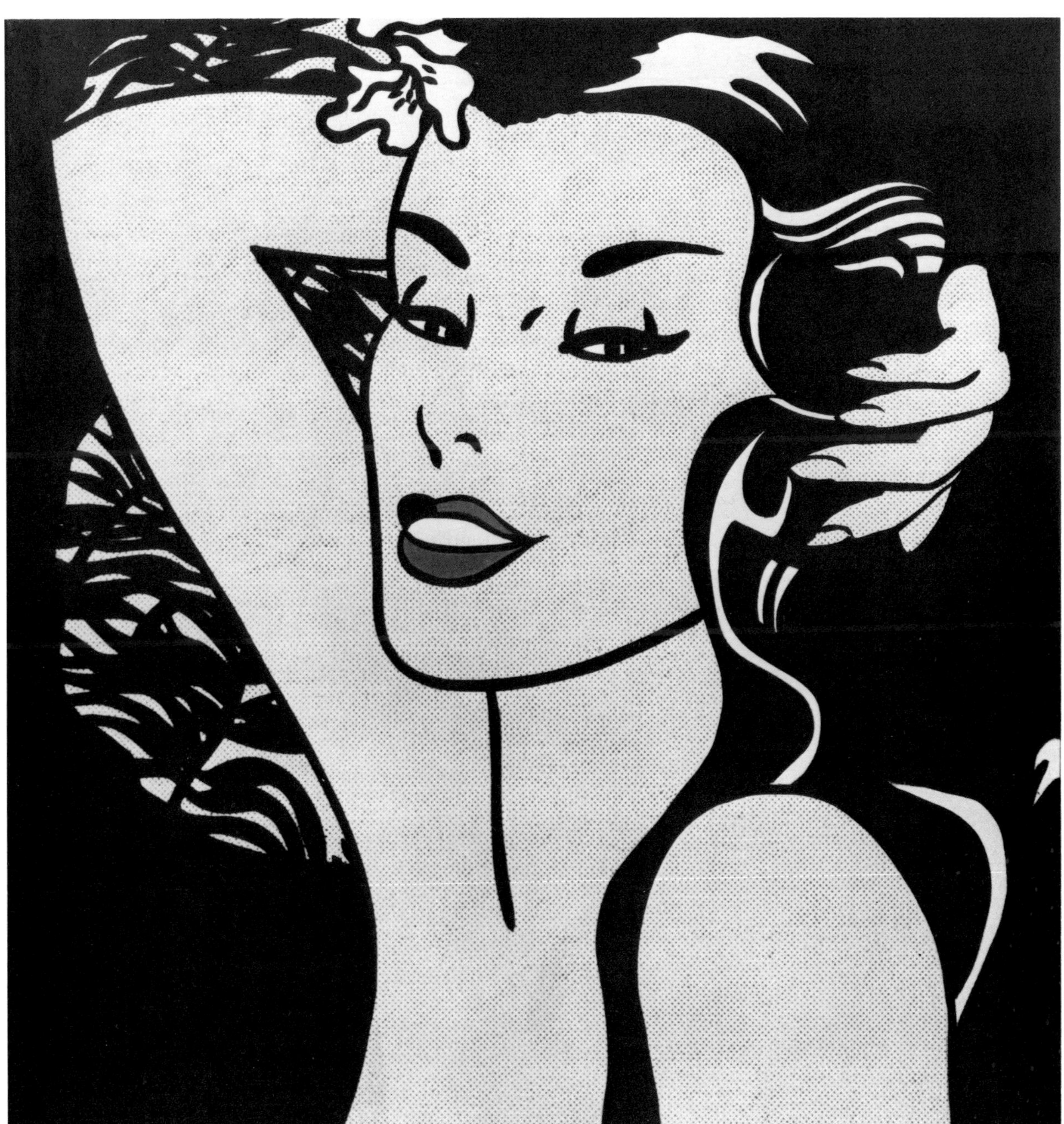

Roy Lichtenstein, *Little Aloha*, 1962, magna on canvas, 44 × 42″. Photograph by Clem Fiori.

paradise suggested by *Little Aloha* of 1962 or adolescent conflict with parental authority, suggested by the *Eddie Diptych*, also of 1962.

The well-known imagery from popular cartoon strips has allowed Lichtenstein to experiment with words as well as with visual content —of prime importance in the *Eddie Diptych*, for example. He has incorporated the caption into

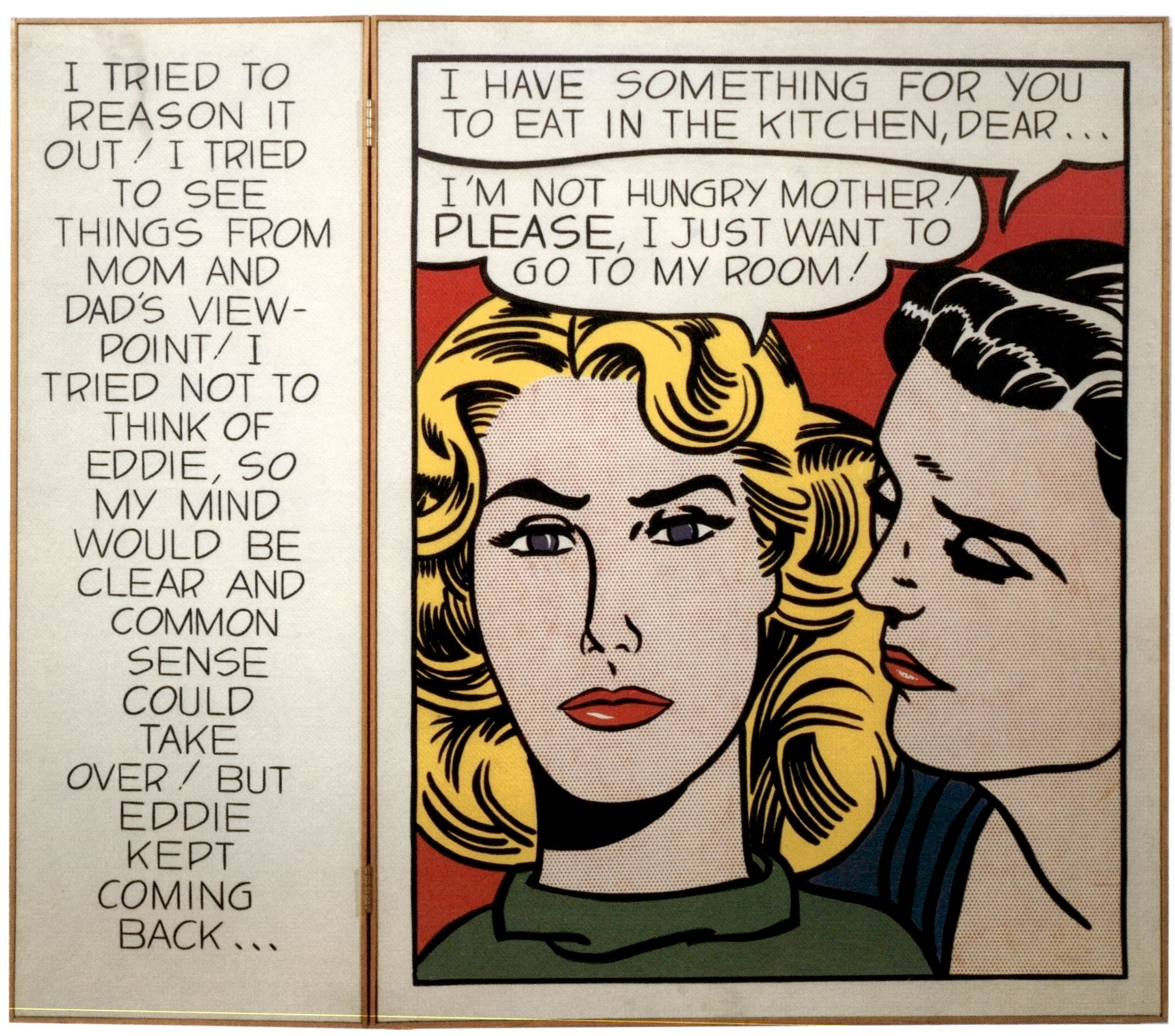

Roy Lichtenstein, *Eddie Diptych*, 1962, oil on canvas, 44 × 52″ (two panels). Photograph by Eric Pollitzer.

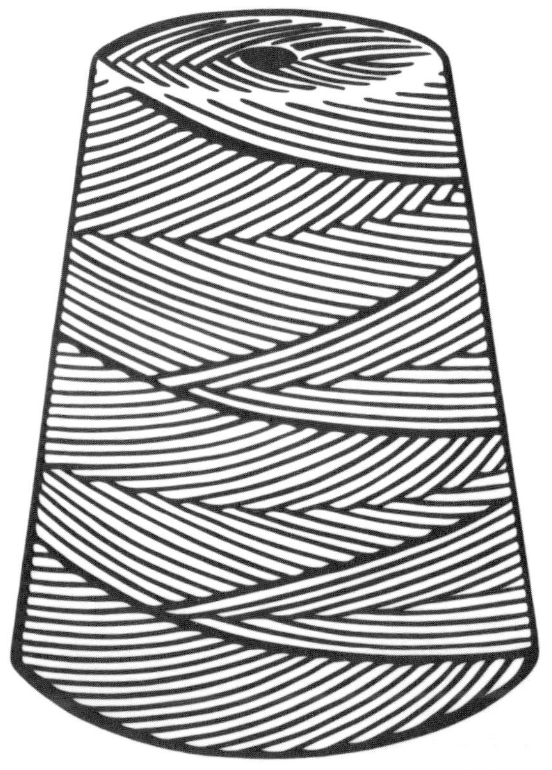

Roy Lichtenstein, *Large Spool*, 1963, magna on canvas, 68 × 56″.

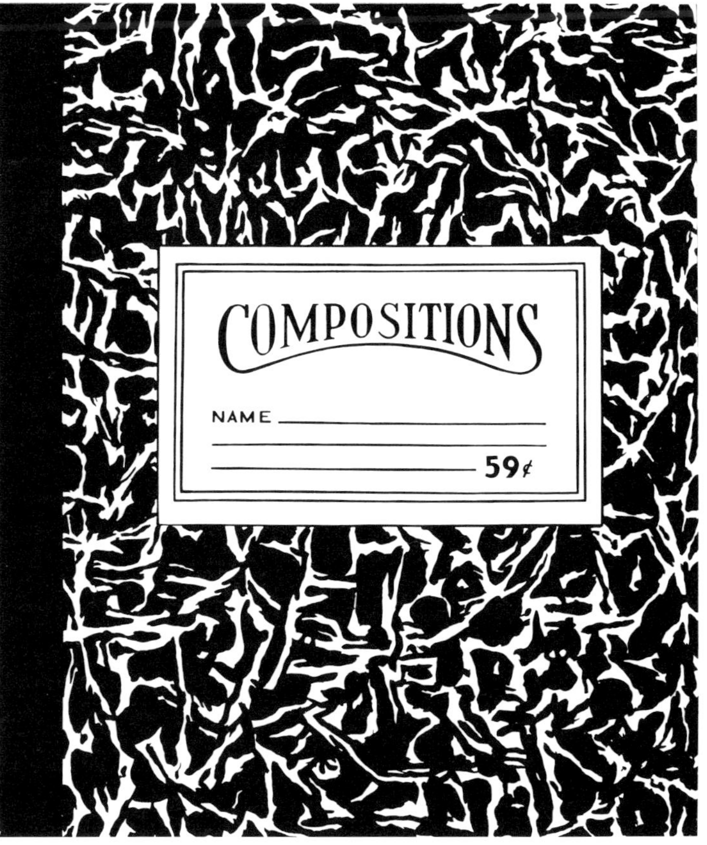

Roy Lichtenstein, *Composition II*, 1964, oil on canvas, 54 × 47″. Photograph by Nick Sheidy.

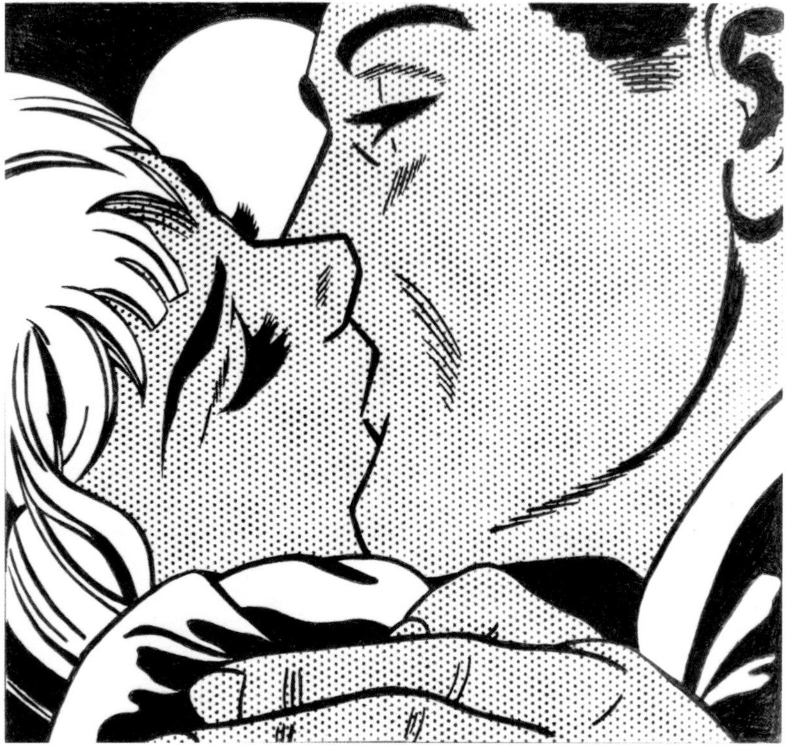

Roy Lichtenstein, *The Kiss II*, 1963, pencil and touche on paper, 16⅝ × 18⅛″ (image size). Photograph by Jon Abbott.

the body of the work rather than relegating it to the position of a blurb or external label; in this way he establishes interesting cross-references between the verbal and the visual. The scale of the caption is proportional to the figurative elements, and the patterned words become cunning and important. Similarly, the emotional tension and ambivalence that the words convey create a striking opposition to their visual boldness and mechanical ordering, much as the coolness of the cartoon style contrasts with emotional subject matter.

After 1963, Lichtenstein began to focus on isolated formal and topical elements that had previously played a marginal role. The crisscross patterning of *Non-Objective II*, 1964, was an offshoot of his experimentation with the Mondrian plus-and-minus graphic system used in earlier works. Lichtenstein also carried the device of unifying foreground and background, seen earlier in the cartoon works, to its logical conclusion by using Mondrian's primary color combinations and emphatic black lines to organize his abstract configuration in large rectilinear areas.

Such abstract works as *Modern Painting* of 1967 focused on yet another form of commercialized subject matter, Art Deco—a newly revived, mildly antiquated decorative and design style inspired by such popular architectural icons as Radio City Music Hall, Rockefeller Center, and the Chrysler Building in New York. The angular and curving shapes on the canvas vibrate with rhythmically disposed concentric arcs set in groups of threes. Such sculptures as *Modern Sculpture with Glass Wave* and *Modern Sculpture with Horse Motif*, both of 1967, balance creative invention with the period flavor of Art Deco. Lichtenstein has explained this historical revivalism in this way: "I'm really involved in a relationship between textures . . . as well as colors and other things; but it's a modern industrial texture . . . that has its own mode and its own sensibility."

Julia Hicks

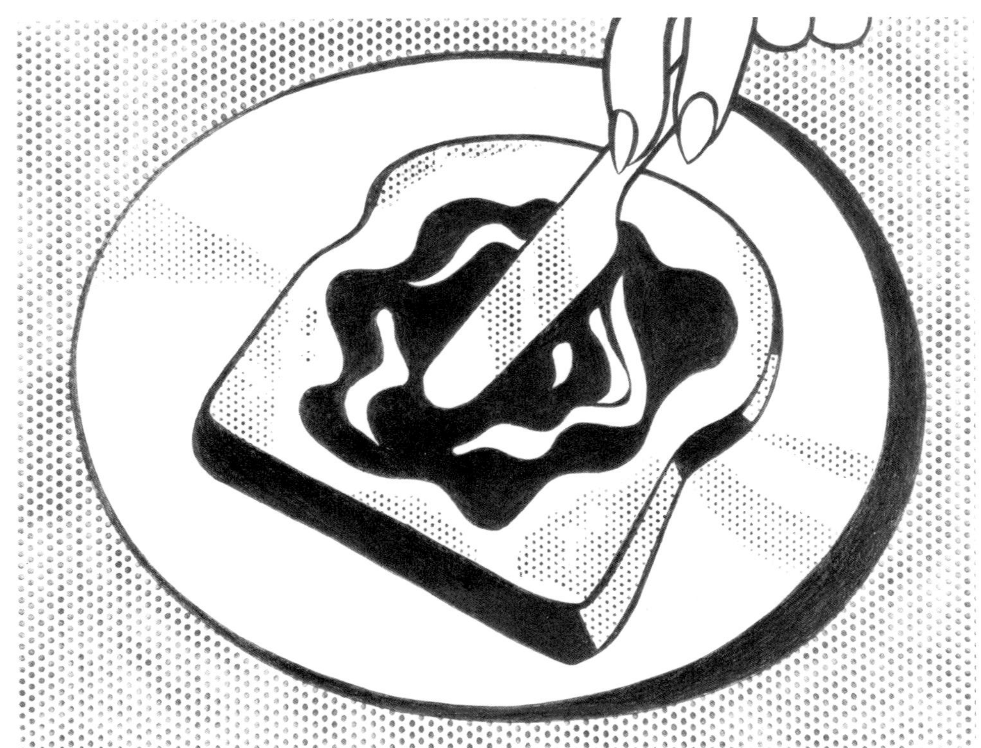

Roy Lichtenstein, *Bread and Jam*, 1963, pencil and touche on paper, 16 × 21⅝″ (image size). Photograph by Jon Abbott.

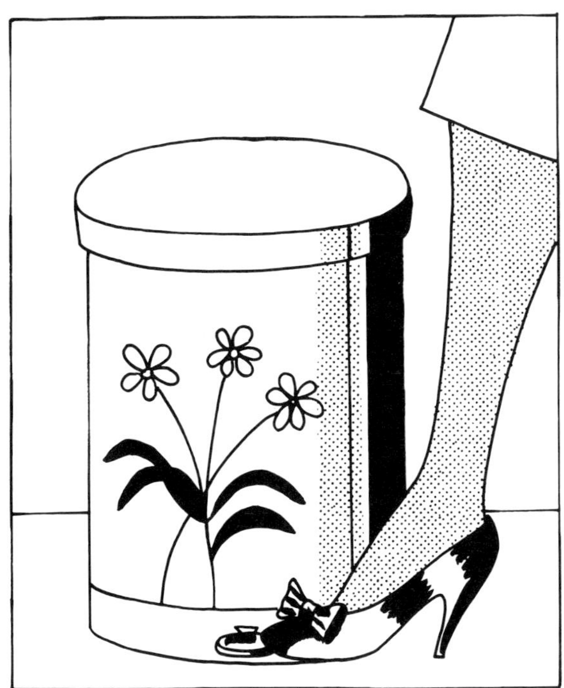

Roy Lichtenstein, *Step-on Can with Leg (Shut)*, 1961, ink on paper, 19⅞ × 23⅛″. Photograph by Jon Abbott.

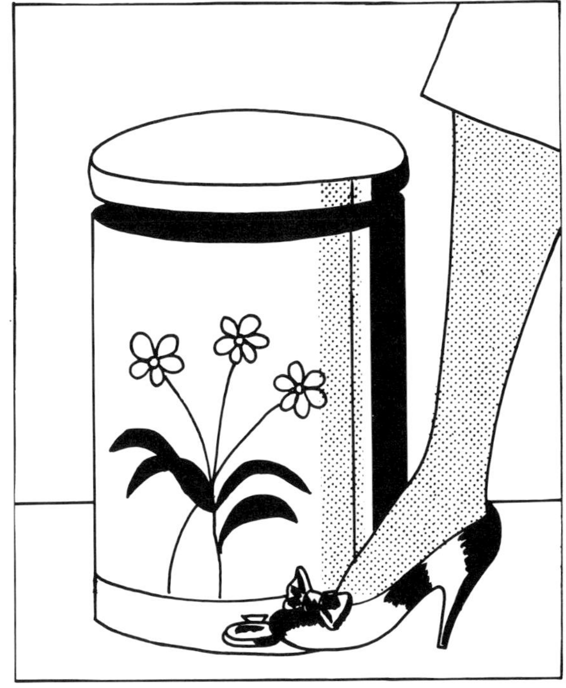

Roy Lichtenstein, *Step-on Can with Leg (Open)*, 1961, ink on paper, 19⅞ × 23⅛″. Photograph by Jon Abbott.

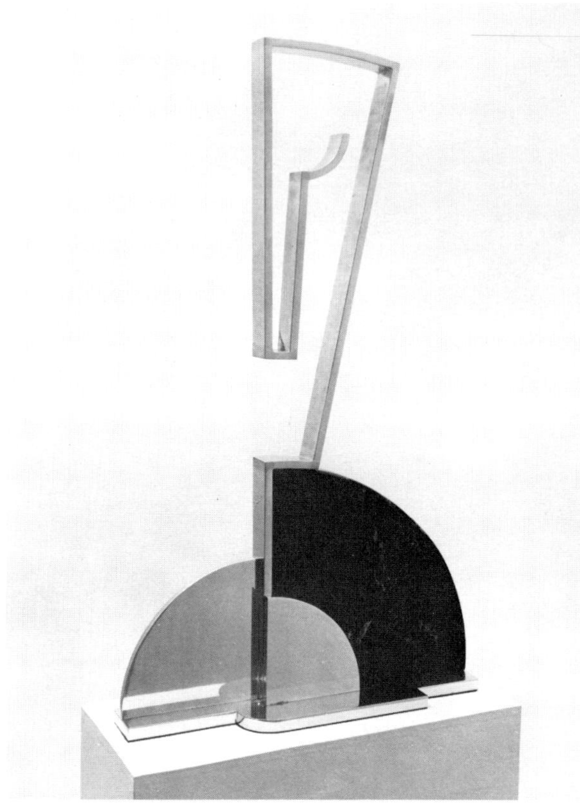

Roy Lichtenstein, *Modern Sculpture with Horse Motif*, 1967, aluminum and marble, 28¾ × 16½ × 5½″ (edition of six). Photograph by Rudolph Burckhardt.

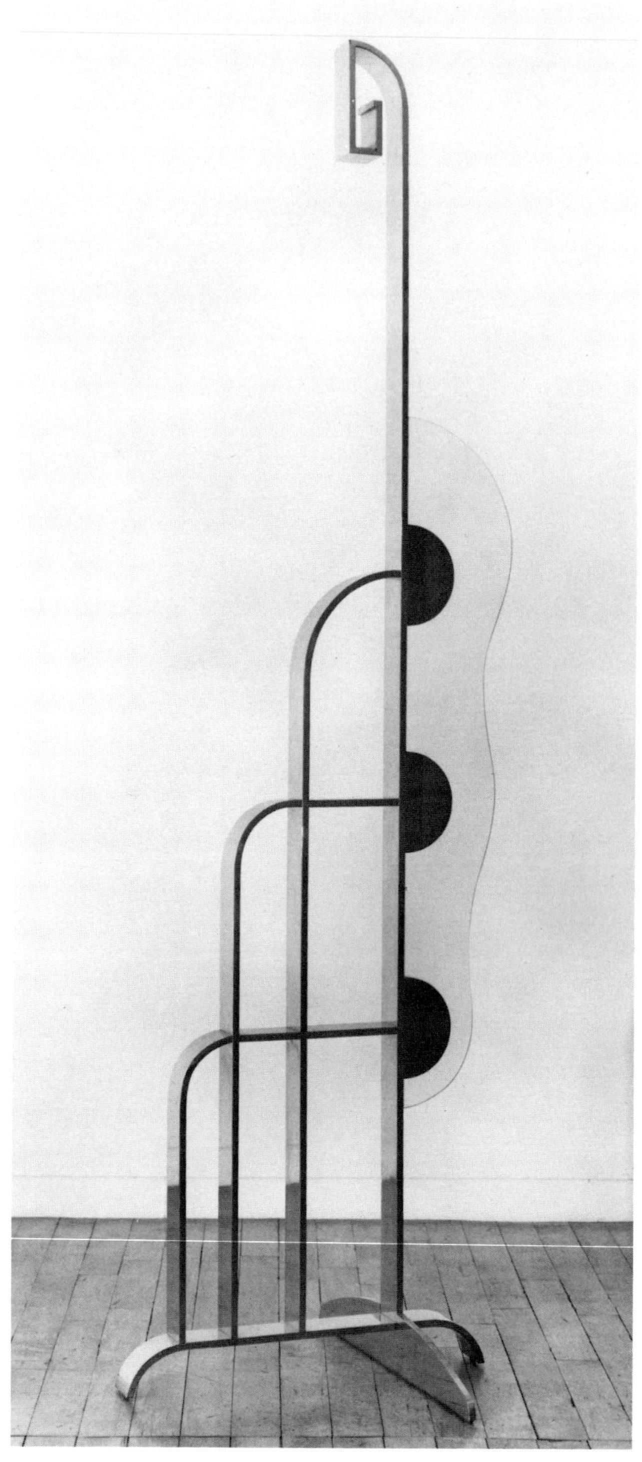

Roy Lichtenstein, *Modern Sculpture with Glass Wave*, 1967, brass and glass, 91 × 26 × 27″ (edition of three). Photograph by Jon Abbott.

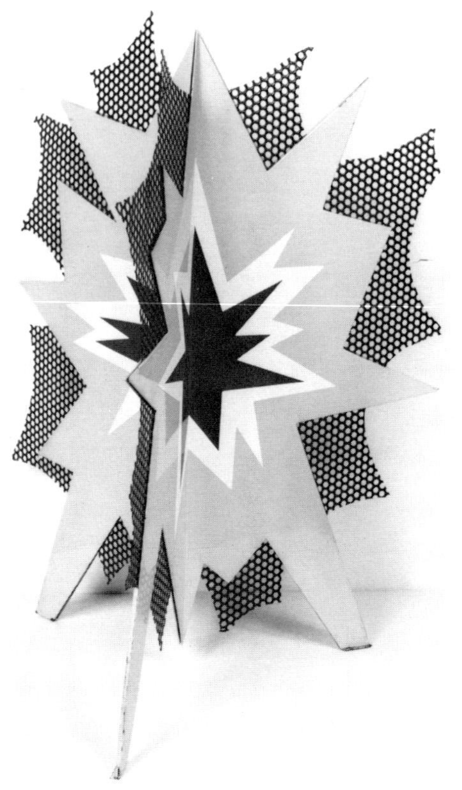

Roy Lichtenstein, *Standing Explosion*, 1966, enamel on steel, 38 × 27 × 25″. Photograph by Jon Abbott.

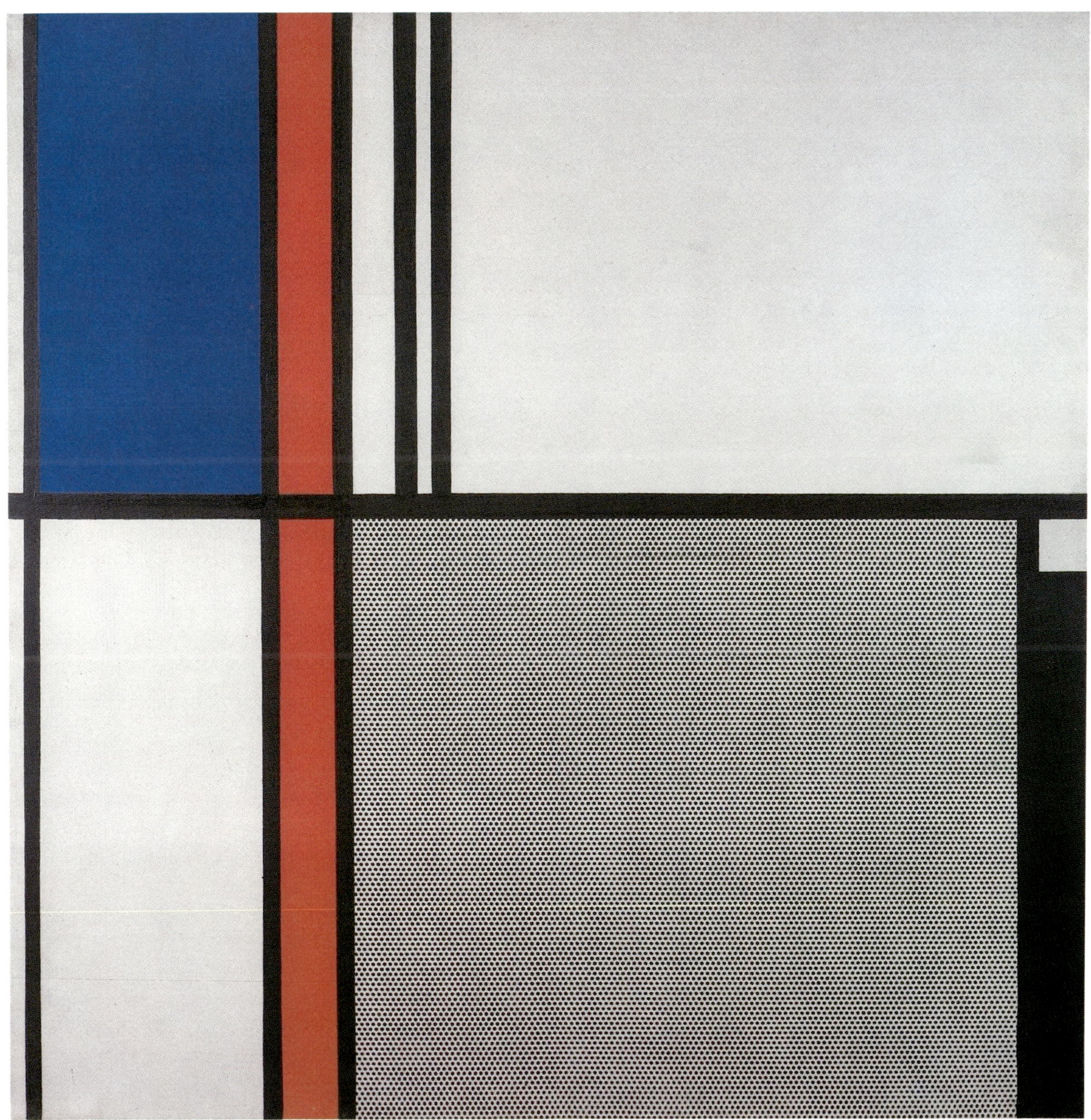

Roy Lichtenstein, *Non-Objective II*, 1964, magna on canvas, 48 × 48″.

Robert Morris

Although he chose sculpture as his dominant medium, Robert Morris began his art career with painting and theatrical improvisations. Born in 1931 in Kansas City, Missouri, he studied art first in Kansas City and then in San Francisco; he began exhibiting his paintings in 1957 and 1958 in San Francisco at the California School of Fine Arts. In 1961 he moved to New York, where he made his first sculptures. From the beginning his work was characterized by concerns expressed through very different and often antithetical forms; hence critics have discussed his successive relationship to Pop Art, Minimal Art, earthworks, and other contemporary styles. But a central and unifying theme has been Morris's questioning of the traditional nature and vocabulary of sculpture.

After making highly reductive and abstract box-like forms related to Minimal Art in 1961 and 1962, Morris began to create small lead constructions with inscriptions that evoked both Duchamp and Jasper Johns. Reflecting Duchamp's intellectual conception of art and his punning, these pieces are the visual embodiment of ideas and of a subversive Dadaist sense of irony. The information they contain often questions the very idea of art itself. Morris's objects are closest in spirit to Duchamp's readymades, and like them they bear few if any traces of the personal intervention of the artist in the execution of the work. This aspect of Morris's work distinguishes his sculpture from Johns's.

"Leave Key on Hook Inside Cabinet" of 1963 raises the issue of the uniqueness of the work of art, apart from the absurdity of the situation presented. As a functional object, the work is illogical, since the cabinet would be locked with the key placed inside, if the instructions of the inscription are correct: "Leave Key on Hook Inside Cabinet."[1] The meaning lies elsewhere. The presence of the inscription seems to imply repeated use by different persons, but in fact the instruction can be satisfied only once. This evident contradiction reflects upon the nature of the sculpture itself, for it is an object which any ordinary person can make (a simple wooden box) but it is, in fact, a unique artistic statement.

Something Else, also of 1963, is one of several sculptures by Morris which utilize rulers and other measuring devices. The idea of measurement was explored earlier by Duchamp in his *Three Standard Stoppages*, where he associated the contradictory notions of measurement and chance, to subvert official standards and rational assumptions. Morris has juxtaposed two rulers, both measuring twelve inches long but actually of slightly different size. They both can be opened as lids to reveal an inner surface with the inscription "Something Else." These words underscore the slight differences, represented by the two unequal ruler lengths, between a theoretical concept and its actualization. In their ambiguous reference these words also take on poetic connotations. The sculpture thus proposes a confrontation between mathematical calculation and poetic statement. It can even be read as the visual metaphor for a traditional form of poetry, in which the poetic content is expressed in regular meter and rhyme. The deliberate relationship between sculpture and poetry, or other literary content, associates Morris with the Dadaists and the Surrealists. Like them, he exploits the visual connotations of language to enrich the content of his sculptures. The invitation to open or close the hinged, movable elements of *Something Else* is reminiscent of Johns's *Target with Plaster Casts*, in which the boxes with body fragments can be concealed or exposed to view. The participation of the viewer became important in Morris's subsequent performance pieces, in which the beholder is encouraged to interact with the work as an environment.

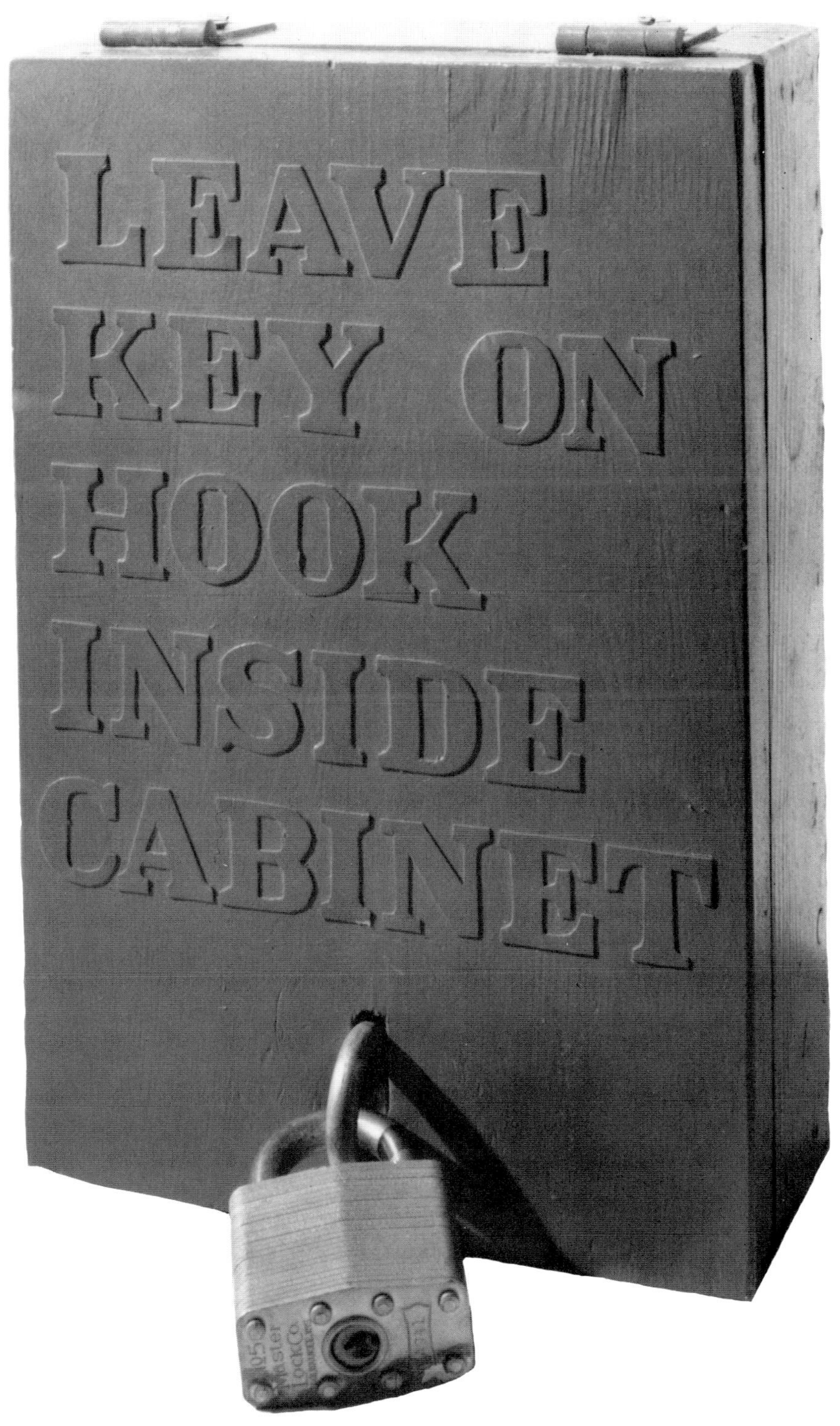

Robert Morris, *"Leave Key on Hook Inside Cabinet,"* 1963, paint on wood with lock, 11 × 7¾ × 3½″. Photograph by Jon Abbott.

Robert Morris, *Battery*, 1963, lead on board, 43 × 12⅛″. Photograph by Clem Fiori.

The Minimalist aspect of Morris's work in the later years of the sixties seemingly offers a sharp contrast to his earlier works. However, they all share the same concern with questions about the nature of sculpture. In the lead pieces with inscriptions, problems of perception and meaning are raised. Despite the simplicity of their forms, as regular polyhedrons, Morris's Minimalist sculptures present paradoxical readings of the complex relationships among scale, proportion, light, space, and surface texture. By reducing the shapes to elementary, given forms, the artist was able to emphasize other aspects of the work. As one example, two identical L-beam forms, placed in different positions, established a contrast between the conceptual identity of the two pieces and their striking perceptual dissimilarity to the eye. Morris's Minimalist sculptures of this kind were permutation pieces, for which he established a program with the different possibilities of compositional arrangement. He thus replaced the single definitive form of the sculpture monolith with a set of variables in potential formal expression.

This idea led him to the theory of "Anti Form," which he developed in an article in *Artforum*[2] in 1968 and carried out in his soft wall hangings of felt. Morris began to make his felt pieces in the summer of 1967, attracted by the idea of soft sculpture, which has antecedents in the soft objects in Surrealist paintings, the stuffed vinyl forms of common contemporary objects, and the earlier work of Joseph Beuys. While Morris's Minimalist sculptures emphasize the variety of perceptions and configurations possible for a single rigid shape, the felt pieces propose an equally ambiguous variety of possible shapes for a work of malleable form. The felt works also have importance as temporal experience, since the disposition of the felt strips is altered each time the work is installed. This focus on new, expressive materials and on the process of making art became characteristic of Morris's work at the end of the sixties. Thus, in one decade Morris had explored a wide variety of formal approaches and had radically reexamined the constituent elements of sculpture—material, space, form, and the relationship to the viewer and to time—as well as the creative process itself.

Isabelle Dervaux

NOTES

1. One hears the key inside while shaking the box.
2. Robert Morris, "Anti Form," *Artforum*, 6 (April 1968), pp. 33–35.

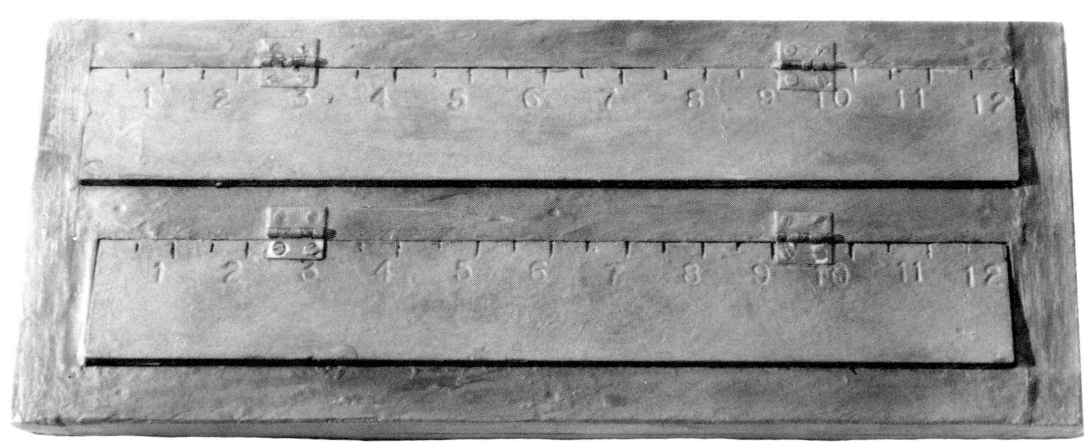

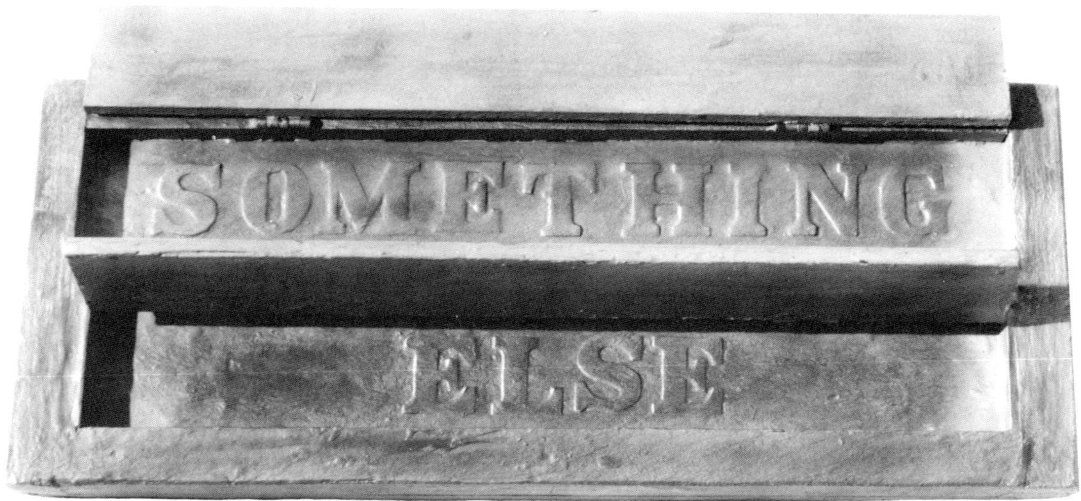

Robert Morris, *Something Else* (closed and open), 1963, painted wood, 5½ × 1¼ × 14¼″. Photograph by Jon Abbott.

Claes Oldenburg

Since the late 1950s, Claes Oldenburg has been one of the most inventive, spirited, and provocative contemporary artists to reexamine the objects and the environments of modern society and to confer a new range of artistic meanings upon them. From his "environments," such as *The Store* and *The Street*, to his large-scale public monuments, his concern has been to manifest, through fantasy and imagination, the physical and psychological possibilities in the common, everyday world. His view of reality is highly personal, and only peripherally related to the more dispassionate and satirical mainstream of Pop Art. His objects, including painted plaster foodstuffs and soft vinyl household appliances, are metamorphosed in form, scale, color, and texture to reveal surprising associations with the natural world and with man himself.

Claes Thure Oldenburg was born in Stockholm on January 28, 1929, the oldest of two sons of a Swedish diplomat then stationed in New York. He came to the United States as an infant and spent his first three years in New York City and Rye, New York. The family moved to Oslo in 1933, only to return to the United States, to Chicago, in 1936. Oldenburg was intensely sensitive to these early changes in environment, and an awareness of the essential characteristics of his physical environment is a distinguishing facet of Oldenburg's work. His fertile child's imagination led him to create "Neubern," an imaginary island between Africa and South America which he documented with drawings, street maps, and scrapbooks. *The Street*, *The Store*, and *The Bedroom* and his mature environmental works are outgrowths of his youthful fantasy.

In 1946 Oldenburg entered Yale University, where he studied art and literature. His interest in writing led to work, upon graduation, as a reporter on the police beat for the Chicago City News Bureau. After 1952, however, he decided to devote himself to art. Between 1952 and 1954 he worked at odd jobs, took occasional art classes, and drew incessantly, a habit he has continued in his fascinating journals. In March 1953 he showed a series of satirical drawings with Robert Indiana. During the next four years he produced hundreds of drawings, including metamorphosed plants and machines, seeking to convey a different psychological state for each season.

Like so many young artists at the time, Oldenburg was drawn to New York by the lure of Abstract Expressionism. He admired the vitality and painterly style of Pollock and de Kooning, both of whom have had a lasting influence upon his art. He continued, however, to paint the human figure, as did a number of his fellow Chicago artists, who were creating an abortive, somewhat grotesque collective style of eccentric humanism. Working part time in the library of Cooper Union, he sketched the street life of the Bowery and the Lower East Side.

His acquaintance with Allan Kaprow, the pioneer of Happenings, and the whimsical Chicago environmental artist Red Grooms inspired Oldenburg to carry the spirit of Abstract Expressionism into evocations of the city. His first one-man show at the Judson Gallery, New York, in May 1959 included abstract sculpture of wood, papier mâché, and string, painted white, which were inspired by the street. About his turning from painting to construction, he has written, "I wanted now to use a technique more expressive of its subject, which was 'the street,' the dominant and most affecting environment for me at that time."[1] Never completely adopting abstraction, Oldenburg probed the aesthetics of the down-trodden in the city life around him. "I am for an art," he wrote, "that takes its form

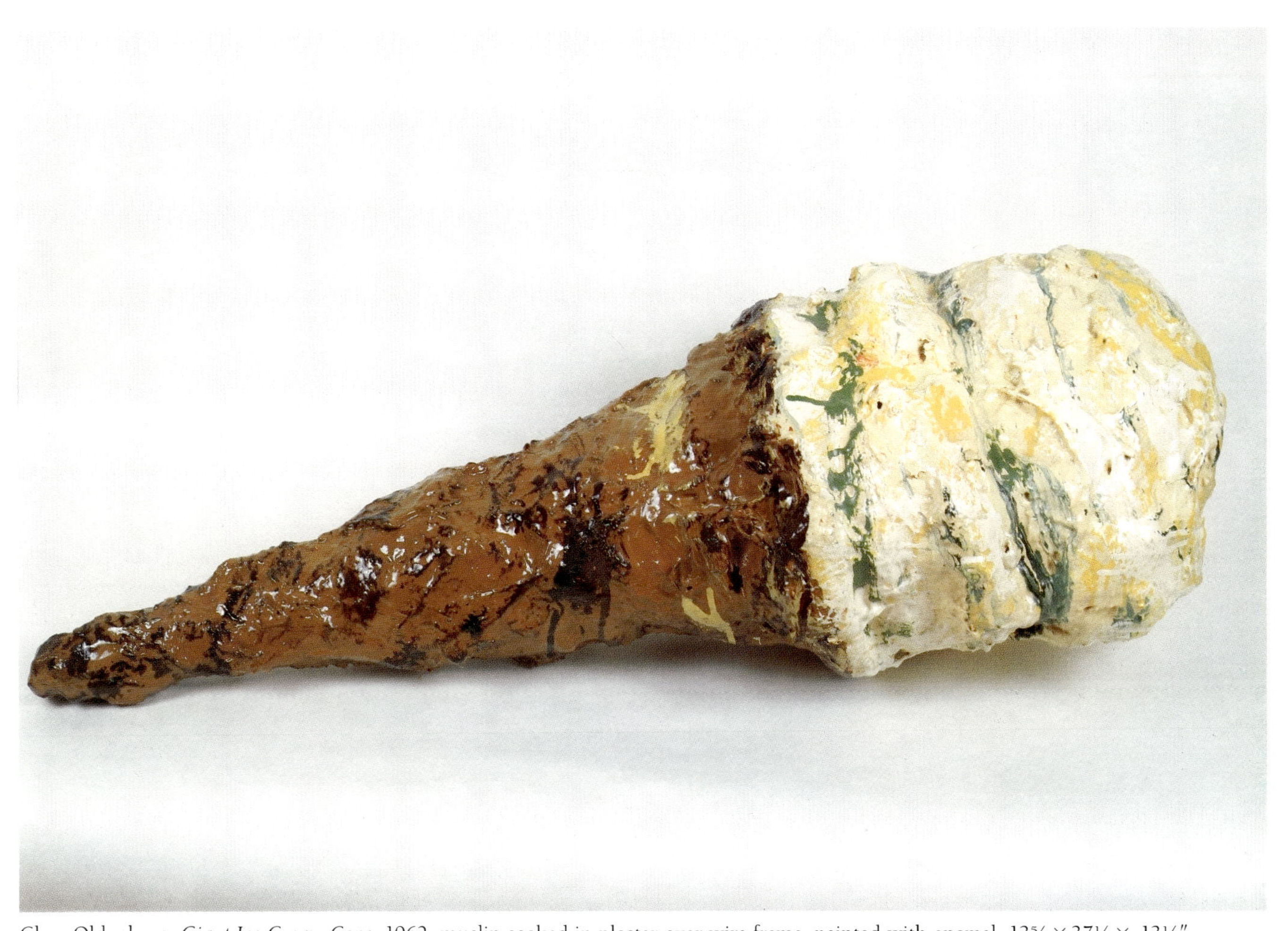

Claes Oldenburg, *Giant Ice Cream Cone*, 1962, muslin soaked in plaster over wire frame, painted with enamel, 13⅝ × 37½ × 13¼″. Photograph by Eric Pollitzer.

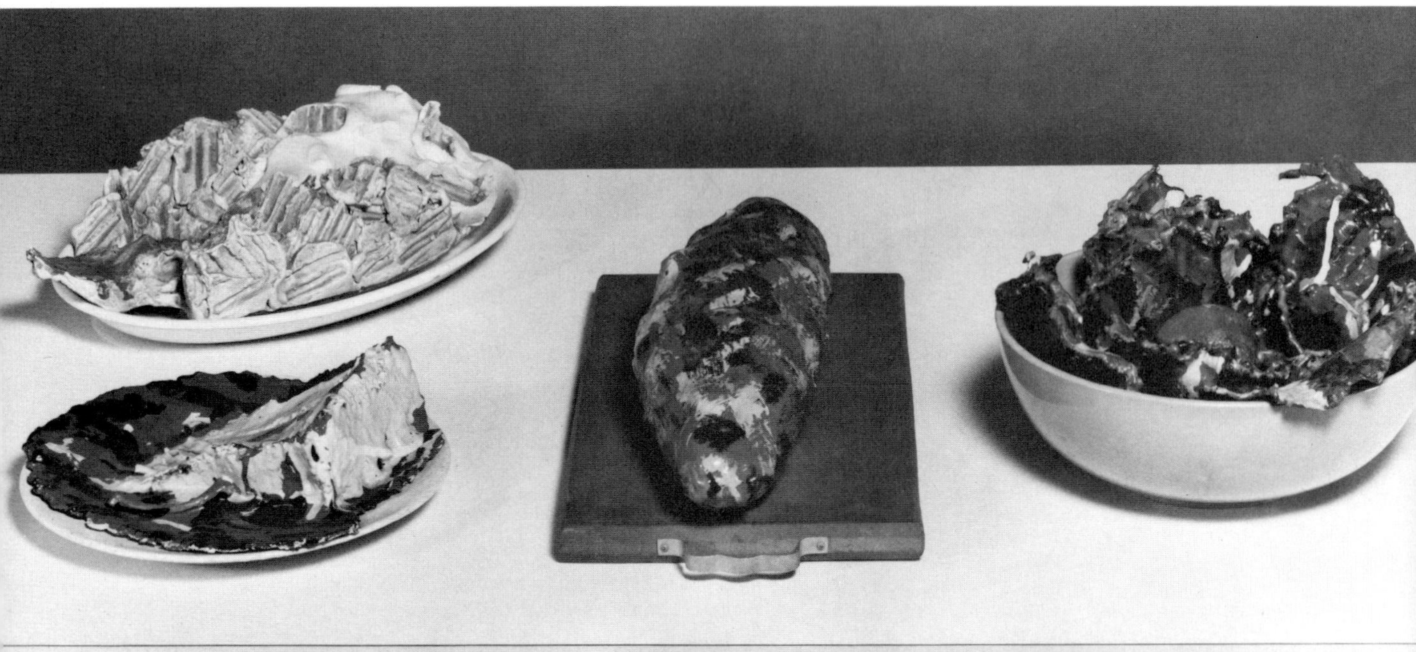

Claes Oldenburg: *Meringue Chantilly*, 1962, muslin soaked in plaster over wire frame, painted with enamel, and plate, 11 × 16 × 4¼″. *Dessert on Plate*, 1962, muslin soaked in plaster over wire frame, painted with enamel, and plate, 10 × 3¼″. *Bread on Breadboard*, 1962, muslin soaked in plaster over wire frame, painted with enamel, and wood, 8½ × 18″. *Salad in Bowl*, 1962, muslin soaked in plaster over wire frame, painted with enamel, and bowl, 6 × 10¾″. Photograph by Clem Fiori.

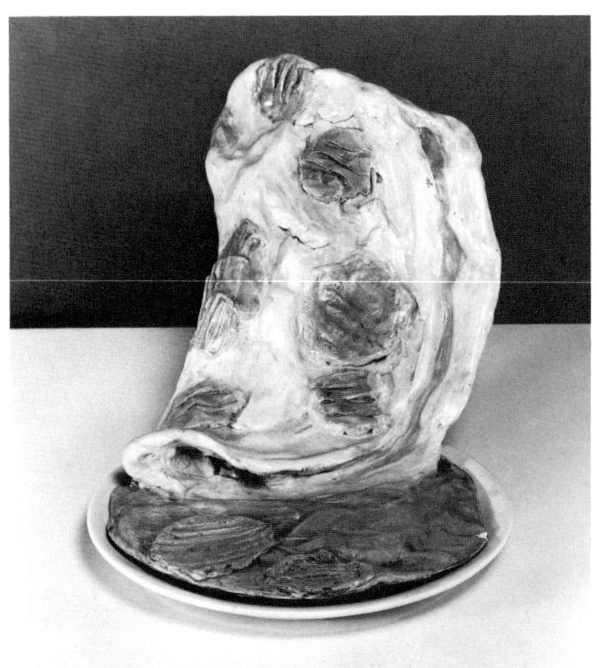

Claes Oldenburg, *Falling Omelette*, 1964, muslin soaked in plaster over wire frame, painted with enamel, and plate, 11 × 12 × 17″. Photograph by Clem Fiori.

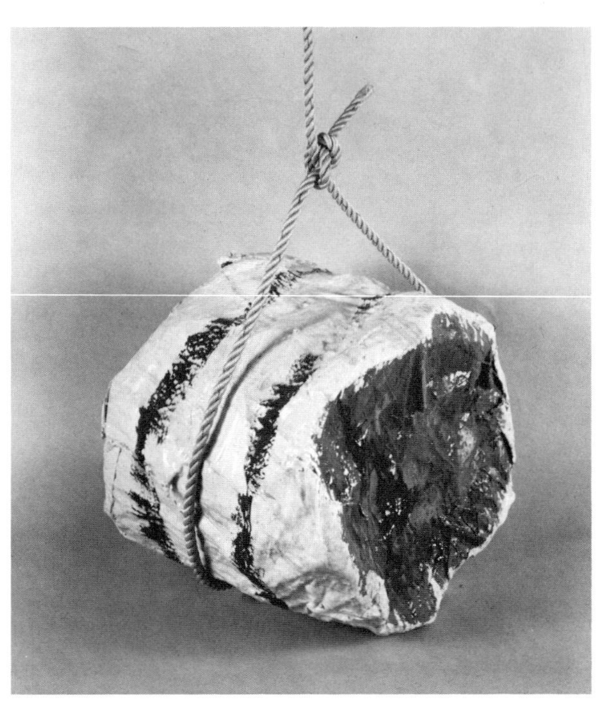

Claes Oldenburg, *Roast Beef*, 1961, muslin soaked in plaster over wire frame, painted with enamel, 14 × 17 × 16″.

from the lines of life. . . ."[2] In street refuse he discerned "elaborate accidental compositions."[3]

The Street was the theme of his second show at the Judson Gallery, in March 1960. Influenced by Dubuffet, the novelist Céline, and the drawings of Jim Dine and Red Grooms, he combined crudely torn cardboard and discarded newspaper with free, graffiti-like scrawl to evoke the decayed, random, and yet vital quality of street life. *The Street* was literal art: drawing was identified with the irregular contours of the torn cardboard. He wrote that his drawing "celebrates irrationality, disconnection, violence, and stunted expression—the damaged life forces of the city streets."[4] *Truck/Pants* (1960) is constructed of and also represents, in an imaginative way, the street life of the Lower East Side. Juxtaposed in a seemingly random manner, the crude truck and pants evoke the human and the man-made aspects of city life, blended together as part of a common degeneration. The blackened edges refer obliquely to the chiaroscuro of traditional modeling, while the gestural handling and human presence seem related to de Kooning's paintings of women.

Oldenburg's next environment, *The Store*, moved from reality to what Oldenburg called "a kind of dream" of American consumerism. It was first shown in "Environments, Situations, Spaces" at the Martha Jackson Gallery, New York, in May 1961. (In December, Oldenburg opened his own store, The Ray Gun Manufacturing Co., at 107 East Second Street in Manhattan.) The store concept enabled Oldenburg to re-create an actual consumer environment, which also provided a museum-like setting for his painted plaster foods and clothing. Color now became a primary formal concern, as he sought to enhance the sensuous, tactile appeal of the objects. The painted plaster foods had been suggested to Oldenburg while he was washing dishes at Provincetown the previous summer. With his metamorphic imagination, Oldenburg unlocked the analogies of form and the erotic associations of common foods. *Salad in a Bowl* (1962), painted in camouflage colors, suggests a tortuous jungle terrain, while *Dessert on a Plate* (1962), becomes a luscious mountain melting into a valley. These pieces reveal his intention "to present the geography of the human imagination."[5] With the giant *Ice Cream Cone* (1962), he created a distinctly phallic object which allied the passion for consumption with eroticism. *Nutella* (1964), Oldenburg's rendering of the European chocolate and peanut-butter spread for a show at the Sonnabend gallery in Paris, is a childishly blunt creation of his erotic fantasy.

Yet Oldenburg's desire to achieve certain formal effects was always an overriding concern. The ice cream cone, for example, was suggested by his desire "to make something flow."[6] *Falling Omelette* (1964) achieves the same dynamic effect by its frozen motion and Oldenburg's fluid, expressive handling of the paint.

The large space of the uptown Green Gallery in New York inspired Oldenburg to create larger objects, such as the ice cream cone, and his first "soft sculptures," for the second version of *The Store*. His soft appliances, made of vinyl stitched together by his wife, Pat, rendered human, harmless, and even erotic the mechanical devices of modern society.

In March 1965 Oldenburg moved into an enormous new studio in New York, and the size of the space, plus his travel by air during the previous months, brought the issue of scale to his attention. At this time he began his "monument" drawings, proposals for both real and imaginary monuments, in which the space became an expansive landscape and the viewpoint was usually from a distance and aerial. In his own works, "The 'monuments'—a conceptual direction—move from simple placement of favorite objects onto the landscape to more studied relations of object and site."[7]

The monuments, many of them humorous, exploit the physical presence and social importance of common, unheroic objects as well as parts of anatomy. *"Dam fall"* (1962), related to a later drawing of a tunnel entrance in the form of a nose, integrates a giant phallus in the natural world in a typically provocative and fantastic manner.

The essence of Oldenburg's art is rooted in everyday life, yet it is infused with a seemingly

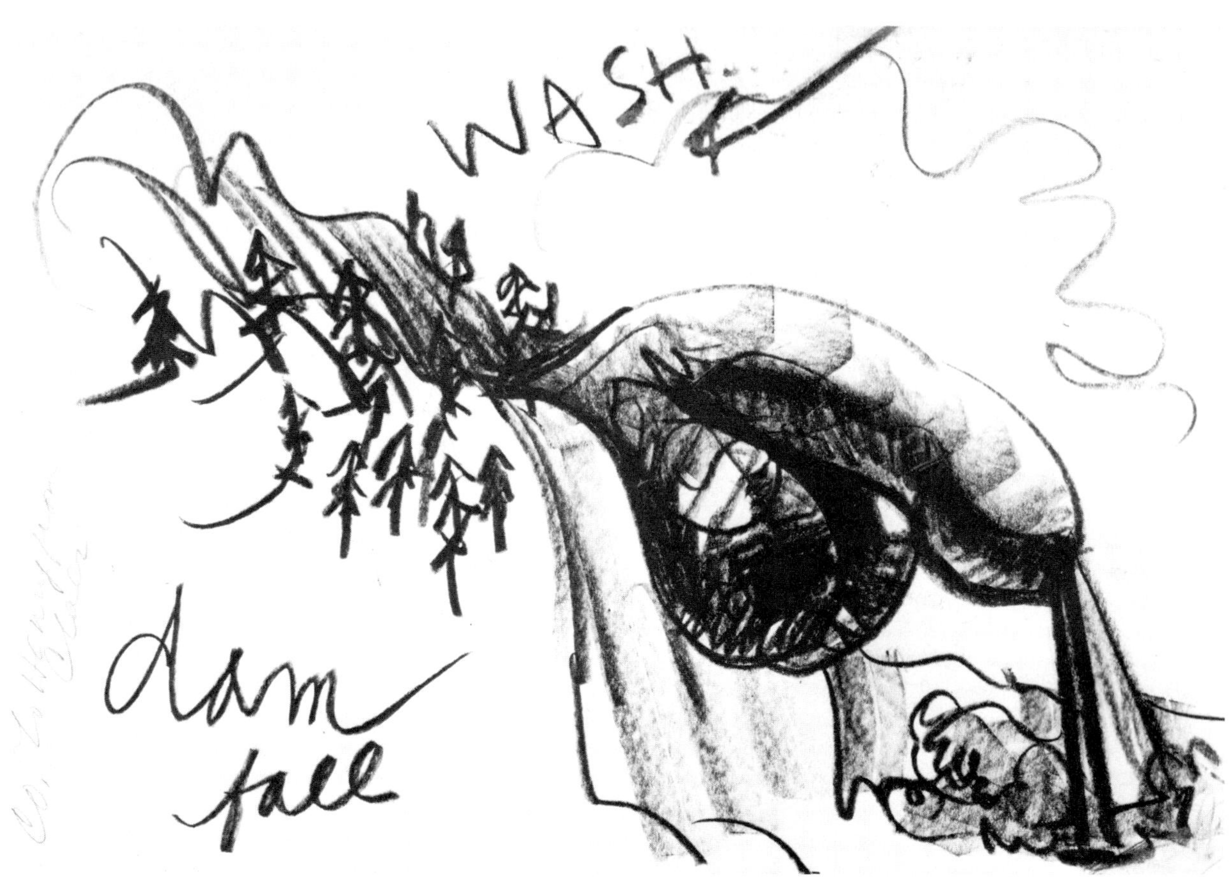

Claes Oldenburg, *"dam fall,"* 1965, litho crayon, 9⅞ × 15″. Photograph by Bevan Davies.

childish fancy and humor which mask its deeper intellectual implications. He shows us, as Gene Baro has observed, that "quite common things, natural or man-made, can now seem to contain the mystery or the poetry of reality."[8] Oldenburg himself has written, however, that his art "gives the (deliberate) impression of being concerned with the outside world . . . but in fact it is simply the personal elaboration of imaginary forms . . . of a limited number . . . in the guise of occasional appearances. . . ."[9]

Jonathan Bloom

NOTES

1. Arts Council, *Claes Oldenburg*, p. 19.
2. Quoted in Ellen H. Johnson, "The Living Object," *Art International*, 7 (January 1963), p. 43.
3. John Rublowsky, *Pop Art* (New York, 1965), p. 62.
4. Gene Baro, *Claes Oldenburg: Drawings and Prints*, London and New York, 1969, p. 15.
5. Gene Baro, "Claes Oldenburg, or The Things of This World," *Art International*, 10 (November 1966), p. 42.
6. "Oldenburg, Lichtenstein, Warhol: A Discussion," moderated by Bruce Glaser, *Artforum*, 4 (February 1966), p. 23.
7. Gene Baro, *Claes Oldenburg: Drawings and Prints* (London and New York, 1969), p. 19.
8. Gene Baro, "Claes Oldenburg, or The Things of This World," *Art International*, 10 (November 1966), p.41.
9. Claes Oldenburg, "Extracts from the Studio Notes (1962–64)," *Artforum*, 4 (January 1966), p. 33.

Claes Oldenburg, *Truck/Pants*, 1960, painted cardboard with charcoal, 22½ × 20½″. Photograph by Jon Abbott.

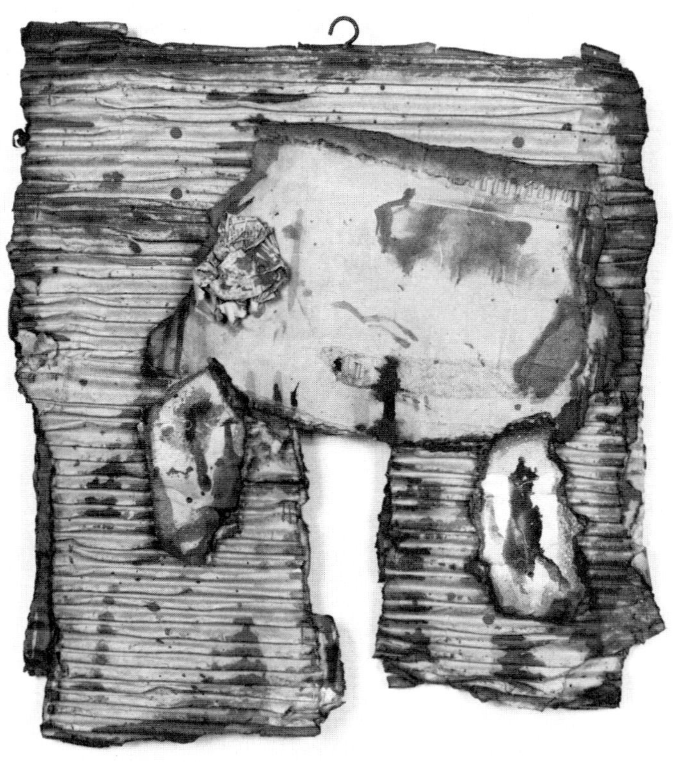

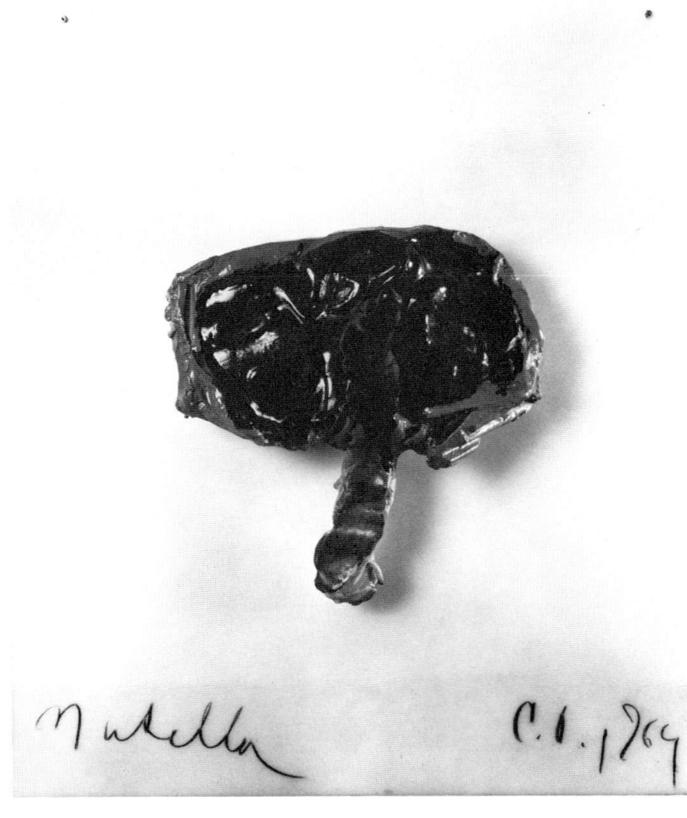

Claes Oldenburg, *Nutella*, 1964, muslin soaked in plaster over wire frame, painted with enamel, mounted to Plexiglas sheet, 15 × 13¾″. Photograph by Clem Fiori.

Robert Rauschenberg

A native of Texas, Rauschenberg became interested in art as a vocation at the age of seventeen, in 1942, and spent the next ten years working through various art schools and approaches in order to find his own interests. Essential to this phase in his development were two periods of study at Black Mountain College, 1948–49 and 1952, where he worked under Josef Albers and encountered the work and ideas of John Cage and Merce Cunningham. Rejecting Albers's formal and methodical instruction, and his concept of expression as the personal will of the artist, Rauschenberg turned eagerly to the ideas of openness and experimentation to which Cage and Cunningham introduced him, and with their support and influence he achieved his own breakthrough.

While he retained such elements as the spontaneity and accidentalism of the Abstract Expressionists' style, Rauschenberg was able to fuse an improvisatory energy with a style that was not anguished or strictly painterly and abstract. He dramatized his rebellion against the dominant aesthetic in 1953 by expunging a de Kooning drawing (given to him by the older artist with the understanding that it would be effaced). *Erased de Kooning Drawing* marked Rauschenberg's break with the Abstract Expressionist ideology of a personally expressive art. In other works of his during this period Rauschenberg seemed to draw on such sources as Picasso's collages and synthetic Cubist painting, both for content and formal structure, and even more obviously he found inspiration in Kurt Schwitters's use of waste materials and street refuse within a Cubist grid.

The collage painting called *Monk*, 1955, not only shows these influences but also prefigures Pop artists' use of popular culture by nearly nine years. Here, Rauschenberg has adapted such elements in a less iconic way than in Pop Art, for there is narrative potential in the relation and repetition of pictorial elements. The work evokes Picasso both in material content and in the grid-like format, which incorporates a filmstrip of Chaplin, a road map, an idyllic landscape accented by the less regular disposition of a cartoon, and an airmail envelope with a Thelonius Monk record-album label. Yet the paint application, the freedom, and the assertive texture recall Abstract Expressionist brushstrokes.

In turning from small and somewhat precious collage paintings to more expansive and ambitious "combine" paintings, Rauschenberg challenged current assumptions about what materials were or were not suitable for art. *Hymnal*, of 1955, is a major combine painting in which the extent of the paint surface has been radically reduced in favor of the assemblage of charged object and material fragments. Rauschenberg covered the canvas with a paisley-patterned shawl, which acts as a decorative paint ground and creates an active and resonant surface that interacts dynamically with the other elements. Although there is no clear narrative message, a kind of thematic consistency emerges in the "Wanted" poster and its catalogue of dangerous and criminal traits, the arrow pointing to an image of a fallen person, a scratched book cover, and a fragment of a Manhattan telephone directory—all suggesting the delinquent and disenfranchised aspects of modern urban existence. The artist's hand and visible touch intrude selectively, but do little to clarify the narrative content, leaving the challenge of deciphering meanings to the viewer. Maintaining this openness to the viewer's response and interaction is a major and controlling element in Rauschenberg's aesthetic.

Opposite page: Robert Rauschenberg, *Dylaby*, 1962, combine painting, 109½ × 87 × 15″. Photograph by Clem Fiori.

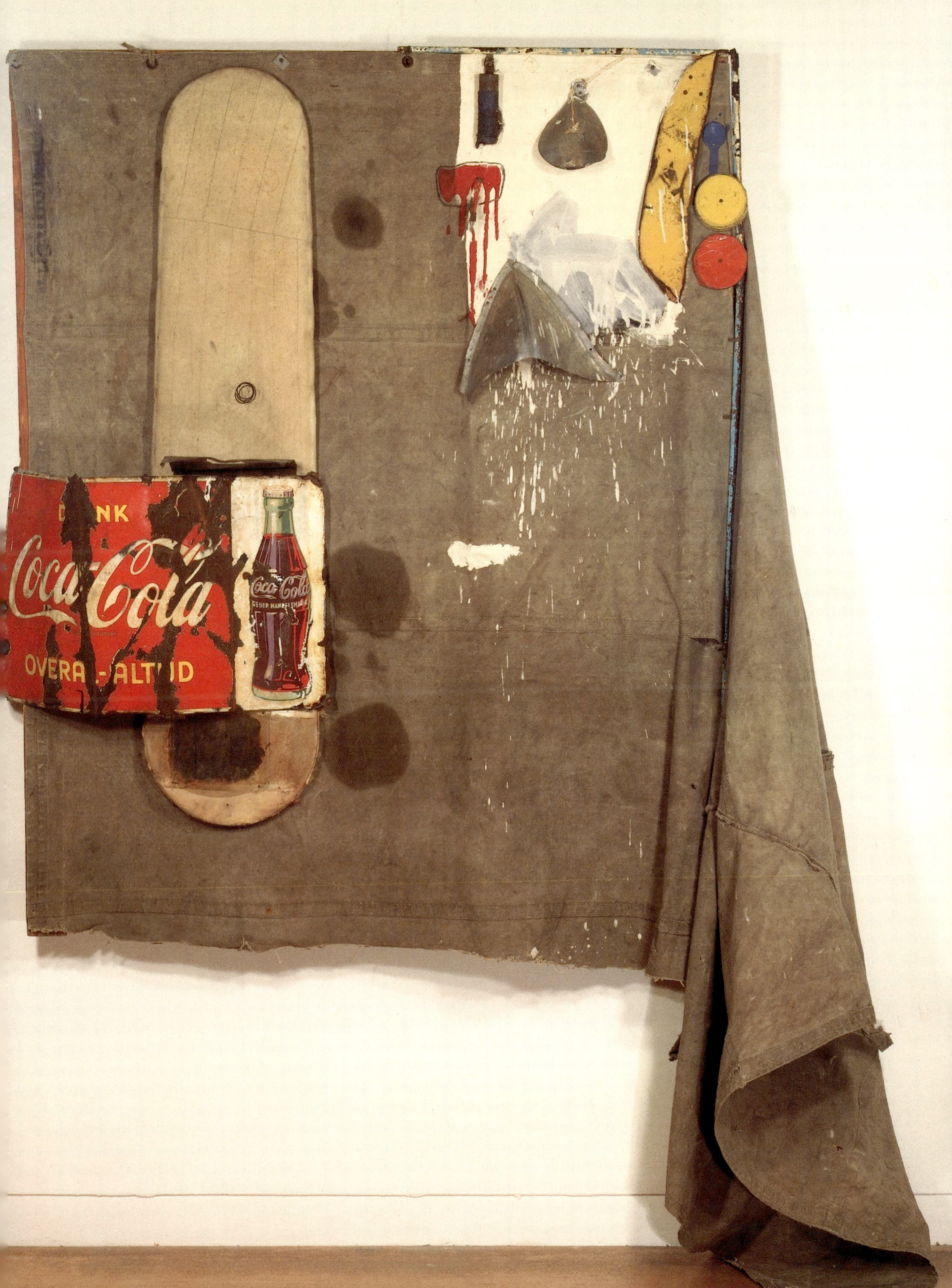

Coca-Cola

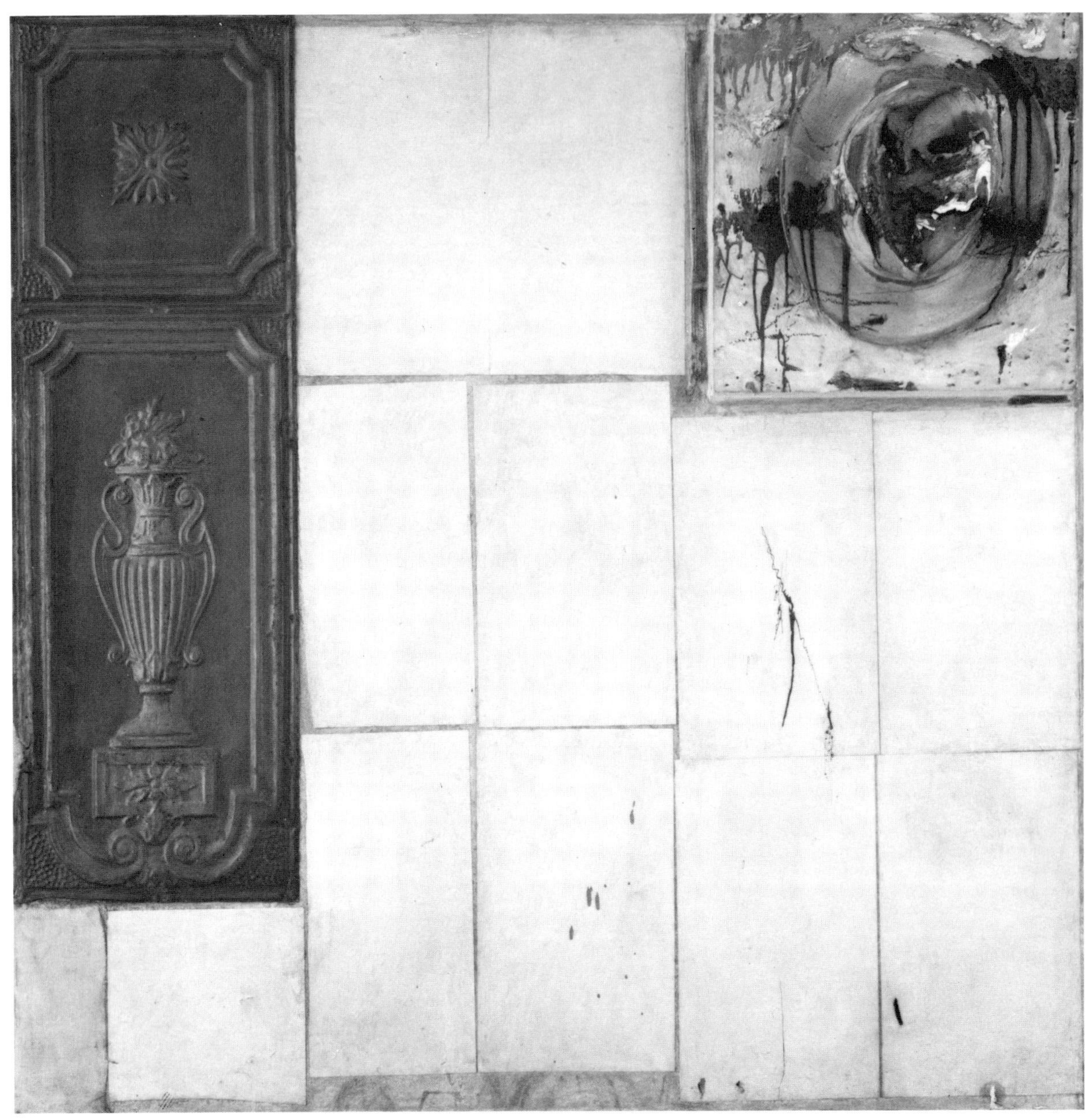

Robert Rauschenberg, *Interior*, 1956, combine painting, 45¼ × 46½ × 7½″. Photograph by Bevan Davies.

Evolved from clues suggested by Schwitters's *Merzbild* trash constructions and de Kooning's energetic paint swipes (and his feeling for popular imagery, especially in his Woman series), Rauschenberg's innovative assemblages were critical influences in the radical changes that took place in American art in the middle and late fifties.

With the combine paintings, Rauschenberg gained recognition both in America and Europe, with regular exhibitions after 1957 at the Leo Castelli Gallery in New York and an important retrospective exhibition at The Jewish Museum, also in New York, in 1963. In Europe there were regular exhibitions at the Sonnabend gallery in Paris in the sixties, and dramatic evidence of his international stature when he was awarded the Grand Prize at the Venice Biennale in 1964. The jury's decision was hotly argued and controversial, but much acclaimed by the younger generation of artists in the United States and abroad.

Even as his combines received international attention, however, Rauschenberg was experimenting with techniques taking him back to a more traditional, flat painted surface. This development first emerged in his delicately shaded and hatched drawings, where he experimented with a technique of "rubbings," to transfer photographic images onto another sheet of paper, instead of attaching the actual photographs to the surface of a work, as he had been doing. He soon began to use photographic images even more freely, and in larger scale, to make photo-silkscreens and then transfer them onto his canvases with both commercial inks and oil paint.

Rauschenberg's technical method required soaking selected areas of a sheet of paper with lighter fluid and then placing a photographic image from a magazine or newspaper face down on the wet paper and rubbing the back of the image with the nib of a dry ball-point pen. The image was thus transferred to the paper, with a grayed and somewhat ghostly quality, yet retaining its identity as a photographic reproduction. Rauschenberg then mediated the mechanical image registration with considerable creative freedom, by brushwork, linear invention, and color application.

Rauschenberg's first major drawing series, the dramatic thirty-four drawings corresponding to the cantos of the *Inferno* of Dante's *Divine Comedy*, depended on this method; the drawings were done in 1959–62. The drawing *Political Folly* of 1968 is a brilliant and subtle later example of the technique, and achieves an unusual combination of privacy, or intimacy of expression, with a public tone. Rauschenberg has a vivid sense of public life and action, and of political events particularly. Here he has depicted Hubert and Muriel Humphrey upside down while showing Eugene McCarthy right side up, but the reversals do not necessarily symbolize a personal preference.

The evident limitations of the transfer technique, since the photograph can be used only once and has to appear in its original published size, could be accommodated in drawing, but posed obvious problems for large paintings. In 1962, probably influenced by Warhol, Rauschenberg began using photo-silkscreens made from published photographs. Gradually these images of persons, events, accidents, and disasters in the world replaced the attached objects and materials of the combines and became the exclusive narrative and iconic substance of Rauschenberg's work.

Sam Hunter

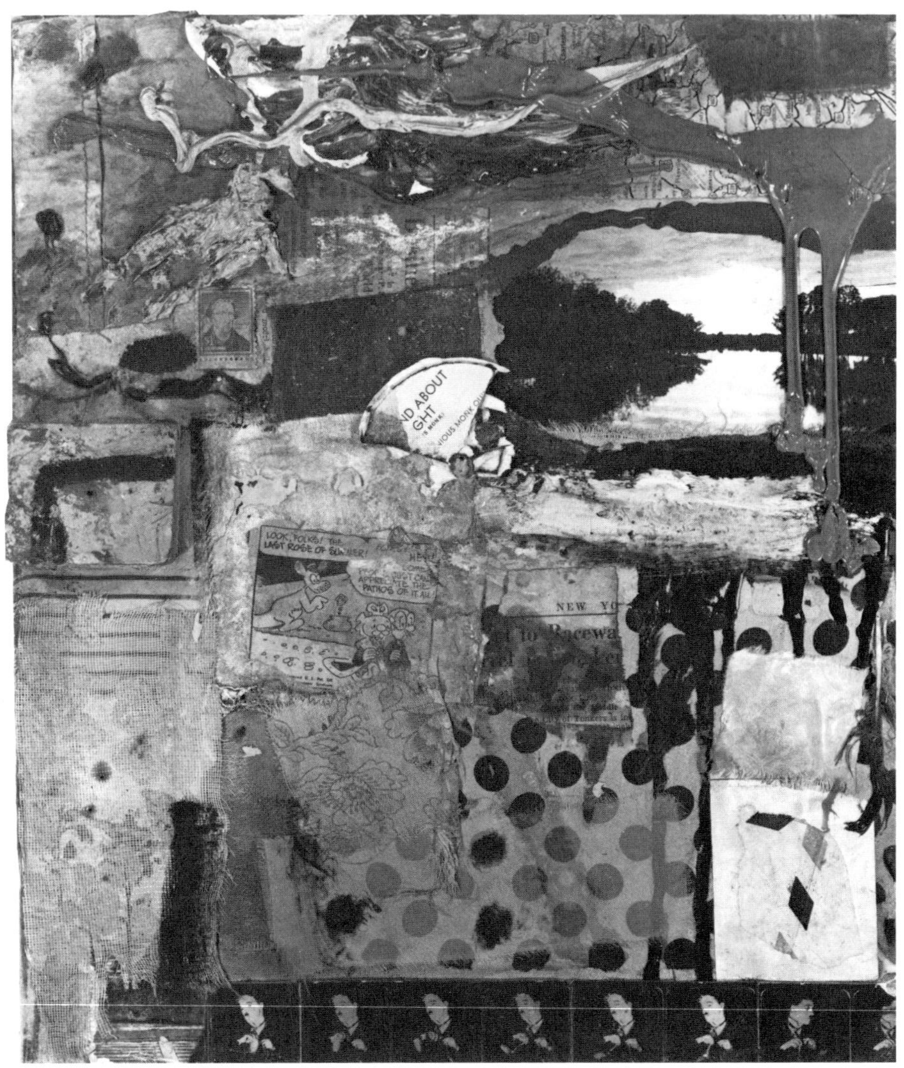

Robert Rauschenberg, *Monk*, 1955, collage and mixed media on canvas, 14 × 12″.
Photograph by Clem Fiori.

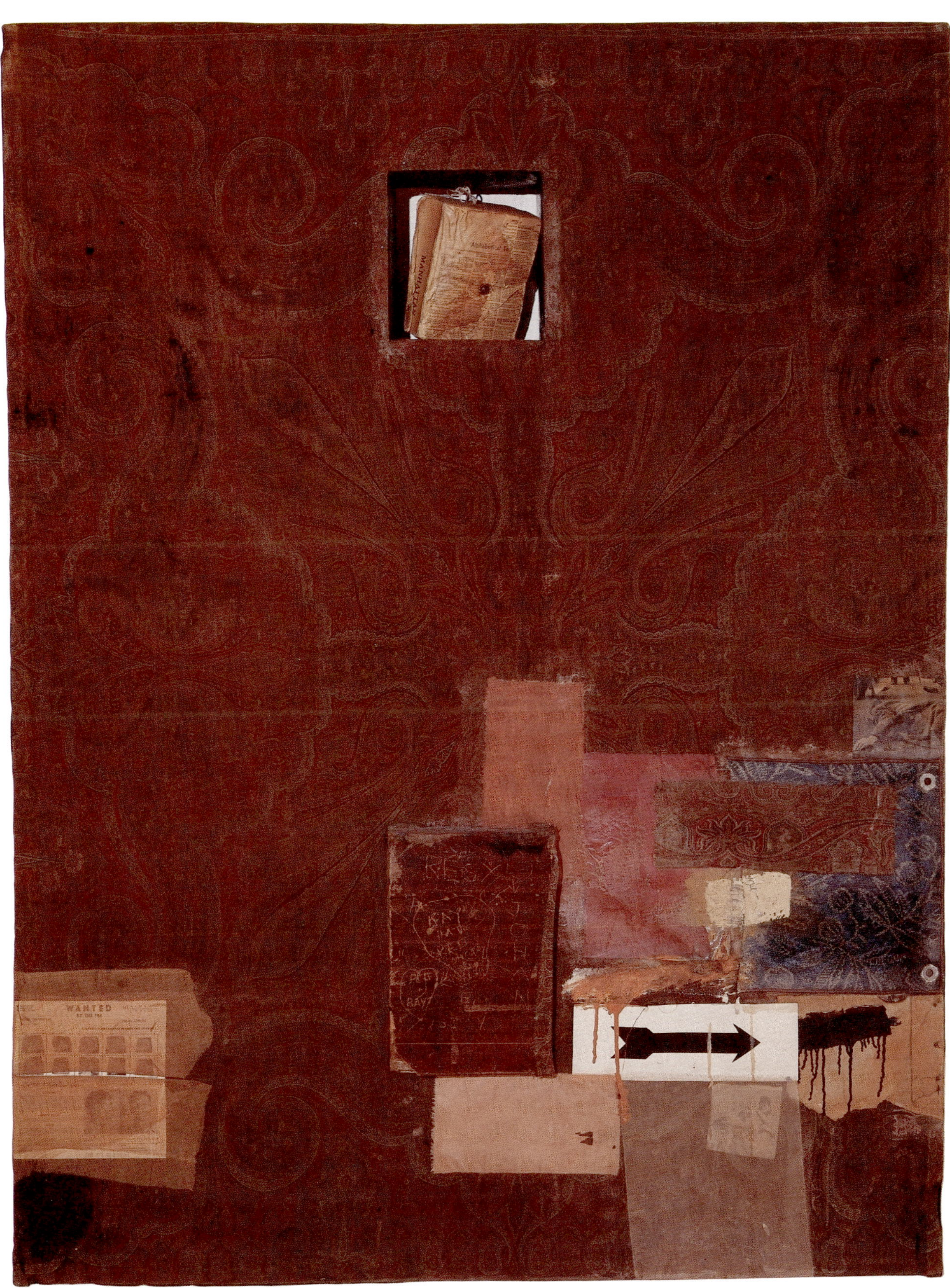

Robert Rauschenberg, *Hymnal*, 1955, combine painting, 64 × 49¼ × 7¼″.

Robert Rauschenberg, *Calendar*, 1962, oil on canvas, 96 × 60¼″. Photograph by Bevan Davies.

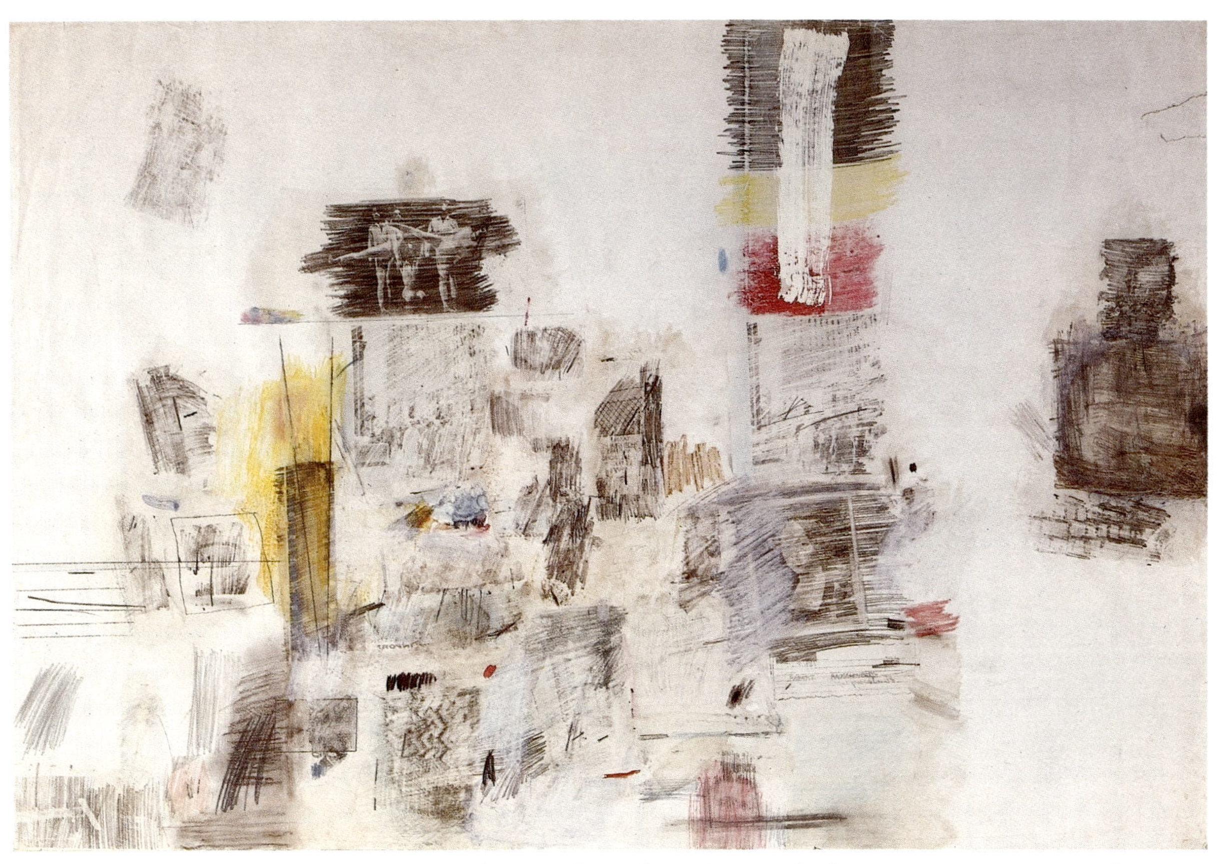

Robert Rauschenberg, *Street Throng*, 1959, pencil, watercolor, and gouache, transfer drawing on paper, 23¾ × 35½″.

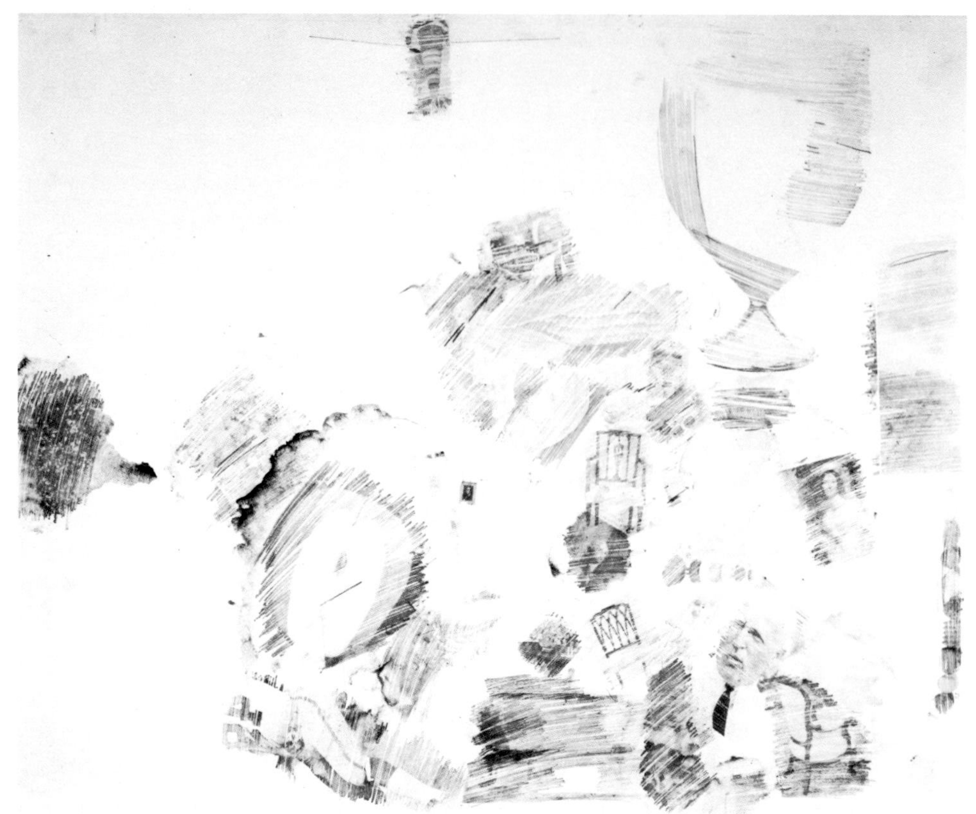

Robert Rauschenberg, *Drawing Room*, 1963, pencil and watercolor, transfer drawing on paper, 22½ × 30″. Photograph by Bevan Davies.

Robert Rauschenberg, *Political Folly*, 1968, pencil and watercolor, transfer drawing on paper, 22½ × 30″. Photograph by Bevan Davies.

James Rosenquist

James Rosenquist was born in Grand Forks, North Dakota, in 1933. His family later moved to Minnesota, where he studied art at the University of Minnesota from 1952 to 1954. While in college, Rosenquist spent his summers painting signs and farm equipment throughout the Midwest. In 1955 he received a scholarship to study at the Art Students League in New York. After leaving the city for six months, Rosenquist returned in 1956 to set up a studio, and became acquainted with Robert Indiana, Jasper Johns, and Robert Rauschenberg.

In 1957 Rosenquist joined the international Picture Painters Union and worked as a billboard painter in New York until 1960. At night he worked on his own paintings, which he executed with commercial paints. These paintings were in the style of Abstract Expressionism; Rosenquist later described them as "wanderings on a Ouija board."[1] In 1959 Rosenquist, through Rauschenberg, did window displays at Bonwit Teller and at Tiffany and Company in New York. In 1960 he stopped working as a professional billboard painter, but began to incorporate commercial subject matter and techniques in his own art. It was at about this time that Rosenquist met Ileana Sonnabend and Leo Castelli. In 1961 he joined the Richard Bellamy Gallery in New York, where he had his first one-man exhibition in January of the following year.

While working as a sign painter, Rosenquist grew sensitive to the role of scale in perception: "After several years of painting large signs ten and twenty stories up and mixing gallons of flesh and gallons of orange whiskey colors, I began to realize scale . . . . I had little interest in images, I was interested in color. But it is because the images were recognizable that I was called a Pop artist."[2] In Rosenquist's paintings, fragments of recognizable objects in exaggerated scale are juxtaposed. Although the images are painted in the illusionistic manner of Photo-Realism, the fragments occupy not a traditional illusionistic space but a flattened, abstract field. "It is pretty clear how much Rosenquist derives from Cubist *collage*, but his combination in one painting seen from a fixed point of view, of things seen from close-up and things seen from far away adds another element not found in conventional *collage*."[3]

In *Balcony* of 1961 Rosenquist has juxtaposed the details of a woman's hair and a man's wrist in different scales on a sky-blue background. By depicting the hair in color and the hand in black and white, Rosenquist plays with the viewer's sensitivity, or indifference, to color. The imagery in *Balcony* is sparse, but Rosenquist has used other devices to explore illusion and reality. The plane of the canvas is interrupted by a sheet of plexiglass and a mirror. The plexiglass, located on the cuff on the hand, is partially painted, but Rosenquist has allowed us to see through the cuff of the shirt sleeve to the wall behind the painting. The plexiglass continues the illusion of the painting, but then destroys it by opening to the space behind the canvas. The mirror also disrupts the continuity of the painting. It serves to select random pieces of visual material from the environment, much as Rosenquist has already done by including fragments of the human body. "Just in case we are trapped into an illusionistic reading of an image (despite everything that has been done to prevent this from happening), we are confronted by a real image to make the distinction clear."[4] A full vision of things seems impossible through any medium—the mass media or the painting media.

In 1963 Rosenquist joined the Leo Castelli Gallery in New York, and was selected *Art in America*'s "Young Talent Painter" of the year. The following year he had his first European show, at the Galerie Ileana Sonnabend in Paris. Rosen-

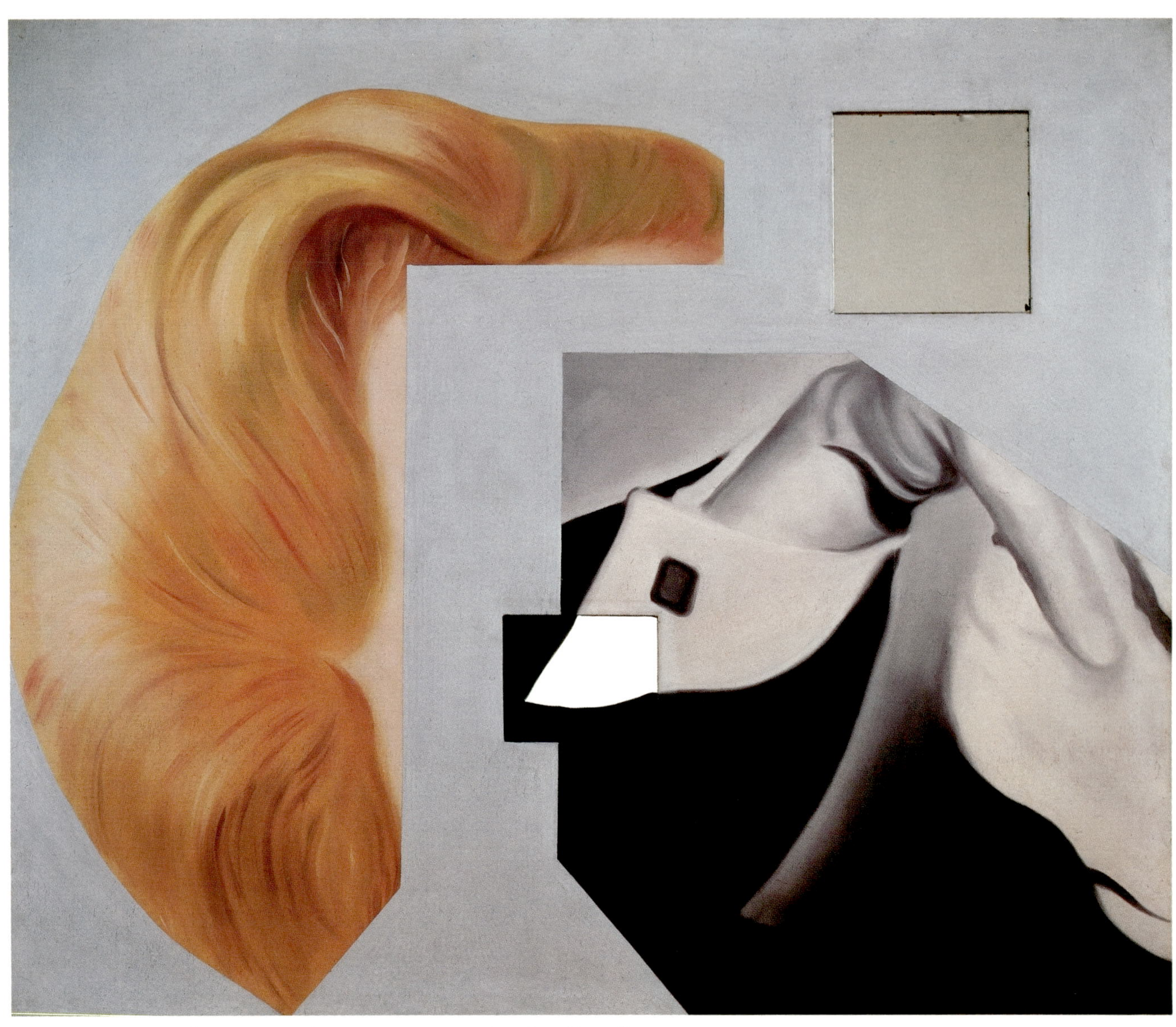

James Rosenquist, *Balcony*, 1961, oil on canvas, mirror, Plexiglas, 60 × 73″

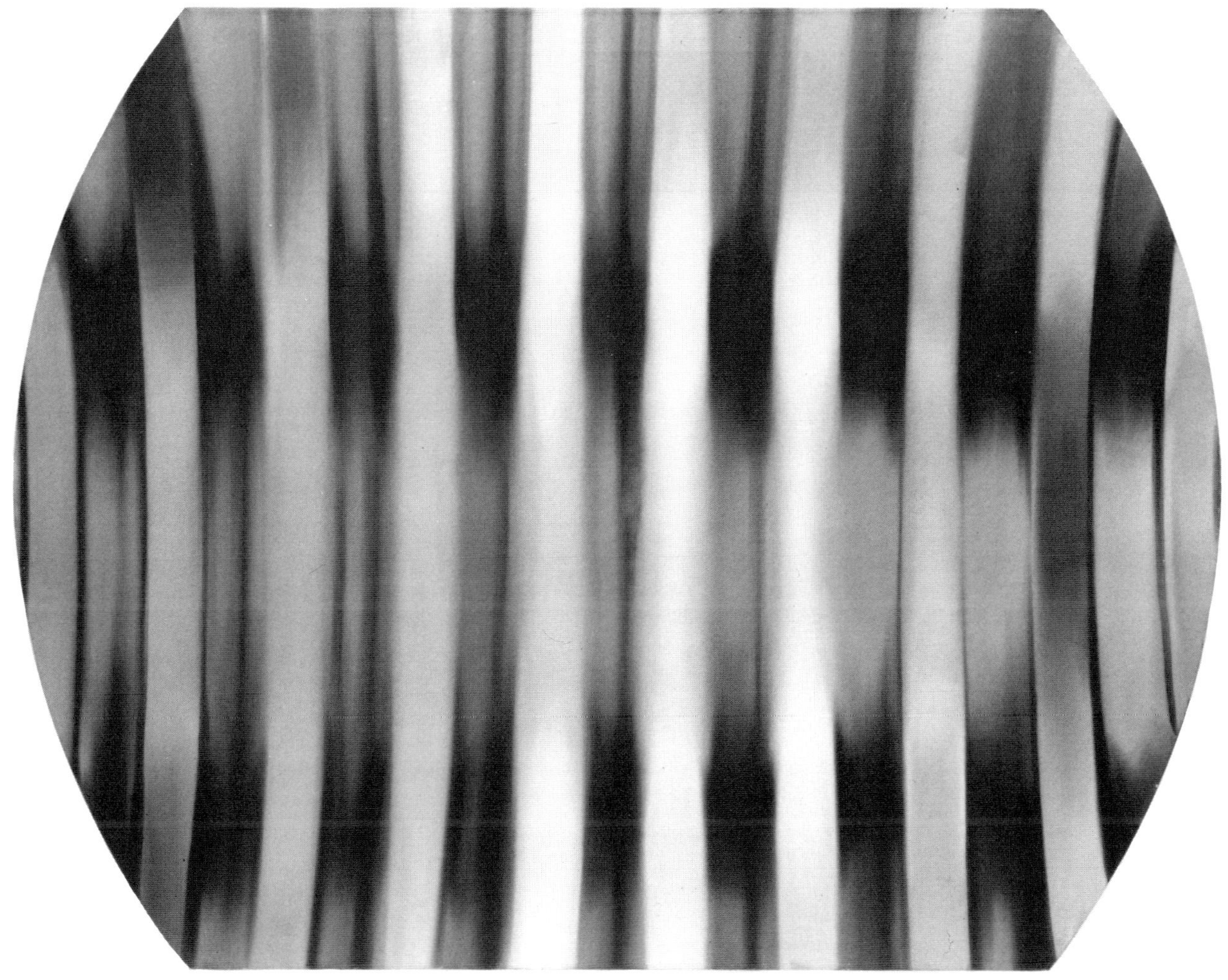

James Rosenquist, *Aspen, Colorado*, 1966, oil on canvas, 48 × 62″. Photograph by Jon Abbott.

quist exhibited *F-111*, probably the most ambitious and monumental of Pop paintings, first at the Castelli Gallery in 1965 and then at The Jewish Museum in New York. *F-111*—the name refers to the jet fighter-bomber the painting partially depicts—was executed in fifty-one panels, and measures eighty-five feet laterally and ten feet in height. Since the public presentation of this immense mural imagery in the mid-sixties, Rosenquist has continued periodically to create other spectacular images of our times, synthesizing disjunctive popular subject matter and abstract illusionistic devices, and drawing on illustrated journalism and TV sources in an imaginative response to the ubiquitous, powerful mass media, and to the artistic and philosophical issues that their insistent presence have raised.

Erica Wolf

NOTES

1. Marcia Tucker, *James Rosenquist* (New York: The Whitney Museum of American Art, 1972), p. 11.
2. Phyllis Tuchman, "Pop! Interviews with George Segal, Andy Warhol, Roy Lichtenstein, James Rosenquist, and Robert Indiana," *Art News*, 73 (May 1974), p. 28.
3. Barbara Rose, "Americans 1963," *Art International*, 7 (September 25, 1963), p. 78.
4. Tucker, p. 25.

Frank Stella

Frank Stella was born in 1936 in Malden, Massachusetts. He attended Phillips Academy in Andover, where he studied art with Patrick Morgan; at Princeton University, 1953–57, he studied under William Seitz and Stephen Greene, who had organized the University's visual-arts studio program. Completing an art history major as well, he wrote a junior research paper on Hiberno-Saxon manuscript illumination, which, it has been suggested, later became a source for his intricate pictorial designs. At Princeton he also formed a close friendship with his classmate, the artist Darby Bannard.

In 1959, Stella had his first one-man show at the Leo Castelli Gallery, New York. Since then, he has exhibited in many group and individual shows throughout Europe, Canada, the United States, and Japan. From 1958 to the present, he has lived and worked in New York.

Stella made his first mature paintings in 1958, shortly after graduating from Princeton and moving to New York. His black monochromatic canvases stunned the art world with their austere presence, symmetry, heroic scale, and limited pictorial means. The first group of works in the black-stripe series consisted of configurations of parallel black bands of uniform width, separated by thin lines of unpainted canvas, which echoed the two perpendicular axes of the support. The image was rigorously contained by the rectangular support, even though the size of the paintings rivaled the open form and heroic mural scale of the Abstract Expressionists. In the second group, the black bands run parallel to the diagonal axes of the support, and thus make the pattern appear to continue, with an expansive energy, beyond the canvas. These early paintings, unlike much later ones, are rather nuanced in paint application and surface, because of the artist's decision to work without tapes or a straightedge. In subsequent works, however, he found these tools appropriate for his shaped canvases and color fields. Stella gave special importance to the thickness of the stretcher bars (more than three inches), which stressed the character of the painting as a real object in real space. Many critics have pointed to Jasper Johns as an early source of visual cues for Stella; Johns's Targets and Flags not only contain concentric bands but also emphasize their nature as objects through the assertive texture and relief of the layered, encaustic surface. Other critics have compared Stella with Pollock, Newman, and Reinhardt, because all have sought non-relational structures outside the Cubist pictorial hierarchy of large and small relational forms, as well as a holistic image.

In 1960, Stella showed his black-stripe paintings in his first one-man show at the Leo Castelli Gallery in New York. The combination of thick, glossy brushstrokes with simple geometric patterns was controversial, winning approval from artists and critics of Stella's own generation but inviting censure from older artists, who viewed the reductive design, apparent vacancy, and monochrome emphasis as either meaningless or, at best, an insult to the visual complexity and energetic handling in the still dominant Action Painting. Later in 1960 Stella began work on his first shaped canvases, known as the aluminum series. In these paintings he extended his interest in the literal painting object by creating a more sculptural presence. He began to compose multiple bands, painted with aluminum pigment, in more intricate geometric patterns, and his interior stripe repetitions were notched and broken so that their patterns could be echoed in the canvas stretcher frames. He boldly left vacant and staggered the painting edges, thereby creating a further ambiguity between the object status of the painting, as a literal thing on the wall, and its now sharply delimited but still existent

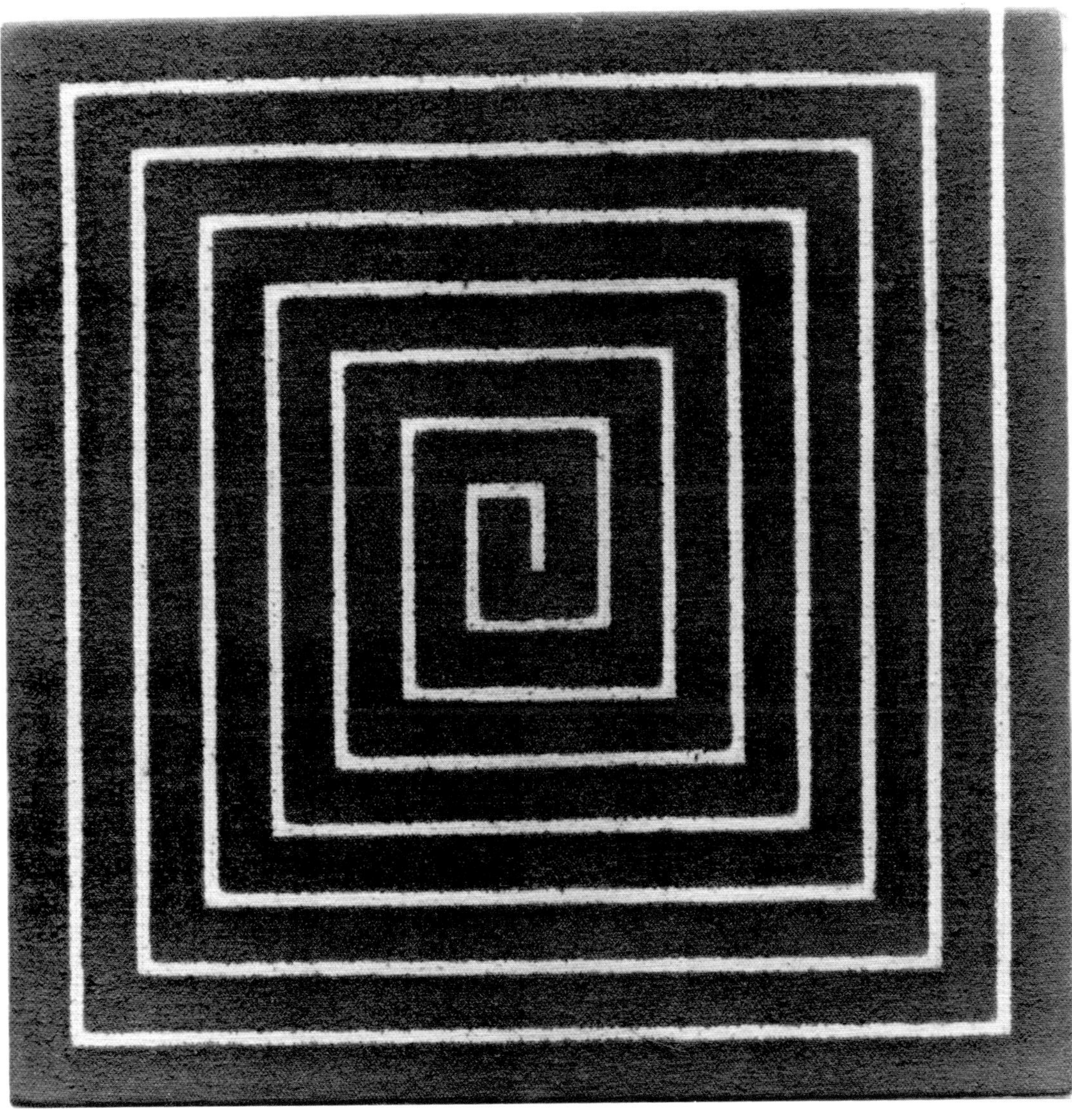

Frank Stella, *Untitled* (Benjamin Moore series), 1961, alkyd on canvas, 12 × 12″. Photograph by Jon Abbott.

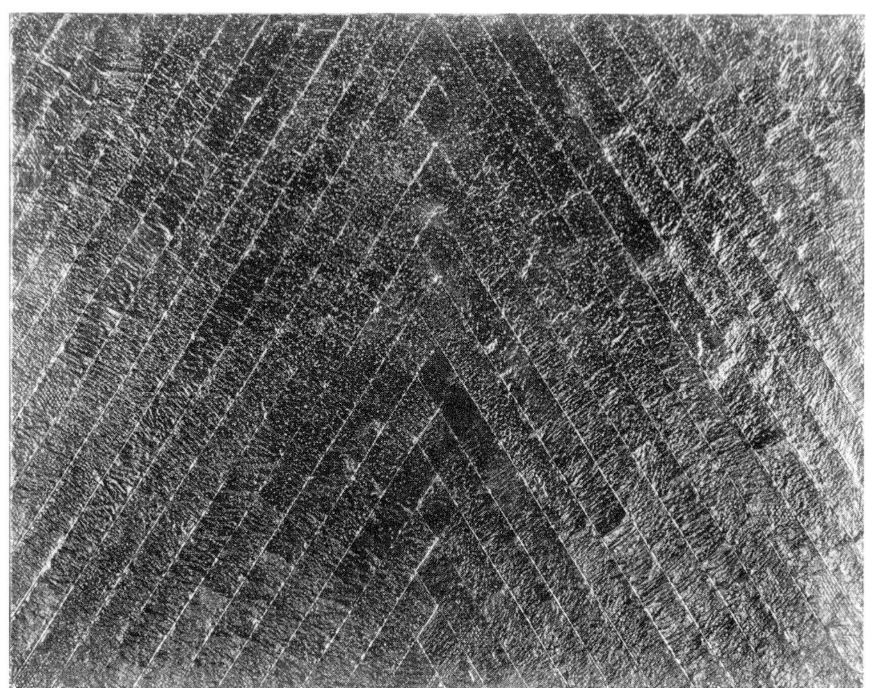

Frank Stella, *Point of Pines*, 1960, metal foil collage on board, 7¼ × 9½″. Photograph by Clem Fiori.

capacity to generate pictorial illusion in a fictive spatial context.

In the copper series of 1961, Stella took an even more radical step in the evolution of the shaped canvas of his own invention. The patterns are simple variations and combinations of right angles, and the shapes are more powerfully accented. The increased scale of these works, in conjunction with the use of metallic pigment over large surfaces, emphasizes the sculptural properties even more than the black-stripe and notched canvases had done. These bare, structurist paintings were later credited with a significant role in the widespread movement of Minimalist sculpture.

From 1962 to 1963 Stella worked steadily on two projects, known as concentric squares and mitered mazes, which, for the first time in his mature work, incorporated more complex color and value combinations. Most of the paintings in this series have single, square formats of concentric bands, although some combine two adjacent visual mazes in diptych form across one large rectangular support. Now, in an unprecedented manner in his work, an illusionistic spatial reading was made possible and even acknowledged by the artist. The diagonal lines, created by the meeting of the corners of these squared fields, clearly function optically, creating perspectival illusion. Lines work together with color and value changes to produce an almost Op Art effect of visual dazzle and dynamic resonance. The art historian William Rubin noted, "The power of the governing pattern was such that it held the pictures together. But the design survived the color more than it was supported by it."[1]

Later in the sixties, Stella developed a number of other painting series: the notched V's, the irregular polygons, and the exhaustive protractor series, all of which were used to further expand upon the ideas that began in the black paintings. As Stella's work developed, his emphasis became increasingly sculptural, an effect achieved not only by the thickness and eccentric shapes of the supports but also because the visual power and physical presence of the works encroached further on the space of the viewer.

John Otte

NOTES

1. William S. Rubin, *Frank Stella* (New York: The Museum of Modern Art, 1970), p. 78.

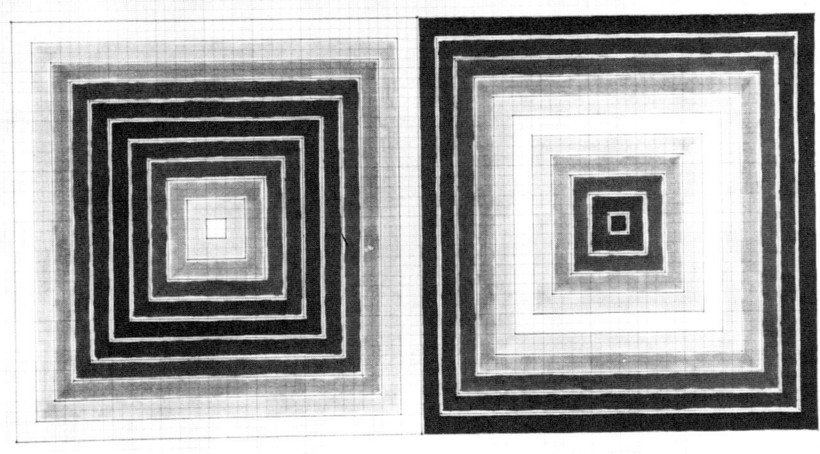

Frank Stella, *Untitled*, 1963, felt-tip pen and pencil on graph paper, 17 × 22″. Photograph by Clem Fiori.

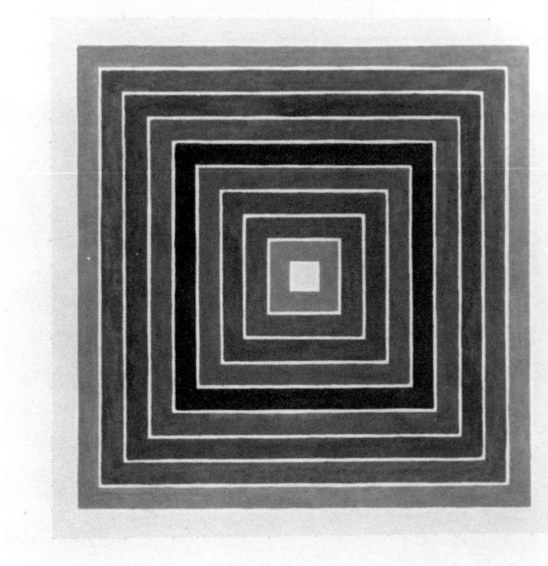

Frank Stella, *Untitled*, 1964, gouache on paper 10¾ × 10″. Photograph by Jon Abbott.

Frank Stella, *Untitled*, 1964, pencil on paper, 10¾ × 10″. Photograph by Jon Abbott.

Cy Twombly

Cy Twombly was born in Lexington, Virginia, in 1929. He has attended Washington and Lee University, The Boston Museum School, The Art Students League in New York, and Black Mountain College. After serving in the United States Army in the 1950s, he traveled with Robert Rauschenberg in Europe and North Africa.

In 1951 his art was given its first public exposure in New York, in a group show at the Kootz Gallery. During the past three decades Twombly has had numerous exhibitions both in Europe and the United States, including a one-man retrospective exhibition of paintings and drawings in 1977 at the Whitney Museum of American Art. Since 1957 Twombly has made his home in Italy, on the outskirts of Rome.

Like his friend Rauschenberg, Twombly began his career during a very transitional period, the late 1940s and early 1950s. Abstract Expressionism was on the wane in the mid-fifties, and many younger artists had begun turning to popular culture and the physical environment for new ideas. But unlike his artist friends, whose environmental interests prophesied Pop Art, Twombly has never comfortably fit in any stylistic category or group, since his art is a composite of contending interests, imagistic and abstract. Twombly's work, in a literal sense, depends upon an obsessive and extended investigation into a private system of visual signs, and their mixed formal and narrative possibilities. In nearly all his work, "calligraphy and the physical act of handwriting"[1] underlie his artistic expression. An important aspect of his art has been the automatic drawing of the Surrealists, which he assimilated in modified form by way of such Abstract Expressionists as Jackson Pollock.

Twombly's characteristic, seemingly undirected doodles and scrawls on canvas or paper expand and contract the surface with a pulsating, intense energy and feeling. Although Twombly has opposed the strongly emotional pictorial rhetoric of Abstract Expressionism and its ponderous existential ideology, he has, in fact, adopted much of the gestural means of such artists as Pollock, de Kooning, and Kline. The powerful immediacy of his creative expression and his concern for spontaneity and the "Creative Moment"[2] also link him to Action Painting. Suzanne Delehanty has accurately described these concerns and Twombly's transformation of the formal devices of the Abstract Expressionists:

> Pencil lines bearing fragments of rectangles, half-born numbers and letters move across the canvas in a manner reminiscent of Pollock's all-over compositions. Unlike Pollock's and Kline's robust drawing, Twombly's line is nervous and swift like Giacometti's: its lively refinement speaks of Klee, its biomorphic vestiges of the surrealist handwriting of Miró and Gorky.[3]

Twombly's passion for Greek and Roman mythology occupies a critical place in his art, further separating him from his American predecessors. Throughout his work Twombly has incorporated many symbols and images from ancient eras of Western culture, which seem to symbolize philosophically and poetically his withdrawal from American life. Twombly's paintings and drawings bear such names as Sperlonga, Galatea, Homer, and Vergil and thus refer to the historical figures or places which inspired them. Twombly also intends the purely visual elements—color, paint, or graphic expression—to establish connections or symbols for places that he has visited or events that have inspired the works. Diagrammatic allusions to landscapes, and even to famous battle scenes, also frequently appear in his art, in the form of maps, plans, or architectural elevations and odd figural forms. The literal and symbolic marks

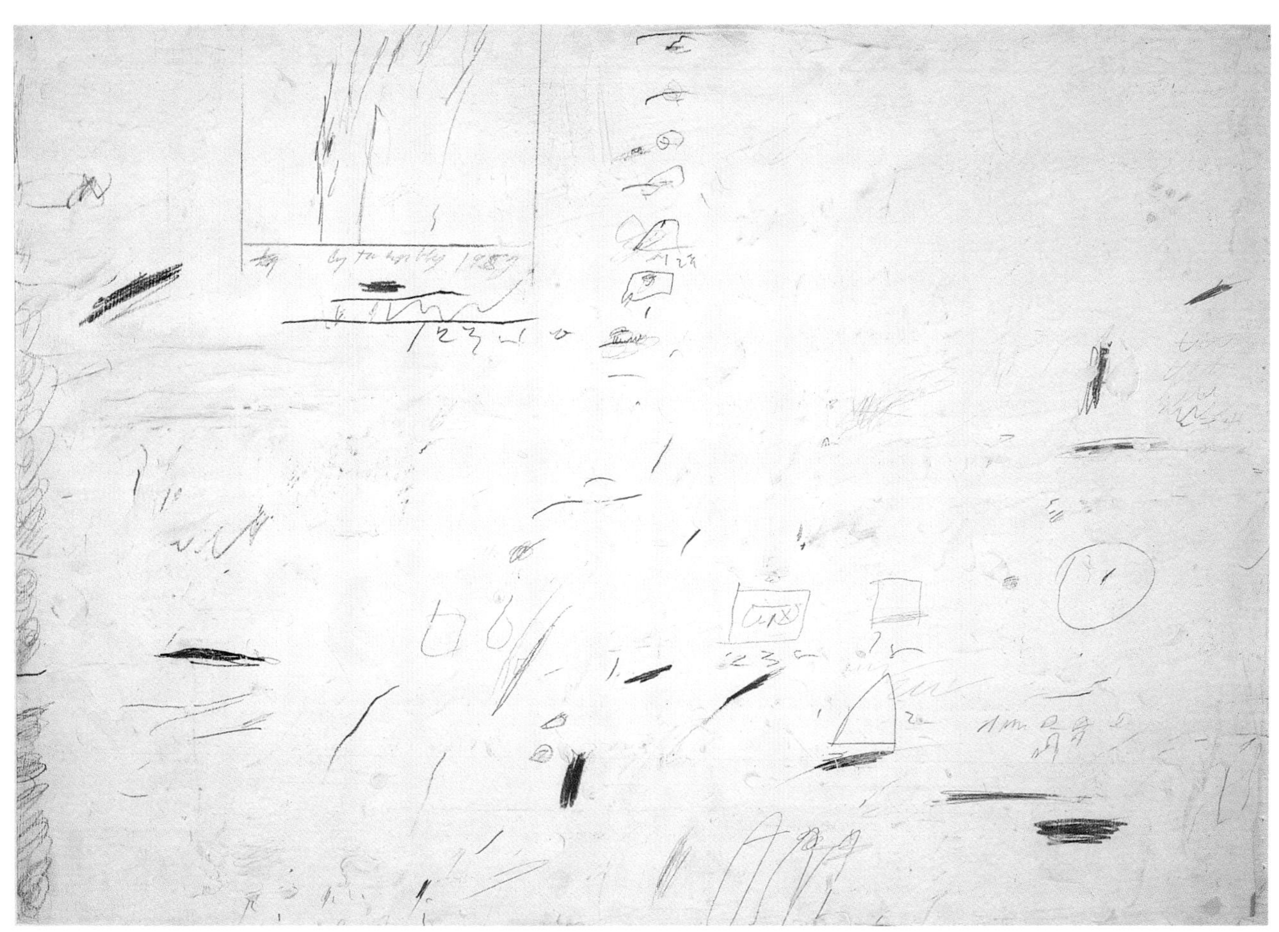

Cy Twombly, *Sperlonga*, 1957, pencil, pastel, and oil on paper, 27¼ × 37¼″ (mat opening).

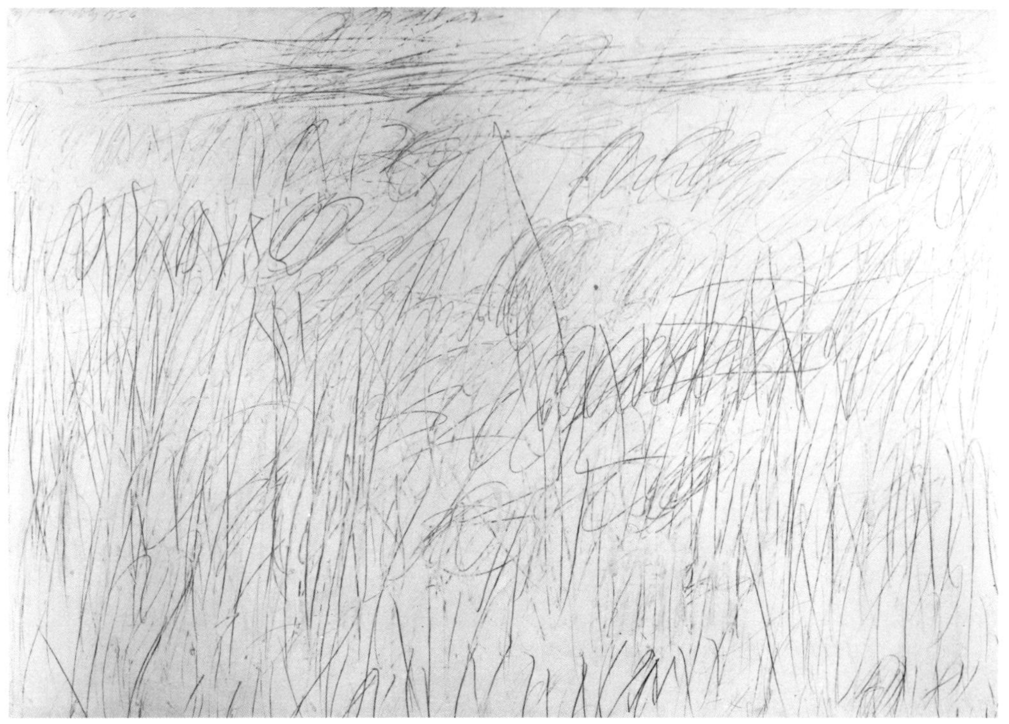

Cy Twombly, *Untitled*, 1956, oil and crayon on canvas, 46⅛ × 62⅞″. Photograph by Bevan Davies.

Cy Twombly, *The Blue Room*, 1957, oil and crayon on canvas, 56¼ × 71½″. Photograph by Bevan Davies.

are both mysteriously private and decipherable; they release the subconscious inspiration of the artist and disclose an "unknown self."[4] Delehanty has observed that useful parallels may be drawn between Twombly's work and French Symbolist poetry:

> Twombly's pictorial system is a-narrative. The relationships among his works, numbers, erotic pictographs and globs of luscious paint are alogical and non-sequential, an order which follows our impressions of felt experiences. Drawing is the convergence of mind, pencil, and hand to distill out of the time of real events single moments of conscious recognition.[5]

Because of the privacy of his signs, Twombly has been likened to an alchemist who seeks the grand transformation from base materials to precious metal. By laying down dense areas of white or gray paint (often a commercial house paint), he creates a sensual ground which then resonates his scrawls and incised scratches, made with a variety of objects, including his fingernails, before the paint dries. His methods are fluid and spontaneous, and depend on the equilibration of numerous visual and psychological factors. Each painting has its own internal history, consisting in visual terms of webs and overlays of curvilinear and jagged lines, superimposed upon one another, until appropriate atmospheric spaces are created and a sense of veiled and discovered narrative meanings is achieved. Twombly's work thus represents a balanced collaboration of eye, hand, paint materials, and personal and cultural memory. All these elements merge to create a personal expression which attains a kind of immanence and credibility as mythology and poetry.

John Otte

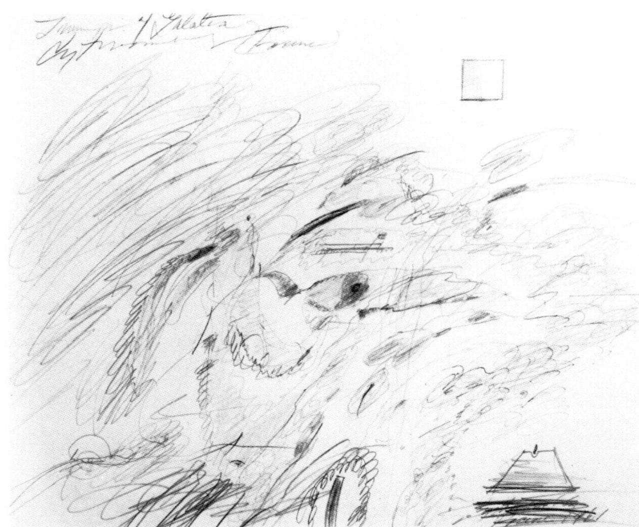

Cy Twombly, *Triumph of Galatea*, 1961, colored pencil on paper, 10½ × 13¾". Photograph by Bevan Davies.

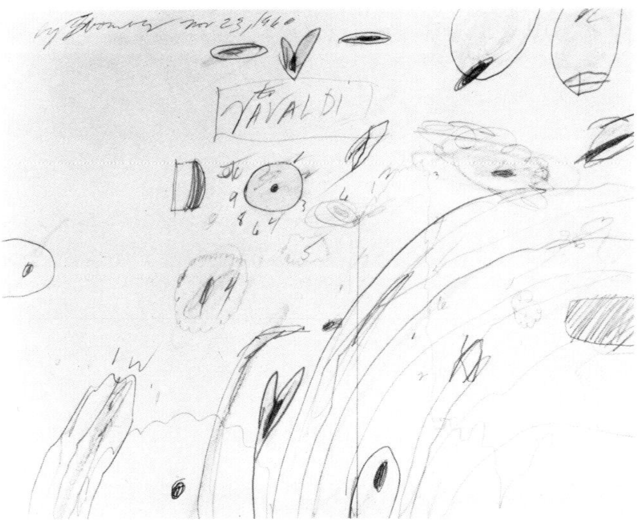

Cy Twombly, *To Vivaldi*, 1960, colored pencil on paper, 10½ × 13¾". Photograph by Bevan Davies.

NOTES

1. Robert Pincus-Witten, "Cy Twombly," *Artforum*, April 1974.
2. Suzanne Delehanty, "The Alchemy of Mind and Hand," *Art International*, March 1946, p. 15.
3. *Ibid.*, p. 15.
4. *Ibid.*, p. 16.
5. *Ibid.*, p. 16.

Andy Warhol

Andrew Warhola, professionally known as Andy Warhol, was born in 1930 to Czechoslovakian immigrant parents in Forest City, Pennsylvania. Warhol studied art at the Carnegie Institute of Technology in Pittsburgh. Upon graduating in 1949 he moved to New York and briefly shared an apartment with the painter Philip Pearlstein, a college friend. Warhol began working as a commercial artist and quickly rose to success through his fashion drawings, which appeared in such magazines as *Vogue*, *Glamour*, and *Harper's Bazaar*. In both 1956 and 1957 he received the Art Directors Club Medal and Award for Distinctive Merit for shoe and hat advertisements for I. Miller. Warhol also did window displays for Tiffany's and Bonwit Teller. While working as a commercial artist, Warhol executed a body of non-commercial drawings and books, most of which were done with a simple monotype process. He drew on non-absorbent paper and then transferred the image to another sheet by pressing them together. The result was a blotted line drawing which could be easily repeated by re-inking the original. The drawings of shoes, children, cupids, and cats were delicate and tenuous, stylistically very distant from both Abstract Expressionism and Pop Art.

By 1960 Warhol had become interested in becoming a successful "serious" artist. He began painting, and adopted a style radically different from his previous work. His first paintings were based on comic strips—"Dick Tracy," "Popeye," and "Nancy." The early works incorporating popular imagery were personalized by drips and smudges, to alter a preselected mass media image and render it unique. In the 1962 drawing *Hedy Lamarr* Warhol utilized a make-up advertisement for his subject matter, but made it personal through his loose drawing style, which is unlike the photographic images of movie stars that we are accustomed to. By 1960 Roy Lichtenstein had also, independently, begun painting comic-strip imagery and, at the Leo Castelli Gallery, was the first to have an exhibition of his work. As a result, since Warhol may have appeared derivative, he was unable to find a gallery in New York to show his paintings, but a number of well-known avant-garde figures, including the dealer Ivan Karp and the critic and curator Henry Geldzahler, became interested in Warhol's work, and subsequent pieces with colder, more generic imagery appeared in two one-man shows in 1962. The Campbell's soup cans, shown at the Ferus Gallery in Los Angeles in July 1962, were the first of Warhol's commercial icons to gain the attention of the art world and the mass media. In November of the same year Warhol had his first New York show, at Eleanor Ward's Stable Gallery. The subject matter in this show included the soup cans, Marilyn Monroe, Elvis Presley, Coca-Cola, and do-it-yourself images.

Warhol's first popular-culture imagery paintings were hand painted, but he soon turned exclusively to the silkscreen process. The Campbell's soup cans and Coca-Cola cap drawings of 1962 reveal the very controlled draftsmanship of which Warhol's hand is capable. The do-it-yourself paintings and drawings of 1962 foreshadow the withdrawal of the artist's hand, and hence evidence of individual authorship, from Warhol's work. The drawing *Do It Yourself* mimics a cheap paint-by-numbers hobby kit or a child's coloring book. Although the content and form of the final product are predetermined, the person executing a paint-by-numbers picture is given the illusion of participating in a creative activity. In this drawing Warhol is commenting on the artistic process and still exercising a degree of creativity in the composition of the image—the kind of creativity that he soon relinquished to the silkscreens of found popular imagery.

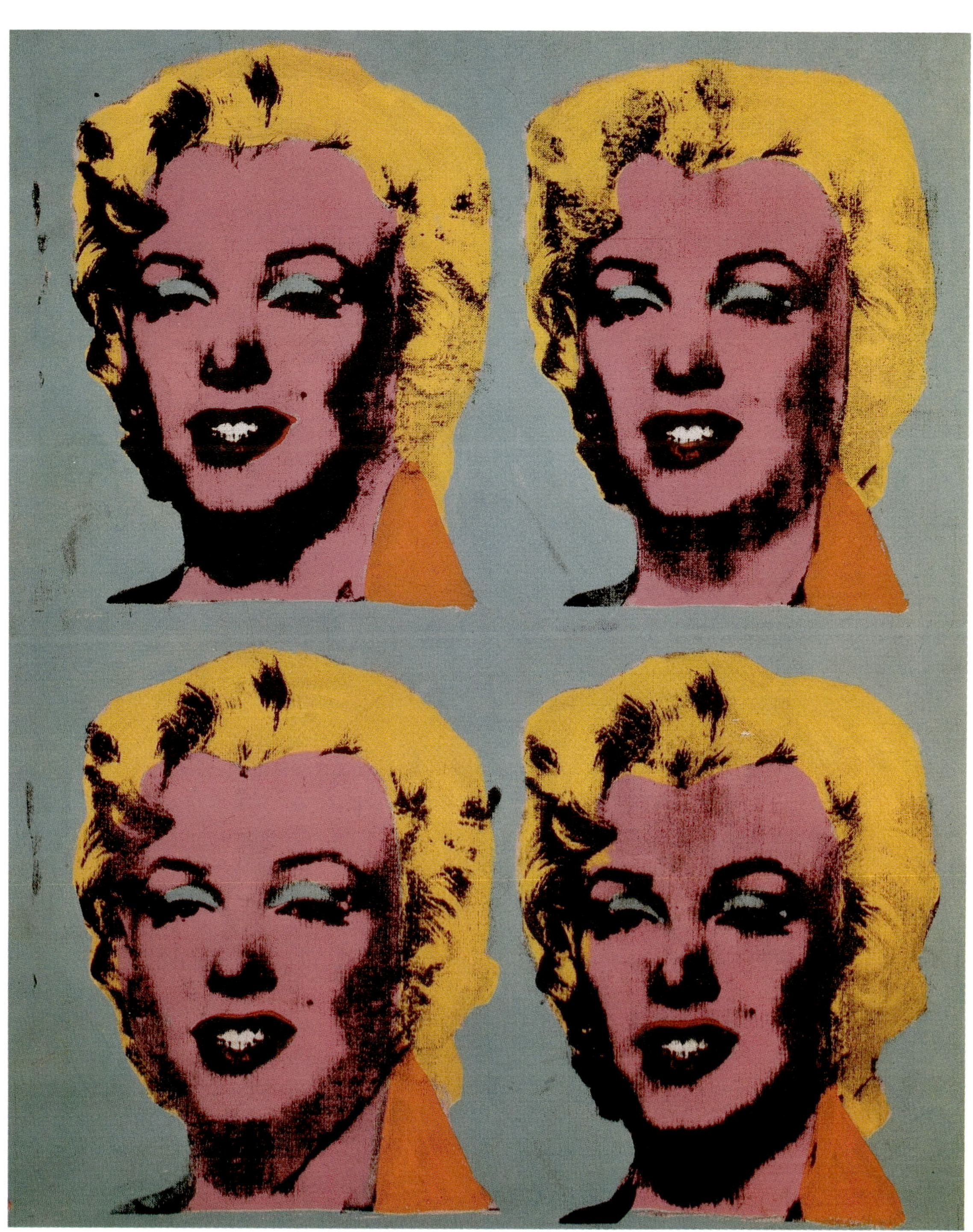

Andy Warhol, *Four Marilyns*, 1962, acrylic and silkscreen enamel on canvas, 74 × 61″. Photograph by Clem Fiori.

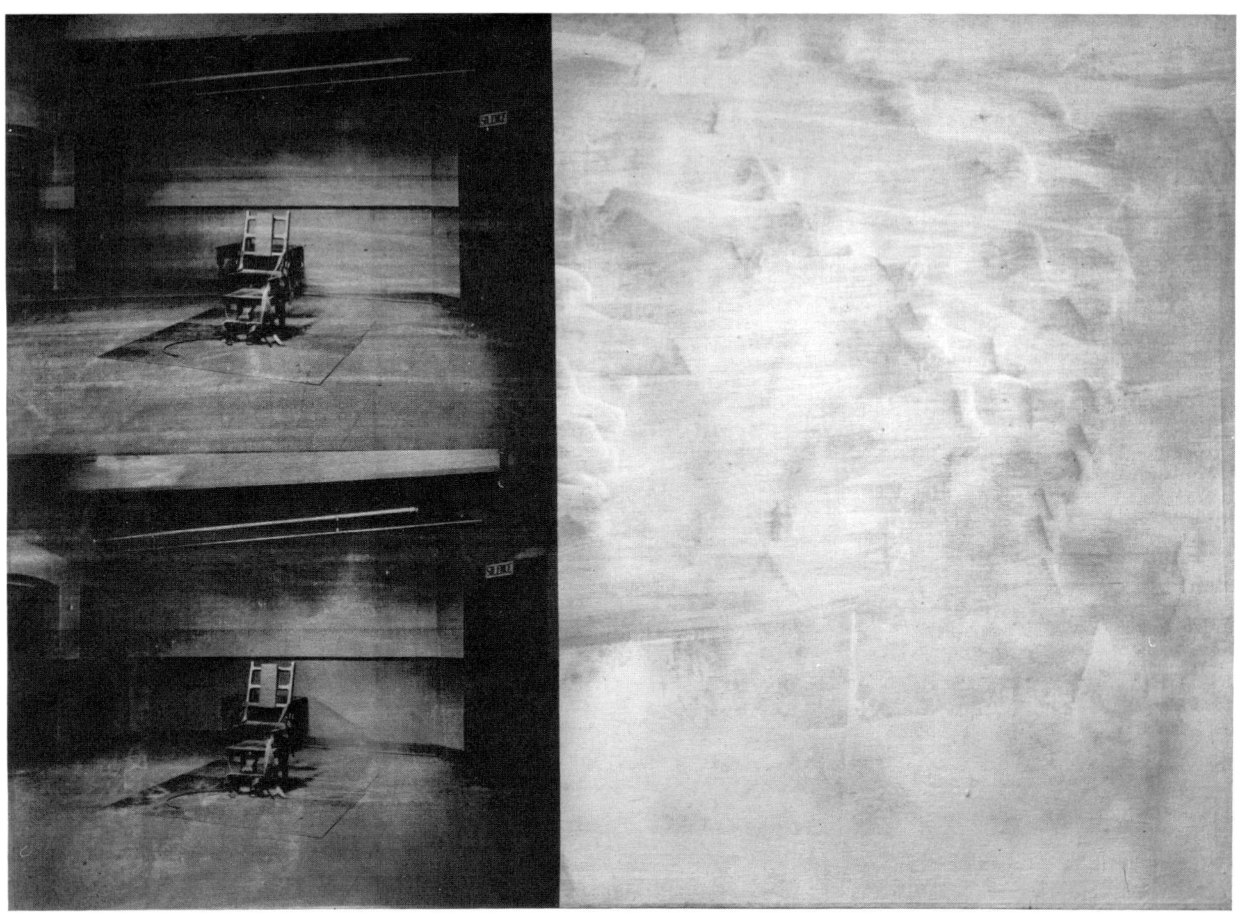

Andy Warhol, *Silver Disaster*, 1963, acrylic and silkscreen on canvas, 42 × 60″.

Four Marilyns of 1962 is one of Warhol's earlier silkscreened paintings. Each of the Monroe images is different due to the unevenness of the silkscreening, but the repetition of her image, in Warhol's work and throughout our culture, makes these differences trivial. Warhol's portraits, both of people and of consumer products, can be seen as the secular icons of a media-saturated culture. *Nine Jackies*, with its somber subject matter and gold-and-black coloration, even resembles a traditional religious polyptych. The flat, gray tonal grounds, combined with the high-contrast silkscreening of Jacqueline Kennedy and the military attendants at President Kennedy's funeral procession, produce, despite the poor quality of the printing, an image of a somber richness reminiscent of early Italian religious paintings.

The silkscreened images that Warhol used in his paintings through 1965 can be categorized into a few major themes: consumer products, deaths and disasters, and famous people. "That Warhol could paint simultaneously Warren Beatty and electric chairs, Troy Donahue and race riots, Marilyn Monroe and fatal car crashes, may seem the peculiar product of a perversely cool and passive personality until we realize that this numb, voyeuristic view of contemporary life, in which the grave and the trivial, the fashionable and horrifying, blandly coexist as passing spectacles, is a deadly accurate mirror of a commonplace experience in modern art and life."[1] Warhol has remained evasive as to what he thinks of his art: "If you want to know about Andy Warhol, just look at the surface of my paintings and films and me, and there I am.

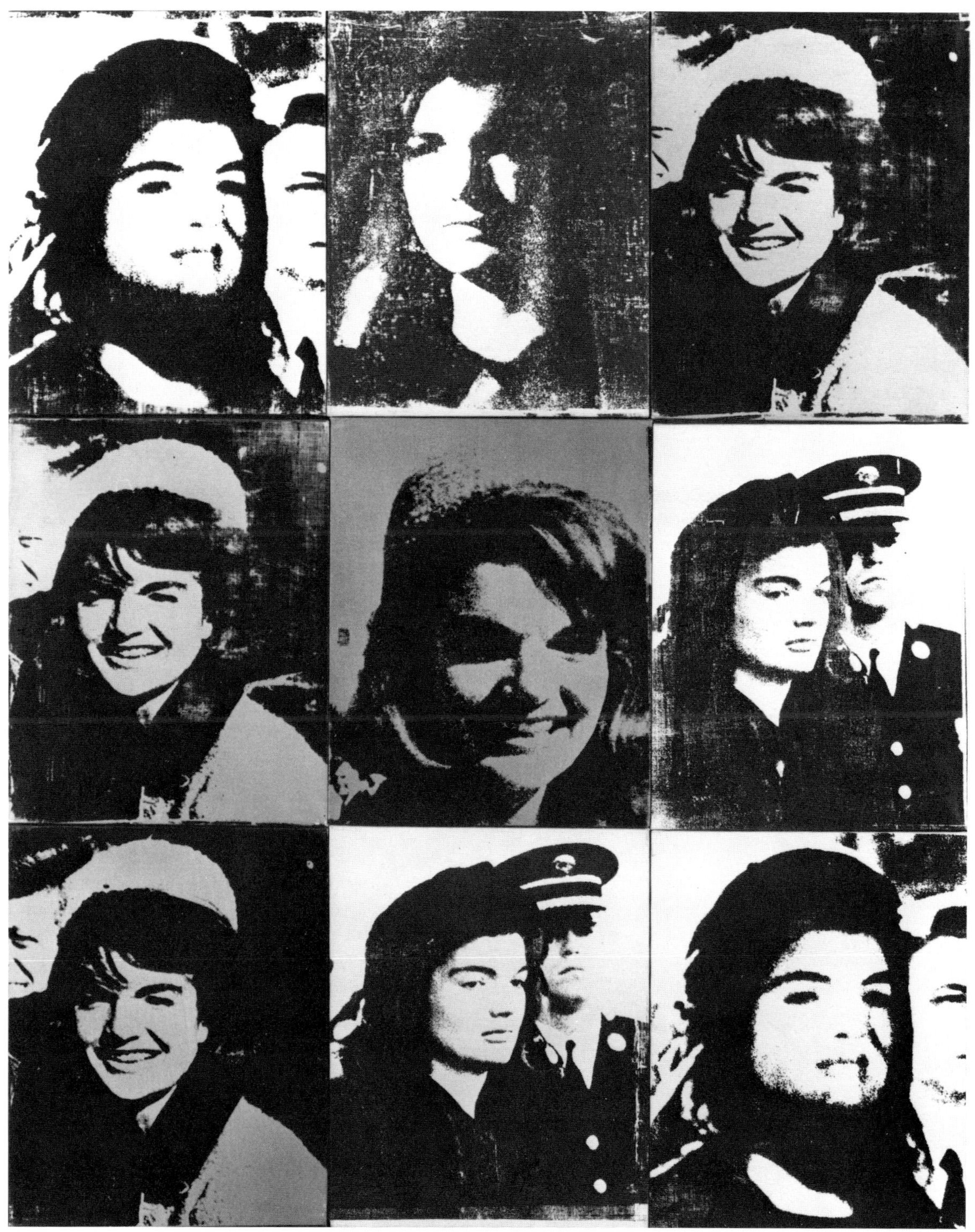

Andy Warhol, *Nine Jackies*, 1964, acrylic and silkscreen enamel on canvas, 60¾ × 48¼″. Photograph by Clem Fiori.

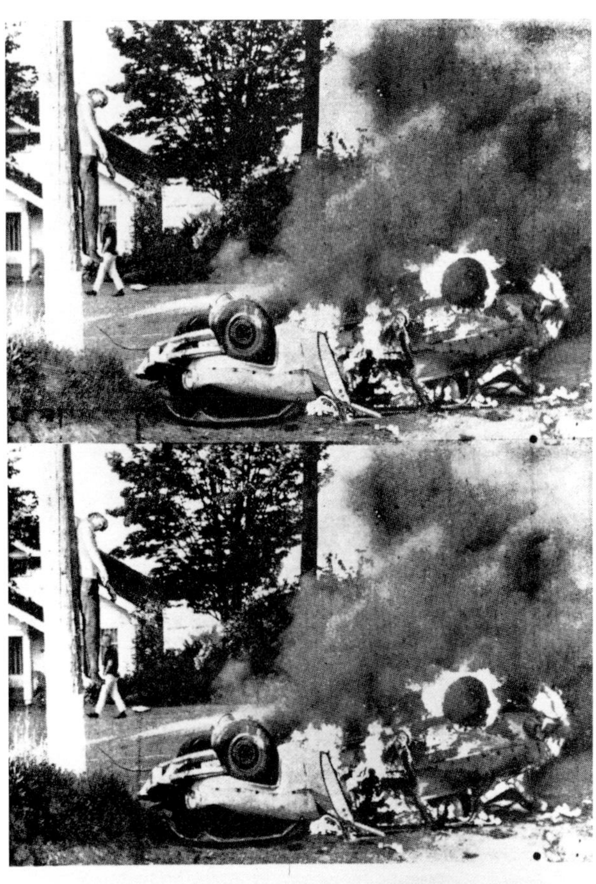

Andy Warhol, *White Burning Car Twice*, 1963, acrylic and silk-screen enamel on canvas, 79 × 42½". Photograph by Clem Fiori.

There's nothing behind it."[2] Warhol incorporates the techniques of mass media and advertising into his painting—the repetition of images, the reappearance of the same product or image in new guises to sustain novelty, the silk-screening process. The four *Campbell's Soup Cans*, 1965, is an example of this sustained novelty; Warhol presents the same icon as in the original 1962 series, but it appears new through a different use of color.

Warhol's fame grew rapidly in the early sixties. In 1964 he had his first European show, at the Galerie Ileana Sonnabend in Paris, and a show at the Leo Castelli Gallery in New York.

In 1965 Warhol announced his "retirement" from painting, while in Paris for his show at the Galerie Ileana Sonnabend, which featured his cow-wallpaper and flower paintings. He insisted he would devote all of his energies to film making, a pursuit which he had begun in 1963. Warhol produced over seventy "underground" films by the close of the decade. However, he did continue to paint and in the seventies executed many portraits. Warhol and his entourage have been very active in the New York subculture and nightclub scene since the early sixties.

The world of Pop Art and pop music effected a brief alliance in 1965 when Warhol designed the ambience for Lou Reed's band, "The Velvet Underground," and Nico, the German actress and model turned singer. In this period Warhol's studio, known as "The Factory," was open twenty-four hours a day to anyone with an interest in its activities or in the "art scene," until 1968, when a disturbed actress wandered in and seriously wounded the artist; the event was front-page news and briefly generated dramatic headlines in the New York press.

Erica Wolf

NOTES

1. Robert Rosenblum, *Andy Warhol: Portraits of the 70s* (New York: Random House, 1979), pp. 12–14.
2. Andy Warhol, Kasper König, Pontus Hultén, Olle Granath, eds., 3rd ed, *Andy Warhol* (Boston: Boston Book and Art Publisher, 1970), n.p.

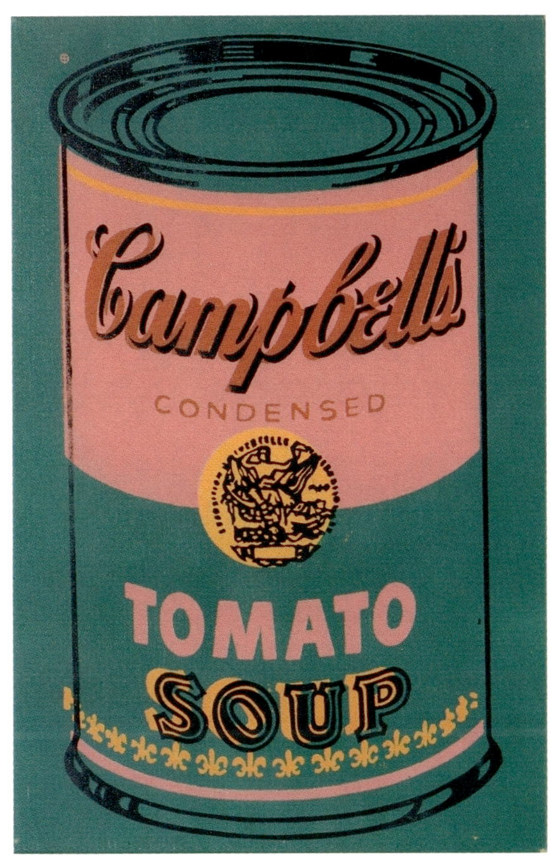

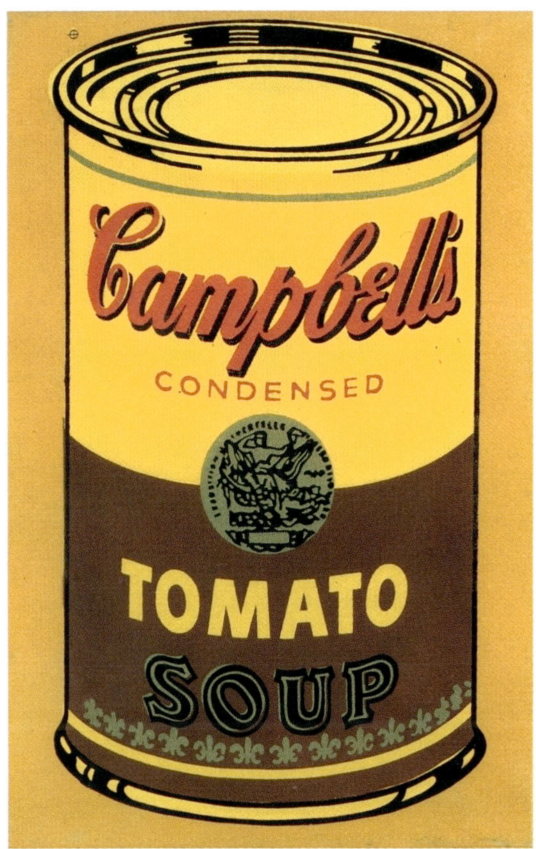

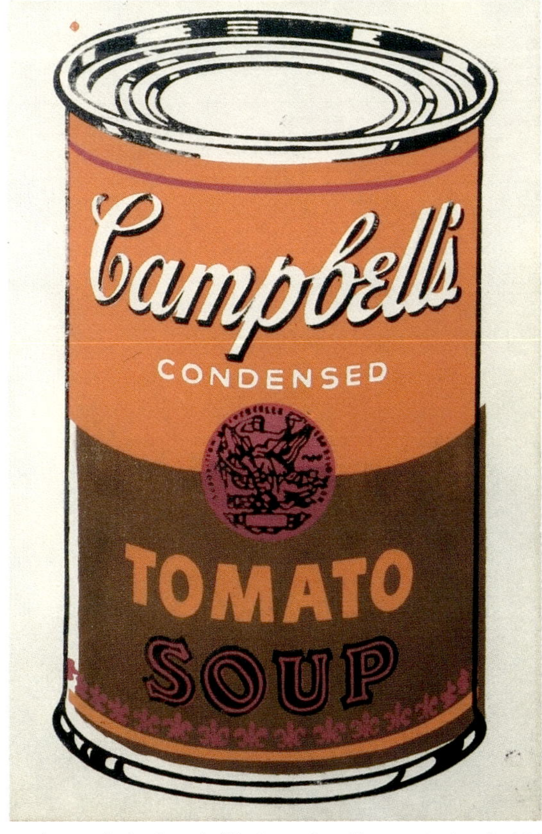

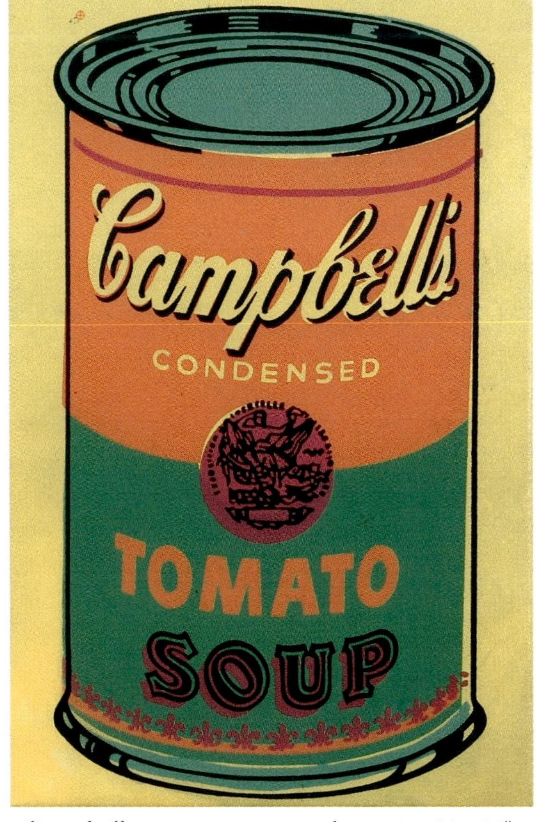

Andy Warhol, *Campbell's Soup Can* (four paintings), 1965, acrylic and silkscreen on canvas, each painting 36 × 24″. Photograph by Clem Fiori.

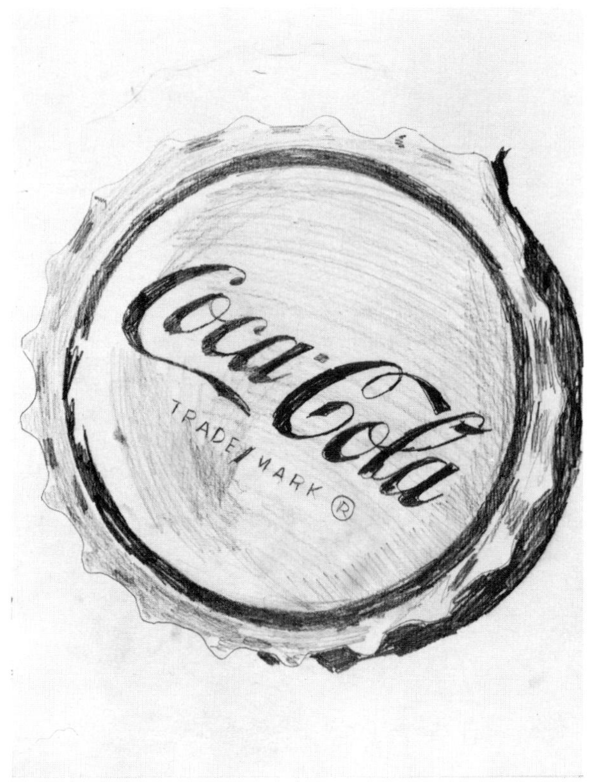

Andy Warhol, *Coca-Cola*, 1962, pencil, 23¾ × 18″. Photograph by Jon Abbott.

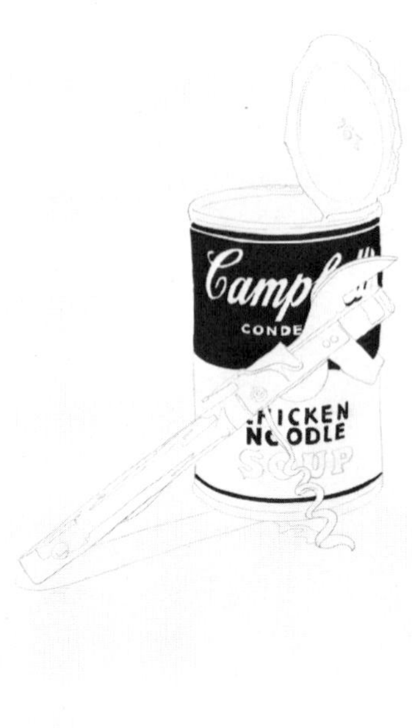

Andy Warhol, *Campbell's Soup Can*, 1962, gouache and pencil on paper, 23¾″ × 18. Photograph by Jon Abbott.

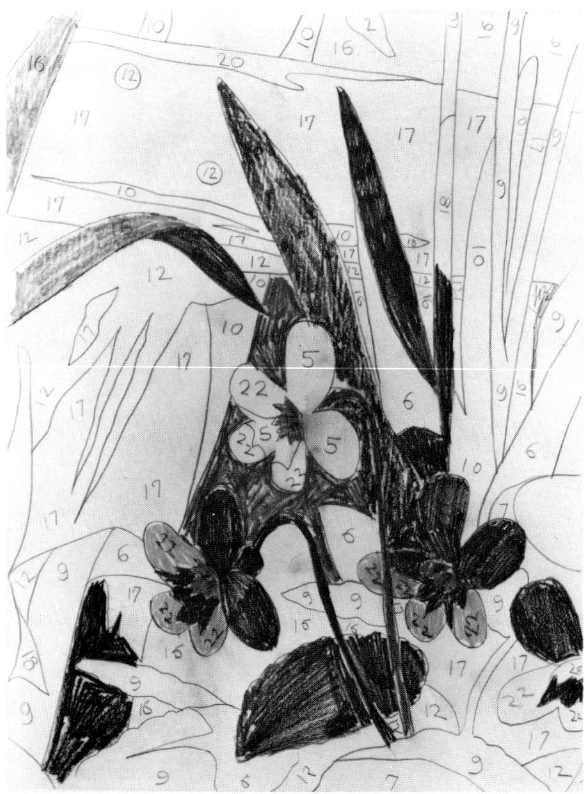

Andy Warhol, *Do It Yourself*, 1962, colored crayon, 25 × 18″. Photograph by Clem Fiori.

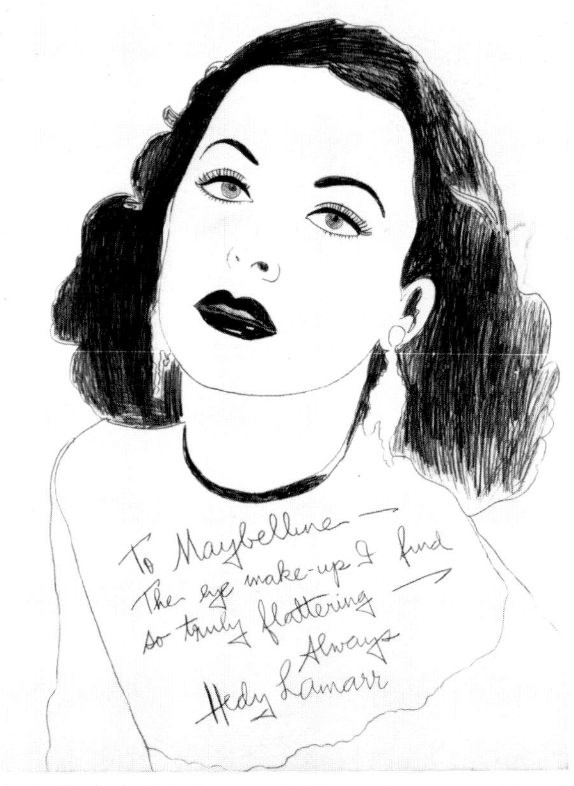

Andy Warhol, *Hedy Lamarr*, 1962, pencil on paper, 40 × 30″. Photograph by Jon Abbott.

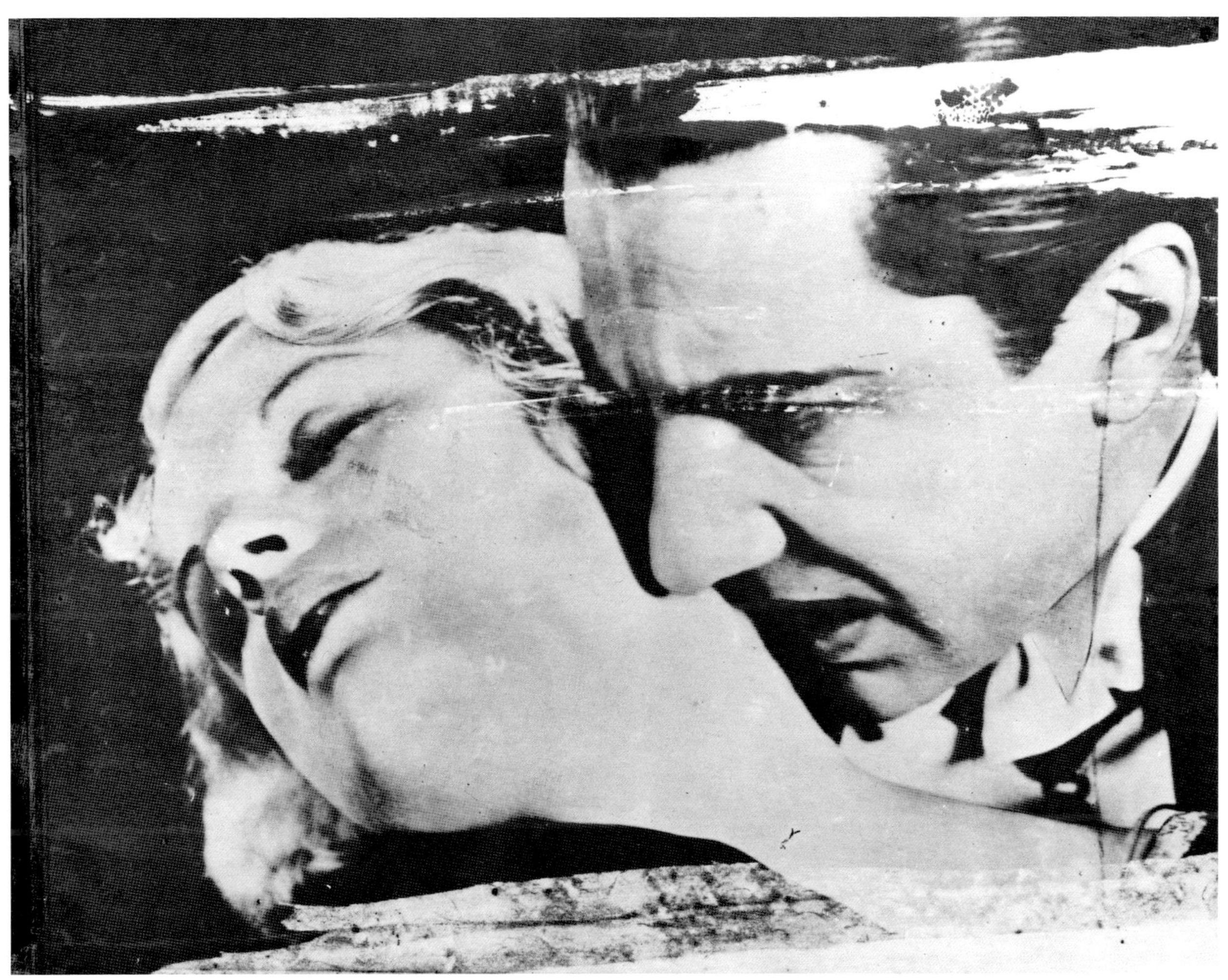

Andy Warhol, *The Kiss (Bela Lugosi)*, 1963, silkscreen on paper handprinted by the artist (edition of eight), 30 × 40″. Photograph by Bevan Davies.

Tom Wesselmann

Born in 1931, Tom Wesselmann, like Jim Dine, was raised and educated in Cincinnati, where he attended the Art Academy—studying cartooning, however, rather than fine art—before transferring to Cooper Union in New York in 1955. In New York, Dine introduced Wesselmann to the avant-garde and was instrumental in arranging a co-exhibition with him in 1956 at the Judson Gallery, a cooperative which Dine and Oldenburg had founded. At this early point in his career, Wesselmann had already turned his attention to collages that combined decorative surfaces and cut-out images taken from magazine advertising with hand-painted human figures or still-life objects. He handled the figures with a deliberate carelessness and expressive vehemence, suggesting the influence of de Kooning's energetic brushstrokes.

As early as 1961 Wesselmann began his most famous series, still continuing today, the Great American Nude, limiting his palette to red, white, and blue, and thus clearly associating an erotic theme with the American flag. In 1962 he executed a still-life drawing with shoes, a proto-Pop Art evocation of the banality and mechanical representation of advertising illustration. Wesselmann's deadpan representation of common objects creates a tone, or attitude, somewhere between celebration and satire in this form of popular realism, whose simplistic forms seem impartially referential to mass-media signs and the depicted objects. A later drawing, *Still Life with Radio*, 1964, is more elementary and also clearly more "abstract." The drastically abbreviated graphic means, so characteristic of Pop Art, create impersonality, minimizing invention and allowing popular culture imagery referential play and impact. At the same time, however, the reductive schema of the drawing can be read as an allusion to the formal tensions of "high art" styles. Like Wesselmann's unmistakable references to Matisse in his early examples in the Great American Nude series, such allusions are combined with equally forceful quotations, or replications, taken from advertising. Pop culture symbols and serious historical art forms thus coexist, and their interaction constitutes a basic and continuing theme in his art.

Wesselmann had his first one-man show in 1961 at the small Tanager Gallery in New York, and the following year he joined the Sidney Janis Gallery, also in New York, and has shown there regularly since then. That year he began to extend his objects into three-dimensional form, incorporating for the first time a sculptured bread loaf taken directly from an advertisement sign. Wesselmann continued to enhance his canvases with a sculptural presence by juxtaposing a variety of competing solid objects and advertising emblems against flat painted areas, using strong colors and textures to achieve his desired expressive effects. In *Still Life #45* of 1962, he explored America's national dish, the turkey, much as Johns had tested new perimeters of signification, with a far more refined pictorial resolution, with his famous *Flag*. Wesselmann, in *Still Life #45*, preferred to emphasize the papier-mâché colors which are echoed in the competing, painted representations of the American Beauty roses, vegetables, and potatoes. The artificial glaze of his colors is reinforced by the orange, red, and yellow "poster-paint" background, standing in direct opposition to his smooth literal rendering of the third dimension, commercial art textures, and the inescapable advertising references.

Wesselmann's interest in singling out and isolating parts of the female body in his Nude series, and other fragmented anatomical subjects elsewhere, transforms commercial signs into a fantastic content that can be linked to Dada

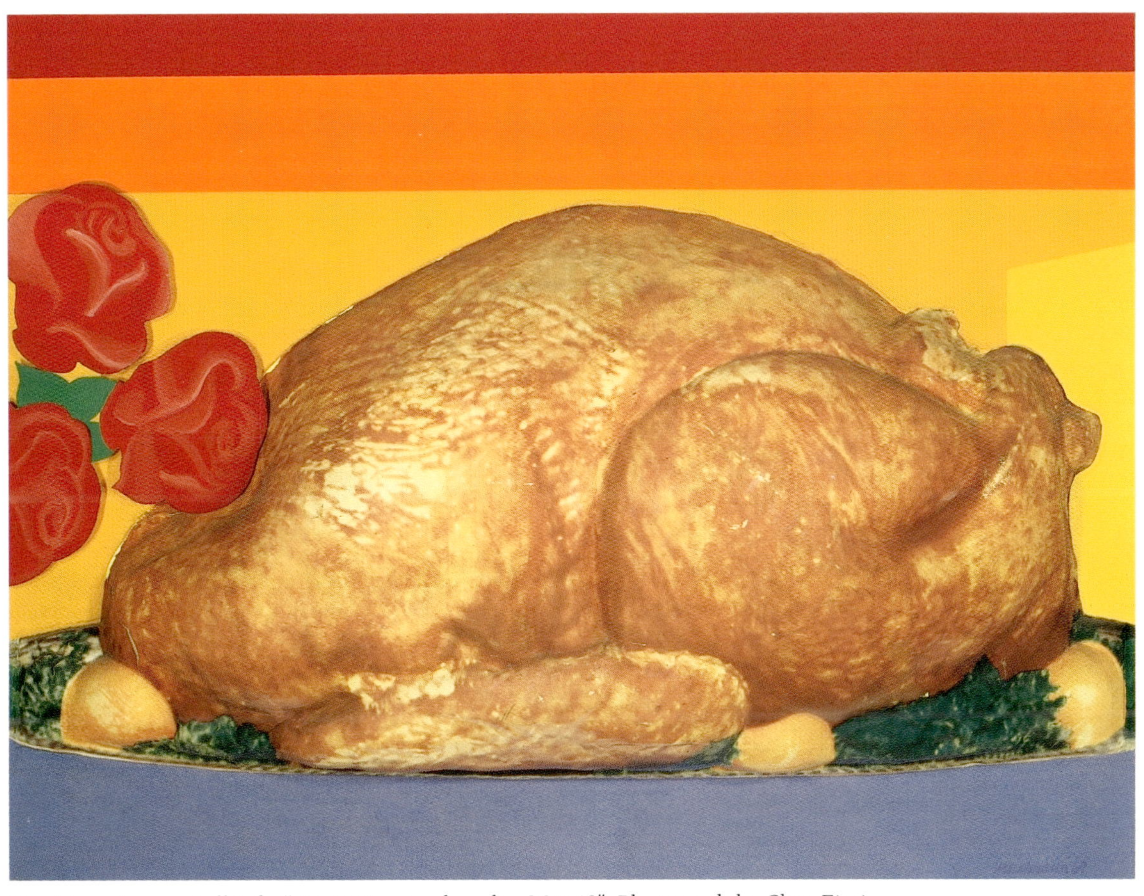

Tom Wesselmann, *Still Life #45*, 1962, mixed media, 36 × 48″. Photograph by Clem Fiori.

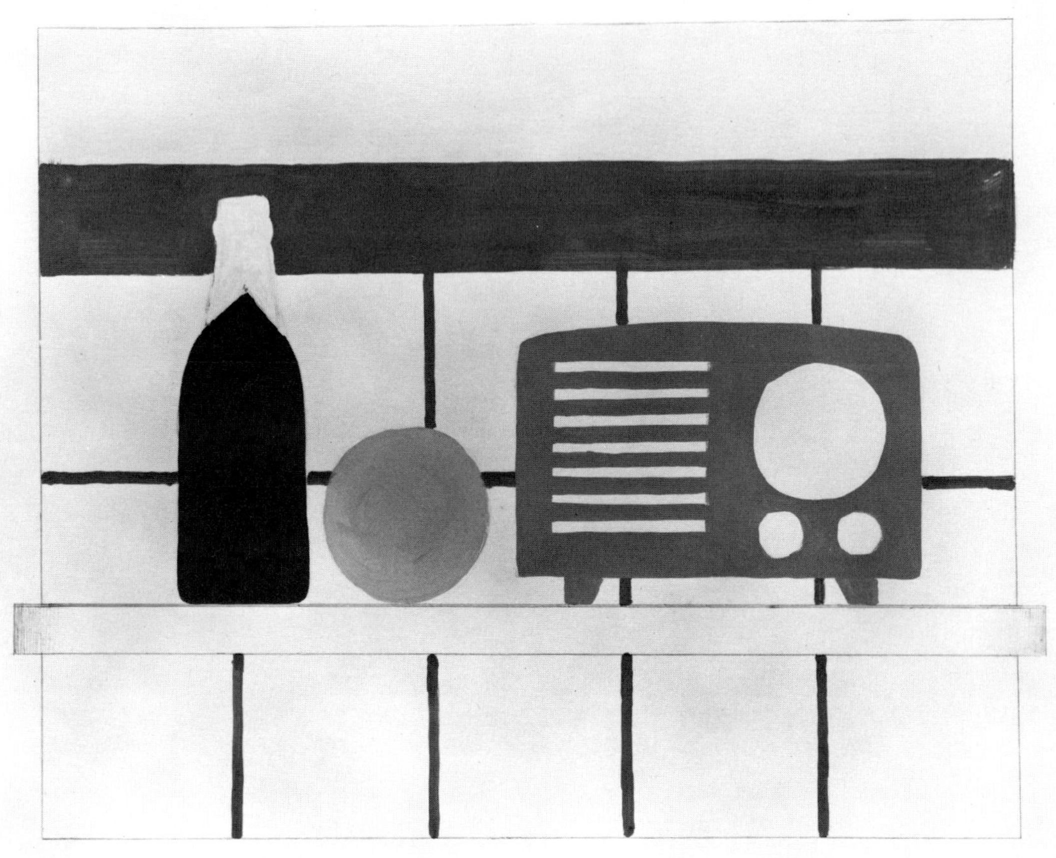

Tom Wesselmann, *Still Life with Radio*, 1964, gouache and pencil on paper, 23 × 31½″. Photograph by Clem Fiori.

and Surrealism. However, no matter how explicitly erotic his imagery might be, it fails to arouse specific associations. Its blandness and rubbery congruence are actually rather sexless, and most clearly recall the tough and blatant presentation of unclothed and semi-clothed forms common in certain contemporary advertising, where the erotic intention is as obvious as it is unimaginative, mechanical, and unavailing, with only a marginal seductive appeal. As his Nude series multiplied, Wesselmann matched its direct impact and shock tactics with more oblique and guarded sexual content, which mingled body parts and landscape. *Seascape No. 14*, 1966, juxtaposes various polarities—a clumsy human foot and scenery, charcoal and white pigment, drawing paper and a softly curving transparent sculptural enclosure of plastic.

Wesselmann's curiously depersonalized but obsessive interest in the female form, whole and in parts, continued in a variety of contexts throughout the sixties, as he abstracted his imagery in monumental and increasingly environmental painted assemblages. An inveterate experimenter with collage juxtaposition, he offset the human imagery with such accessories as finger rings, car keys, and lipsticks, or focused on a detached mouth, magnified into a yawning orifice of vast scale, waiting to receive a lighted cigarette or expelling a sinuous cloud of three-dimensional smoke.

Julia Hicks

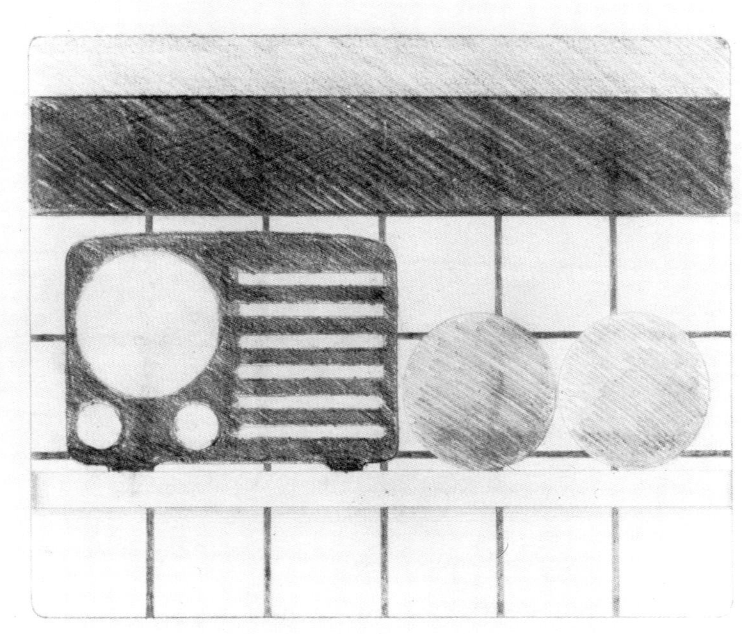

Tom Wesselmann, *Still Life with Radio*, 1964, pencil on paper, 15¾ × 23″. Photograph by Jon Abbott.

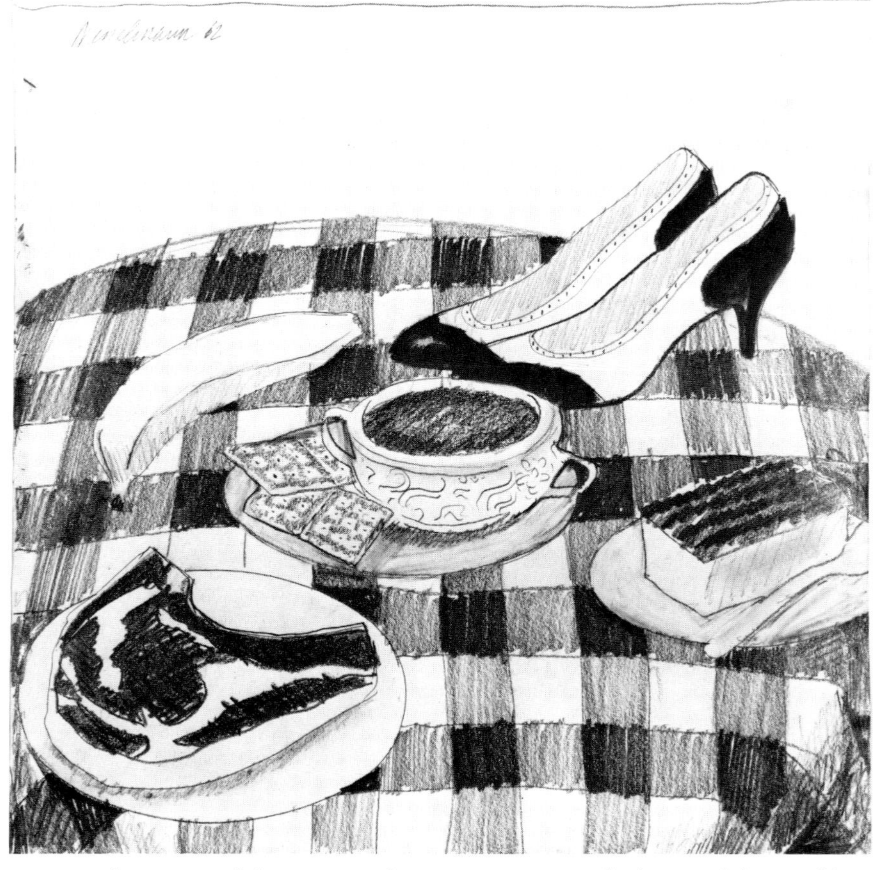

Tom Wesselmann, *Untitled*, 1962, pencil on paper, 16½ × 16⅞″. Photograph by Jon Abbott.

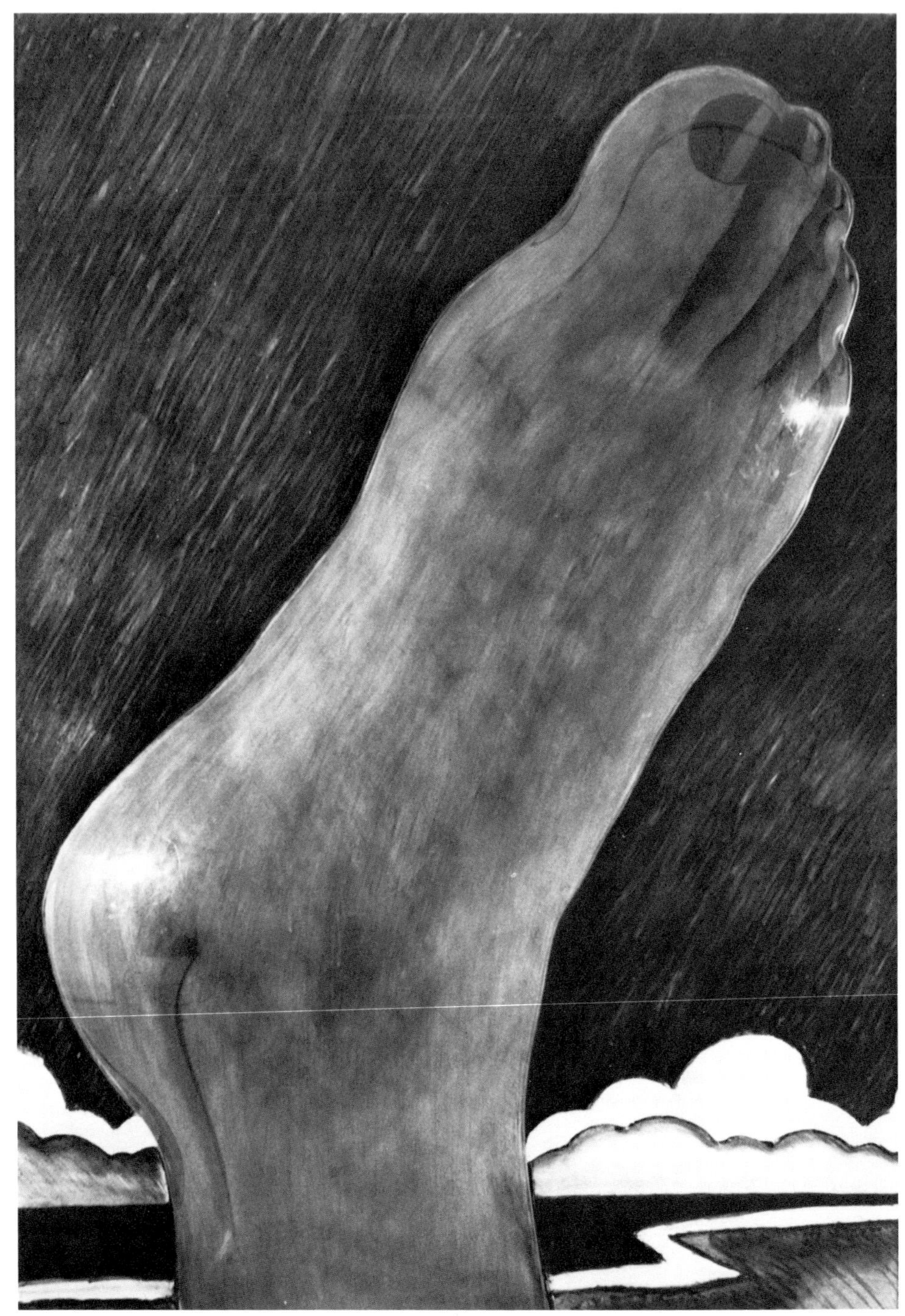

Tom Wesselmann, *Seascape #14*, 1966, charcoal, oil on Plexiglas, 66 × 39½″.

Checklist

Arman

1. *Infinity of Typewriters and Infinity of Monkeys and Infinity of Time = Hamlet*, 1962, typewriters in wood encasement, 72 × 69 × 12″.

John Chamberlain

2. *Untitled* (Colonel Splendid), 1964, painted metal, 25 × 23 × 25″.

Christo

3. *Le Diable* (Hand Cart), 1963, fabric, plastic, metal, hand cart, 48 × 40 × 26″.

Jim Dine

4. *Proposed Still Life*, 1962, oil on canvas, mixed media, 84 × 36″.
5. *Four Soap Dishes*, 1962, oil on canvas with objects, 49 × 41 × $1\frac{1}{2}$″.
6. *Bedroom Light over Flesh Square*, 1965, oil and graphite on canvas, mixed media, 72 × 36″.
7. *Landscape*, 1963, oil on canvas with objects, $27\frac{1}{2}$ × 126 × 6″, each panel 24 × 18″.
8. *Tie*, 1962, charcoal and oil on paper, 26 × $19\frac{3}{8}$″ (mat opening).
9. *Bow Tie*, 1961, pencil and wash on paper, 24 × 18″.
10. *Black Door*, 1962, painted door, oil on wood, $84\frac{1}{2}$ × $136\frac{1}{2}$″.
11. *A Black on White Tie / A White on Black Tie*, 1962, oil on canvas, diptych, each panel $50\frac{1}{4}$ × 40″.
12. *Untitled*, 1963, collage on paper, 11 × $8\frac{1}{2}$″.
13. *French Pants*, 1962, oil on paper, $30\frac{3}{4}$ × $22\frac{1}{2}$″.
14. *A Nice Pair of Boots*, 1965, painted bronze, each boot 16 × 11 × 4″.

Jasper Johns

15. *Number 8*, 1959, encaustic on canvas, 20 × 15″.
16. *Flashlight*, 1958, sculpmetal over flashlight and wood, $5\frac{1}{4}$ × $9\frac{1}{8}$ × $3\frac{7}{8}$″.
17. *Sketch for Flashlight*, 1958, pencil on envelope, $4\frac{1}{4}$ × $9\frac{1}{2}$″.
18. *Flag*, 1954, pencil on paper, $4\frac{1}{2}$ × $3\frac{3}{4}$″.
19. *Target*, 1960, pencil with paint brush and dry watercolor cakes, wood frame, $7\frac{3}{4}$ × $3\frac{3}{4}$″.

*20. *Flag Above White*, 1954, encaustic on canvas, $23\frac{1}{4}$ × 20″.

*21. *Gray Target*, 1958, encaustic and collage on canvas, 42 × 42″.

22. *Hook*, 1958, crayon and charcoal on paper, 17 × $20\frac{3}{4}$″.
23. *Numbers*, 1960, oil on board, $8\frac{1}{4}$ × 6″.

Roy Lichtenstein

24. *Little Aloha*, 1962, magna on canvas, 44 × 42″.

*25. *Eddie Diptych*, 1962, oil on canvas, 44 × 52″ (two panels).

*26. *Composition II*, 1964, oil on canvas, 54 × 47″.

27. *Large Spool*, 1963, magna on canvas, 68 × 56″.
28. *The Kiss II*, 1963, pencil and touche on paper, $16\frac{5}{8}$ × $18\frac{1}{8}$″ (image size).
29. *Bread and Jam*, 1963, pencil and touche on paper, 16 × $21\frac{5}{8}$″ (image size).
30. *Step-on Can with Leg (Shut)*, 1961, ink on paper, $19\frac{7}{8}$ × $23\frac{1}{8}$″.
31. *Step-on Can with Leg (Open)*, 1961, ink on paper, $19\frac{7}{8}$ × $23\frac{1}{8}$″.
32. *Modern Sculpture with Horse Motif*, 1967, aluminum and marble, $28\frac{3}{4}$ × $16\frac{1}{2}$ × $5\frac{1}{2}$″ (edition of six).
33. *Standing Explosion*, 1966, enamel on steel, 38 × 27 × 25″.
34. *Modern Sculpture with Glass Wave*, 1967, brass and glass, 91 × 26 × 27″ (edition of three).

*35. *Non-Objective II*, 1964, magna on canvas, 48 × 48″.

Robert Morris

36. *"Leave Key on Hook Inside Cabinet,"* 1963, paint on wood with lock, 11 × $7\frac{3}{4}$ × $3\frac{1}{2}$″.

37. *Battery*, 1963, lead on board, 43 × 12⅛″.

38. *Something Else*, 1963, painted wood, 5½ × 1¼ × 14¼″.

Claes Oldenburg

*39. *Giant Ice Cream Cone*, 1962, muslin soaked in plaster over wire frame, painted with enamel, 13⅝ × 37½ × 13¼″.

40. *Meringue Chantilly*, 1962, muslin soaked in plaster over wire frame, painted with enamel, and plate, 11 × 16 × 4¼″.

41. *Dessert on Plate*, 1962, muslin soaked in plaster over wire frame, painted with enamel, and plate, 10 × 3¼″.

42. *Bread on Breadboard*, 1962, muslin soaked in plaster over wire frame, painted with enamel, and wood, 8½ × 18″.

43. *Salad in Bowl*, 1962, muslin soaked in plaster over wire frame, painted with enamel, and bowl, 6 × 10¾″.

44. *Falling Omelette*, 1964, muslin soaked in plaster over wire frame, painted with enamel, and plate, 11 × 12 × 17″.

45. *Roast Beef*, 1961, muslin soaked in plaster over wire frame, painted with enamel, 14 × 17 × 16″.

46. *"dam fall,"* 1965, litho crayon, 9⅞ × 15″.

47. *Truck / Pants*, 1960, painted cardboard with charcoal, 22½ × 20½″.

48. *Nutella*, 1964, muslin soaked in plaster over wire frame, painted with enamel, mounted to Plexiglas sheet, 15 × 13¾″.

Robert Rauschenberg

49. *Magician II*, 1959, combine painting, 65½ × 38¼ × 16¼″. (Frontispiece.)

50. *Dylaby*, 1962, combine painting, 109½ × 87 × 15″.

51. *Interior*, 1956, combine painting, 45¼ × 46½ × 7½″.

52. *Monk*, 1955, collage and mixed media on canvas, 14 × 12″.

53. *Hymnal*, 1955, combine painting, 64 × 49¼ × 7¼″.

54. *Calendar*, 1962, oil on canvas, 96 × 60¼″.

55. *Street Throng*, 1959, pencil, watercolor, and gouache, transfer drawing on paper, 23¾ × 35½″.

56. *Drawing Room*, 1963, pencil and watercolor, transfer drawing on paper, 22½ × 30″.

57. *Political Folly*, 1968, pencil and watercolor, transfer drawing on paper, 22½ × 30″.

James Rosenquist

58. *Balcony*, 1961, oil on canvas, mirror, Plexiglas, 60 × 73″.

59. *Aspen, Colorado*, 1966, oil on canvas, 48 × 62″.

Frank Stella

60. *Untitled* (Benjamin Moore series), 1961, alkyd on canvas, 12 × 12″.

61. *Point of Pines*, 1960, metal foil collage on board, 7¼ × 9½″.

62. *Untitled*, 1963, felt-tip pen and pencil on graph paper, 17 × 22″.

63. *Untitled*, 1964, gouache on paper, 10¾ × 10″.

64. *Untitled*, 1964, pencil on paper, 10¾ × 10″.

Cy Twombly

65. *Sperlonga*, 1957, pencil, pastel, and oil on paper, 27¼ × 37¼″ (mat opening).

66. *Untitled*, 1956, oil and crayon on canvas, 46⅛ × 62⅞″.

*67. *The Blue Room*, 1957, oil and crayon on canvas, 56¼ × 71½″.

68. *Triumph of Galatea*, 1961, colored pencil on paper, 10½ × 13¾″.

69. *To Vivaldi*, 1960, colored pencil on paper, 10½ × 13¾″.

Andy Warhol

70. *Four Marilyns*, 1962, acrylic and silkscreen enamel on canvas, 74 × 61″.

*71. *Silver Disaster*, 1963, acrylic and silkscreen on canvas, 42 × 60″.

72. *Nine Jackies*, 1964, acrylic and silkscreen enamel on canvas, 60¾ × 48¼″.

73. *White Burning Car Twice*, 1963, acrylic and silkscreen enamel on canvas, 79 × 42½″.

74. *Campbell's Soup Can* (pink and blue-green on blue-green background), 1965, acrylic and silkscreen on canvas, 36 × 24″.

75. *Campbell's Soup Can* (yellow and brown on ocher background), 1965, acrylic and silkscreen on canvas, 36 × 24″.

76. *Campbell's Soup Can* (orange and brown on white background), 1965, acrylic and silkscreen on canvas, 36 × 24″.

77. *Campbell's Soup Can* (orange and green on yellow background), 1965, acrylic and silkscreen on canvas, 36 × 24″.

78. *The Kiss (Bela Lugosi)*, 1963, silkscreen on paper handprinted by the artist (edition of eight), 30 × 40″.

79. *Coca-Cola*, 1962, pencil, 23¾ × 18″.

80. *Do It Yourself*, 1962, colored crayon, 25 × 18″.

81. *Campbell's Soup Can*, 1962, gouache and pencil on paper, 23¾ × 18″.

82. *Hedy Lamarr*, 1962, pencil on paper, 40 × 30″.

Tom Wesselmann

83. *Still Life #45*, 1962, mixed media, 36 × 48″.

84. *Still Life with Radio*, 1964, gouache and pencil on paper, 23 × 31½″.

85. *Still Life with Radio*, 1964, pencil on paper, 15¾ × 23″.

86. *Untitled*, 1962, pencil on paper, 16½ × 16⅞″.

87. *Seascape #14*, 1966, charcoal, oil on Plexiglas, 66 × 39½″.

* Works on loan indefinitely to The Baltimore Museum of Art.